Integrated Engine Transmission Systems

Proceedings of the Institution of Mechanical Engineers

ISBN 0 85298 593 2

IMechE 1986–7

INTEGRATED ENGINE TRANSMISSION SYSTEMS

Conference Planning Panel

F J Wallace, DSc, MSc, PhD, FEng, FIMechE (Chairman)
School of Engineering
University of Bath

C R Burrows, BSc, PhD, CEng, FIMechE
University of Strathclyde
Glasgow

R J Varley, BSc, CEng, MIMechE
Self-Changing Gears Limited
Coventry

R M Richardson, BSc(Eng)
Ford Motor Company Limited
Basildon
Essex

N Watson, PhD, DSc(Eng), CEng, FIMechE
Imperial College of Science and Technology
London

INTERNATIONAL CONFERENCE ON
INTEGRATED ENGINE
TRANSMISSION SYSTEMS

IMechE CONFERENCE PUBLICATIONS 1986–7

Sponsored by
The Power Industries Division of
The Institution of Mechanical Engineers

Co-sponsored by
The Automobile and Railway Divisions of
The Institution of Mechanical Engineers

8–9 July 1986
The University of Bath
Avon

Published for
The Institution of Mechanical Engineers
by Mechanical Engineering Publications Limited
LONDON

ISBN 0 85298 593 2

Printed by Waveney Print Services Ltd, Beccles, Suffolk

CONTENTS

The Institution of
Mechanical Engineers

The primary purpose of the 76,000-member Institution of Mechanical Engineers, formed in 1847, has always been and remains the promotion of standards of excellence in British mechanical engineering and a high level of professional development, competence and conduct among aspiring and practising members. Membership of IMechE is highly regarded by employers, both within the UK and overseas, who recognise that its carefully monitored academic training and responsibility standards are second to none. Indeed they offer incontrovertible evidence of a sound formation and continuing development in career progression.

In pursuit of its aim of attracting suitably qualified youngsters into the profession — in adequate numbers to meet the country's future needs — and of assisting established Chartered Mechanical Engineers to update their knowledge of technological developments — in areas such as CADCAM, robotics and FMS, for example — the IMechE offers a comprehensive range of services and activities. Among these, to name but a few, are symposia, courses, conferences, lectures, competitions, surveys, publications, awards and prizes. A Library containing 150,000 books and periodicals and an Information Service which uses a computer terminal linked to databases in Europe and the USA are among the facilities provided by the Institution.

If you wish to know more about the membership requirements or about the Institution's activities listed above — or have a friend or relative who might be interested — telephone or write to IMechE in the first instance and ask for a copy of our colour 'at a glance' leaflet. This provides fuller details and the contact points — both at the London HQ and IMechE's Bury St Edmunds office — for various aspects of the organisation's operation. Specifically it contains a tear-off slip through which more information on any of the membership grades (Student, Graduate, Associate Member, Member and Fellow) may be obtained.

Corporate members of the Institution are able to use the coveted letters 'CEng, MIMechE' or 'CEng, FIMechE' after their name, designations instantly recognised by, and highly acceptable to, employers in the field of engineering. There is no way other than by membership through which they can be obtained!

C187/86

A comparative assessment of truck transmissions by computer simulation of vehicle performance for typical road routes

N D VAUGHAN, BSc(Eng), PhD, CEng, MIMechE and **K BANISOLEIMAN**, BSc, PhD
School of Engineering, University of Bath, Avon

SYNOPSIS The use of a suitably controlled continuously variable transmission (CVT) in a heavy goods vehicle would provide a fully automatic transmission as an alternative to a conventional stepped ratio gearbox. This paper describes a computer based study to examine the fuel consumption and performance differences between a hydrostatic CVT and a stepped ratio transmission over a range of heavy goods vehicle duty cycles. Results are presented for three route categories and indicate comparable performance in all cases with a fuel saving potential for the CVT in urban operation.

INTRODUCTION

The use of automatic or semi-automatic gear-boxes in heavy goods vehicles as a replacement for stepped ratio transmissions has been considered desirable for a number of reasons. Filsell (1) comments that one of the most frequent causes of failure in a conventional transmission is the dry friction plate clutch and Hatfield (2) demonstrates a reduction in servicing costs if the clutch could be eliminated. Such automatics would also be easier to drive and help considerably in reducing driver fatigue (1). However these benefits are generally offset by a reduction in fuel consumption and both higher initial costs and repair costs (3).

The use of a continuously variable transmission (CVT) in such an application also offers the benefits associated with automatic transmissions. In addition there is the potential for optimising the overall engine-transmission efficiency if the system is suitably controlled (4). It is the purpose of this paper to predict by computer simulation, the effects on fuel consumption which result from the use of this optimisation. The particular transmission chosen was a hydrostatic split power type in one of its simpler forms (5). This configuration has a higher efficiency than a simple hydrostatic transmission but still lower than that of comparable stepped transmissions. The effectiveness of this overall system optimisation to compensate for lower efficiency has been examined for a wide range of operating conditions. These have been represented by duty cycles typical of operation from the stop/start of city centres to the steady speed of motorways. To provide a reference, similar techniques have been applied to a stepped ratio transmission and allow direct comparisons to be made of both fuel consumption and vehicle performance.

The modelling approach adopted here for both transmissions requires consideration of the physical components contributing to both energy losses and system dynamics. The modelling techniques are described below in conjunction with the hardware details for each major component in the system. This is followed by a discussion of the control logic necessary when running these models over representative duty cycles and a brief description of the routes used. Typical results of the simulations are presented for both the transmissions considered.

SYSTEM COMPONENTS AND MODELLING

The components described below have all been selected as suitable for operation in a 32.5 tonne gross weight heavy goods vehicle but they do not represent a particular manufacturer's design. Wherever possible the data used have been based on commercially available items and either taken from manufacturers literature or experimental information.

Stepped Ratio Transmission

The stepped ratio transmission used for the modelling was a constant mesh, twin layshaft arrangement shown schematically in Fig. 1. This has six ratios in the primary section and in series a two speed range change. After the elimination of duplicate ratios this gives a total of nine forward speeds the ratios for which are shown in Table 1.

In modelling this transmission it was assumed that the transmitted torque was equally divided between the twin layshafts. The losses in the gearbox were defined in terms of a torque dependent and a speed dependent loss coefficient for all the bearings and gears in the assembly. Values of these coefficients were assigned on the basis of the physical dimensions and type of each item. The total loss then depended on the ratio selected and components transmitting torque as well as their speeds. The overall speed and torque dependent coefficients are given in Table 1, based on the input shaft torque and speed. In a similar manner the total inertia of each shaft within the gearbox was estimated and the total inertia referred to the output shaft is given in Table 1 for each gear ratio. The equation defining the torque transmitted is given below:

$$M_{out} = M_{in} \frac{R(1-c)}{1+c} - f\omega_{in}$$

where M = output and input torques
  R = overall gear ratio
  ω_{in} = input shaft speed
  c = torque dependent coefficient
  f = speed dependent coefficient

A clutch model was required for this transmission to allow simulation at slow speeds and starting from rest. A simple model was used considering a dry friction plate clutch which permitted engine torque to be transmitted during clutch slip. When both clutch members reached the same speed then the clutch was considered as a solid shaft.

Continuously Variable Transmission

The CVT considered is shown in Fig. 2 and is of the input differential split power type, using a hydrostatic transmission as the variable speed element. As the name implies the input to this transmission is made to the annulus of the fully floating epicyclic gear and the output taken from the geared combination of the planet carrier and one side of the hydrostatic transmission. The hydrostatic units are variable capacity and reversible, and are used to give control of the overall transmission ratio, which includes a neutral and reverse output.

The components of the CVT were sized to give a representative vehicle top speed of 89 km/h and a fully laden gradient capability of 16% (1). The design procedure minimised the peak power transmitted through the hydrostatic path and was calculated to be 136 kW. This gave the basic CVT a ratio range of 3:1 and hence required the use of a series, two speed range change to give the required overall ratio range of 8.5:1. In performance terms this gave a zero gradient top speed of 95 km/h and a gradient restart capability of 16%. Details of the selected components are given in Table 2.

As with the stepped ratio transmission, the losses were treated as speed and load dependent. In this case however suitable bearings and gear sizes had first to be selected to represent a realistic transmission design. In addition the hydrostatic units also experience flow losses, and these were modelled by use of a pressure dependent coefficient and an allowance for oil compressibility. The selection of a representative coefficient was based on experimental results for a unit similar to that selected for the transmission. Typical results for this are shown in Fig. 3 as a variation of flow loss with pressure at constant speed for a unit acting as a pump. This approach shows a reasonable correlation between the experimental and modelled loss with the modelling erring on the pessimistic side at lower pressures.

Engine

A description of the thermodynamic processes within the engine using a filling and emptying model could be adapted for use with the transmission models described above. However such models provide considerably more information

than is required in this work. For vehicle simulation an adequate engine model would provide only information on the engine torque developed and the fuel used to produce it. In steady state operation such data can be readily obtained from the engine operating map with superimposed details of experimentally measured fuel flow. However it was questionable whether such information could describe accurately the operation during an engine transient when obvious discrepancies can occur with effects such as turbocharger lag.

Direct comparisons were made between actual transient fuel flow and calculated fuel flow using a well instrumented test rig fitted with a turbocharged truck diesel engine. Experimental measurements had initially established a steady state map with details of fuel rack position and actual fuel flow. To make direct comparisons with a typical transient the engine was subjected to the sequence shown in Fig. 4. The actual engine fuel consumption during this transient was measured by a load cell as the reduction in weight of a fuel supply vessel. The variation of total fuel used with time is shown in Fig. 5 by the full line; the staircase effect arises from the resolution due to digitisation in the data logging.

This sequence was also simulated using the same methods employed for the overall vehicle simulation, and these results are shown by the dashed lines in both Figs. 4 and 5. As can be seen the simulation overestimates the engine torque produced and hence predicts a more rapid engine acceleration to the final speed. The lower output and acceleration of the experimental results are ascribed to turbocharger lag. The totalised fuel used in Fig. 5 show less than 2% difference during the acceleration sequence itself even though the computed total finishes by being 5% optimistic. The majority of this error occurring during the initial part of the deceleration phase of the sequence. The slopes of both the computed and actual results, representing steady state conditions, were identical throughout the sequence to within the experimental accuracy.

It was felt these results showing small errors for free engine acceleration would have a negligible effect for full vehicle simulation and fully corroborated the methods used for both fuel consumption calculation and performance prediction. It is pertinent to note that the stepped ratio transmission experiences very many more engine transients, due to gear changes, than occur with the CVT for the same number of vehicle transient events. This suggests that if anything there would be a tendency to overestimate the acceleration capability and underestimate the fuel consumption figures obtained for the stepped ratio transmission at the expense of the CVT.

The engine controller used with the CVT scheduled the engine operating conditions to lie on the locus of minimum specific fuel consumption. Thus from the scheduled line of operation and the demanded power the required engine governor setting and the required engine speed were calculated. The submodel also anticipated transmission speed restrictions, namely over speeding of the hydrostatic units.

The engine control model detected these conditions and avoided their occurrence by operating the engine away from the scheduled operating conditions whilst the conditions persisted.

Vehicle Characteristics

The complete vehicle model must also include representative information on mass and power losses. In this case it was based on typical data for a 32.5 tonne heavy goods vehicle with the main details given in Table 3. The important parameters in modelling terms are the vehicle mass, its contribution on gradients and the resistance to motion. The total resisting torques acting on the vehicle have been discussed by Williams (6) and consist of aerodynamic drag as well as rolling resistance. Experimental work (6) on a range of vehicles for their coast down characteristics enabled representative coefficients to be selected (Table 3) for use in this model.

In addition the effect of losses in a rear axle have been treated in an identical way for both transmissions; as an efficiency for torque transmission of 98%.

DRIVER-VEHICLE-ROAD INTERACTION

The interactions which occur in practice between a driver, the vehicle and the road information are very complex. However, some recognition of the important factors in this process is necessary to produce a valid simulation over a variety of road routes. These factors have been discussed by Watson (8) for light vehicles, and are equally appropriate for heavy vehicles. These may be summarised under the headings of vehicle, driver, and road/traffic characteristics. A realistic simulation will depend on the route information available, the way it is specified, and a suitable model of driver behaviour.

Route Classification and Specification

To examine the vehicle models in realistic situations it is important to use duty cycles which are representative of the spectrum of operation experienced in practice. This is most conveniently achieved by classifying the operation under the headings of motorway, rural and urban routes (9). This follows a trend from almost steady operation on motorways to the stop-start motoring of a congested city centre. As an extreme example of stop-start operation the SAE urban cycle (10) was selected as well as a less severe urban route through Southampton (9).

The most important information to be specified for route simulation are the speeds and gradients. Provided sufficient speed information is available then approximations to the realistic gradients can usually be specified along a route.

In the work reported here the route data were specified as realistic speed limits for defined distances along the route. This was assumed to include the influence of both traffic and road features (8). This method required the development of some driver logic to

control the vehicle speed during transients.

Driver Modelling

The driver model controlled the vehicle speed along the route by comparing the instantaneous vehicle speed with the route speed limit and eliminated the speed error by either accelerating or decelerating the vehicle. Steady speed operation was achieved when the vehicle speed was within a small speed tolerance band about the route speed limit. The driver model was able to select from acceleration, deceleration or steady speed modes of operation according to the logic detailed below.

During the acceleration mode for the stepped transmission only the maximum demand was considered, which implemented the maximum governor set speed for the engine. Full fuel-rack torque was developed by the engine to accelerate the vehicle and the gears were changed every time the engine speed reached its maximum. The relationship between the governor set speed and the driver demand was modelled using linear calibration so that partial demands could be used during steady speed operation to operate at a specified route speed.

For the CVT the driver model was assumed to demand an engine power. To investigate the performance and fuel economy potential of the CVT demands of less than the full power were considered. This was implemented through the use of a demand factor and modified the engine power demanded during acceleration using the relationship

$$H_D = H_L \times \frac{100}{df}$$

where H_D = demanded power
H_L = power required to give steady state operation at the next route speed limit
df = demand factor as a percentage.

Thus during a transient a power will be selected which should give vehicle acceleration to exceed the next route speed limit. This was then reduced to the steady speed requirements when the vehicle speed entered the tolerance band.

For steady speed operation the driveline output was matched to the prevailing route conditions of gradient and speed limit. In the case of the stepped transmission a gear was selected to give the most favourable engine efficiency. If a severe down gradient meant that vehicle speed could be maintained without engine power then this also could be implemented. For the stepped transmission the engine was motored and appropriate adjustments made to fuel consumption. For the CVT the engine was run at idle and the speed maintained by an appropriate braking torque considered to come from the vehicle service brakes. In practice it would be possible to use the CVT to give engine braking at greater levels than a stepped transmission.

The driver model also included some anticipation of the route speed limit and the road gradients ahead of the vehicle, by a distance which was assumed to be equal to that of the "allowable headway" (8). In reality, the allowable headway is not easily quantified, it was therefore assumed that a driver must at least anticipate the changes in the road speed limit and gradients by a distance within which the vehicle could be brought to rest safely. Although minimum deceleration requirements for heavy goods vehicles are specified, Smith (7) suggests that a constant rate of 0.12 g typifies the average deceleration for this class of vehicle. For the purposes of the simulation the allowable headway was calculated assuming the constant average deceleration rate suggested by Smith. The algebraic sum of the total distance travelled by the vehicle and the allowable headway was termed the 'horizon distance' and this was used as the reference for the retrieval of route data from the appropriate sub-routine. This horizon distance was used to determine the point at which a deceleration should be initiated to ensure that the vehicle was within the next specified speed limit. Operation in braking was carried out as an extension of the method used for the steady state operation on a downward gradient.

COMPUTER SIMULATION RESULTS

The simulation was used to compare the vehicle performance and fuel consumption for the two transmissions over all the route types described above and a range of vehicle weights.

SAE urban cycle

Fig. 6 shows the computed fuel consumptions of the two transmissions specified against vehicle mass for this driving cycle. The simulations for the CVT were repeated with different demand factors of 10% to 40%. As seen from this diagram for a demand factor of 40% the CVT used 20% and 12% less fuel than the stepped transmission at the unladen weight and the maximum weight respectively.

The effect of the demand factor on fuel consumption and vehicle speed can be shown by indicating the fuel used at the different sectors of the driving cycle on engine maps. This has been shown on Fig. 7, with labels A to D indicating the progressively more severe sections of the route. The subscripts tr and ss after the labels represent the fuel consumption during the transient and the steady speed operation for each section. Figs. 7a to 7c show the effect of the demand factor on the engine operating conditions. As seen from these diagrams for increasing demand factor the power developed by the engine during the accelerations reduces. For a demand factor of 10% acceleration is mainly under full engine power and for a demand factor of 40% intermediate engine powers are developed for acceleration. This means that in the latter case the majority of fuel is used at engine operating conditions with better thermal efficiency. Hence a better fuel economy but at the expense of a slower vehicle response. On the other hand, in the former case the majority of fuel is used at full power effecting a rapid vehicle response but at the expense of fuel efficiency. This meant that at an intermediate demand factor between 10% and 40% the relative fuel consumptions of the transmissions could be compared based on equal average speeds to complete the route.

Fuel consumption and the average speed of the CVT were plotted against the demand factor. Fig. 8a shows the average speed plotted against demand factor and Fig. 8b the fuel consumption against the demand factor. In fact both the fuel consumption and the average speed figures used to generate the diagrams were themselves averaged for the range of vehicle weights considered in the simulations. Superimposed on Fig. 8a is the mean of the average speeds obtained with the conventional transmission, arbitrarily plotted at zero demand factor. Extrapolation of this point to cut the locus of CVT values gives the demand factor which would give equal average speeds, a figure of about 23%. Examination of Fig. 8b shows that the fuel consumption of the CVT at this demand factor is slightly better than that of the conventional transmission, showing an improvement of just over 8%.

Southampton city route

The fuel consumption of the CVT was computed for demand factors of 10% and 40% in a similar way to that above. In this case the CVT showed a better fuel consumption than that of the stepped transmission at the unladen vehicle weight where a 4.9% improvement was achieved by the CVT at the demand factor of 40%. However in comparison with the stepped transmission this improvement in fuel consumption was at the expense of 4.1% slower average speed. For the demand factor of 10% and the unladen weight the CVT completed the journey with an average speed which was marginally (2.4%) higher than the stepped transmission, whilst using 2.2% more fuel.

The same procedure described above was used to determine a demand factor to give an equivalent average speed. In this case the fuel consumption was virtually identical with the CVT showing only 0.5% better economy.

Overall Comparison

The fuel consumption and vehicle speed for all route types considered are shown as a bar chart on Fig. 9. The CVT was controlled over the remaining routes with a very small demand factors, thus giving maximum power for all acceleration sequences. Also superimposed on this diagram are the numbers of stop starts per kilometre of the route. As can be seen, on the rural and motorway routes the CVT consistently showed a higher fuel consumption than the stepped transmission. This was caused by the relatively poor efficiency of the CVT in comparison with the stepped transmission. However the CVT showed potential for fuel saving with comparable performance relative to the stepped transmission for driving environments with a larger number of stop-start and major slows (9). The Southampton city route and the SAE urban driving cycle having respectively 2.03 and 3.72 acceleration sequences per kilometre.

The relative improvements in the fuel consumption of the CVT come about because during a stop-start mode of operation the CVT is free from the tractive effort deficiencies of the stepped transmission at the gear changes. For example in the SAE urban cycle the fully laden stepped transmission performed 45 gear changes. The computer simulations show that for typical urban driving conditions the tractive effort deficiencies of the stepped transmission offset the poor efficiency of the CVT, thus giving a net improvement in fuel consumption for the CVT.

For the rural and motorway routes the CVT shows a consistent fuel consumption penalty. In all cases however, comparable or higher average speeds were achieved providing some operational improvement. The CVT was not designed for high speed operation and fuel economy could have been improved with alternative designs, for example an additional ratio in the range change. However, major fuel savings which could be achieved by the CVT implies operation confined to urban and city centre driving.

CONCLUSIONS

A simple split power transmission using typical hydrostatic unit efficiencies shows an overall deterioration in fuel consumption relative to a conventional stepped ratio transmission. However this is accompanied by an increase in vehicle performance and the potential for an increase in average speeds and a reduction in journey times.

If vehicle operation is confined to the urban region then the CVT would show consistent benefits in fuel consumption and performance potential with an accompanying reduction in driver fatigue when automatically controlled.

Alternative configurations of split power transmission have been shown in other work (5) to have higher overall efficiency and if adapted to this application it is likely that the CVT would show greater benefit.

REFERENCES

(1) FILSELL, M.K. The use of automatic and semi-automatic gearboxes in maximum weight articulated vehicles engaged in short haul work. Instn. Mech. Engrs. Conference, Solihull 1978, 9-20.
(2) HATFIELD, R. Maintenance experience with automatic and semi-automatic gearboxes fitted to aircraft ground handling equipment. Instn. Mechn. Engrs. Conference, Solihull 1978, 21-32.
(3) MANNING, W. Problems appertaining to the installation of automatic transmissions as regular production options into truck production. Instn. Mechn. Engrs. Conference, Solihull 1978, 85-88.
(4) BANISOLEIMAN, K. and VAUGHAN, N.D. Control of a heavy vehicle continuously variable transmission for fuel economy. Int. Conf. on Fluid Power Transmission and Control, Zheijang Univ., Hangzhou PRC, 1985, 1490-1506.
(5) DOREY, R.E. and VAUGHAN, N.D. Computer aided design of split power hydrostatic transmissions. Proc. Instn. Mech. Engrs., 1983, 1984, 61-69.
(6) WILLIAMS, T. Energy losses in heavy commercial vehicles. TRRL, SR329, 1977.
(7) SMITH, G.L. Commercial vehicle performance and fuel economy. SAE 700194, 1970.
(8) WATSON, H.C. Vehicle driving patterns and measurement methods for energy and emission assessment. Australian Govt. Pub. Service, Occ. paper 30, 1978.
(9) RENOUF, M.A. Prediction of the fuel consumption of heavy goods vehicles by computer simulation. TRRL, SR453, 1979.
(10) Anon. Fuel economy measurement test procedure. SAE J1082, 1974.

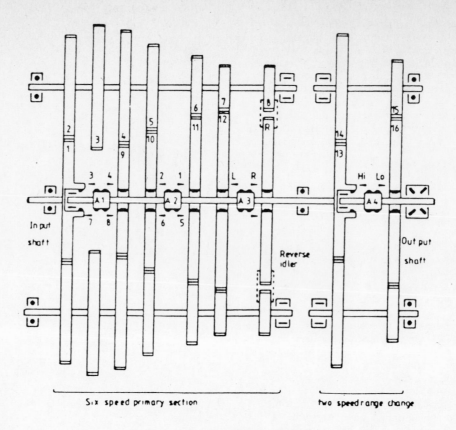

Fig 1   Stepped ratio transmission

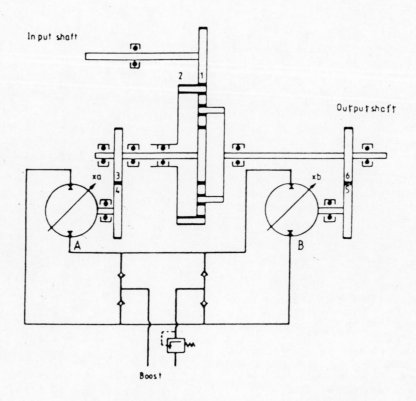

Fig 2   Continuously variable split power transmission

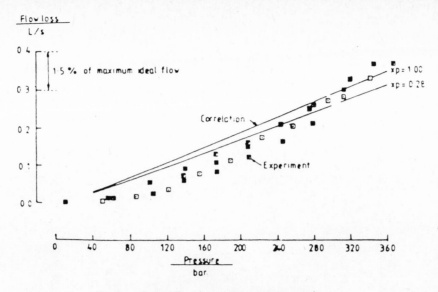

Fig 3   Pump flow losses at constant speed

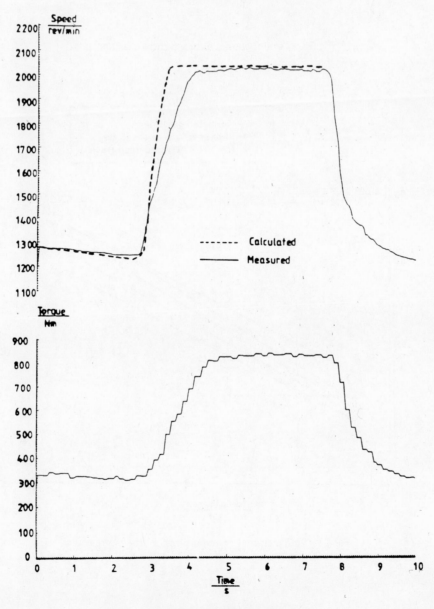

Fig 4   Engine torque and speed transient

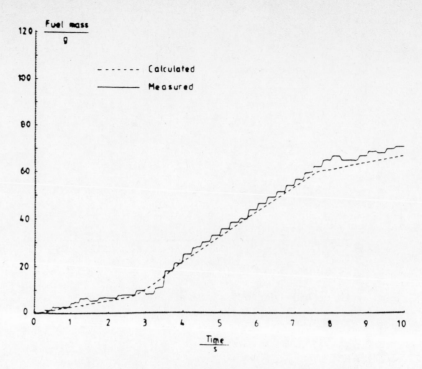

Fig 5   Total fuel used during transient sequence

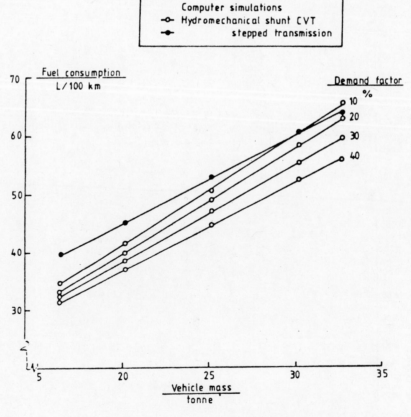

Fig 6   Predicted fuel consumption for city centre route

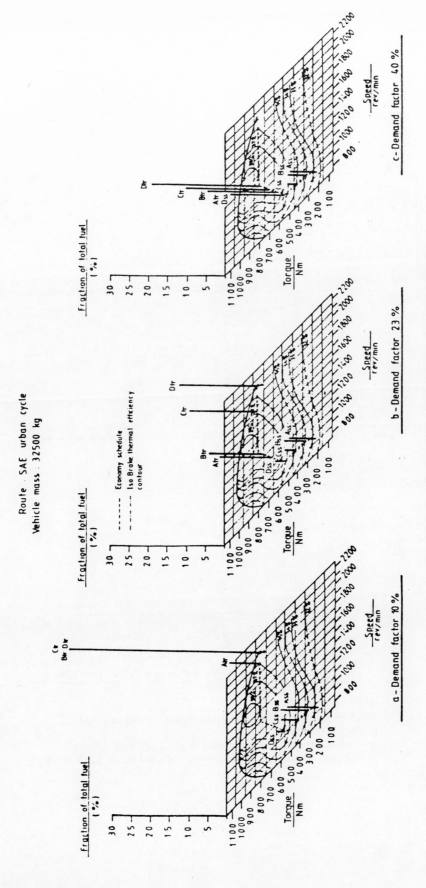

Route : SAE urban cycle
Vehicle mass : 32500 kg

a - Demand factor 10 %

b - Demand factor 23 %

c - Demand factor 40 %

Fig 7   Engine operating conditions for different demand factors
(a) demand factor 10 per cent (b) demand factor 23 per cent
(c) demand factor 40 per cent

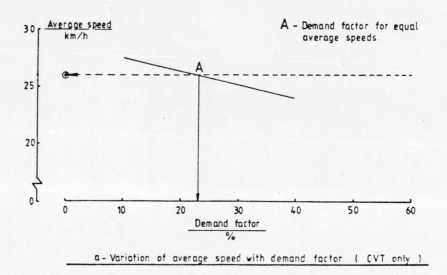

a - Variation of average speed with demand factor (CVT only)

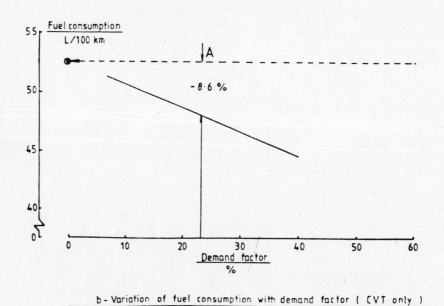

b - Variation of fuel consumption with demand factor (CVT only)

Fig 8   Effect of demand factor on continuously variable transmission
(CVT) performance
(a)   variation of average speed with demand factor (CVT only)
(b)   variation of fuel consumption with demand factor (CVT only)

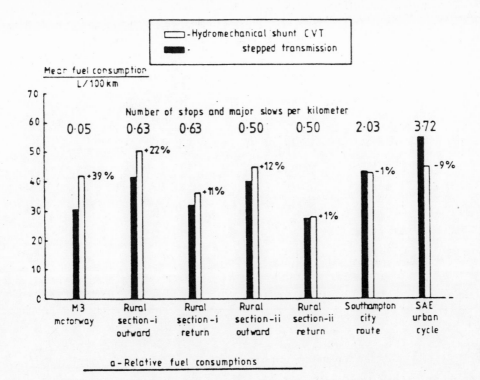

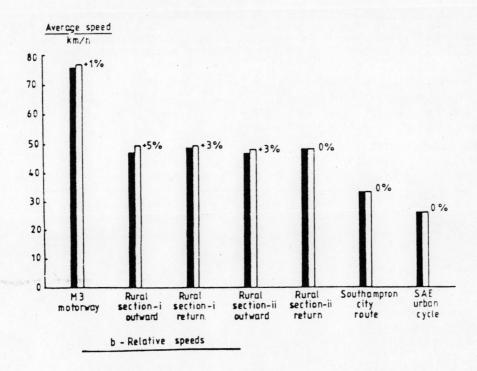

Fig 9   Relative transmission performance for all routes considered
           (a)   relative fuel consumptions
           (b)   relative speeds

Table 1 Data for the stepped ratio transmission

Gear	Ratio	Inertia kg m^2	Torque dependent coefficient (c)	Speed dependent coefficient (f) Nm/(rad/s)
low	8.87:1	9.707	0.0323	0.00181
1st	5.92:1	4.504	0.0314	0.00192
2nd	4.37:1	2.551	0.0301	0.00203
3rd	3.24:1	1.536	0.0241	0.00218
4th	2.40:1	0.433	0.0301	0.00238
5th	1.83:1	4.504	0.0129	0.00192
6th	1.34:1	2.551	0.0117	0.00203
7th	1.0 :1	1.536	0.0057	0.00218
8th	0.74:1	0.433	0.0117	0.00238

Rear axle ratio 5.69:1

Table 2 Data for the continuously variable transmission

Hydrostatic unit capacity	26.4×10^{-6} m^3/rad
Maximum pressure	350 bar
Maximum speed	2400 rev/min
Inertia	0.019 kg/m^2
Flow loss coefficient	1.137×10^{-9}
Coulomb friction loss coefficient	3.066×10^{-2}
Viscous friction loss coefficient	6.207×10^{-5}
Epicyclic ratio	2:1
Range change ratios	2.87:1 & 1:1
Rear axle ratio	4.23:1

Table 3 Vehicle data

Maximum weight	32.0 tonne
Minimum weight	15.0 tonne
Height	3.36 m
Width	2.02 m
Drag coefficient	0.7
Rolling resistance coefficients	0.0077
	0.00012 s/m
Maximum engine power	177 kW @ 2100 rev/min
Maximum engine torque	970 Nm @ 1300 rev/min

C193/86

Secondary speed controlled hydrostatic units on quasi-constant pressure systems

F METZNER, Dr-Ing
Mannesmann Rexroth GmbH, Lohr, West Germany

SYNOPSIS   Beginning with the fundamentals of the secondary speed control hydrostatic system, the function is shown by two configurations: a hydraulic and an electro-hydraulic valve actuation of the adjustable secondary unit.
In a short digression on the advantages of this speed control it will be compared with the conventional hydrostatic system. Based on simulation with a non-linear and discontinous model for the dynamic behaviour, it is possible to show the influence of the system parameters and, as a result of that, to determine the stability of the system control. The application of the system is illustrated by an experimental vehicle and a combustion-engine test equipment.

1   INTRODUCTION

An excellent alternative to the conventional hydrostatic or electric drives will be shown in this paper by explaining the secondary speed control system /1,2,3/.
It is realized with slightly modified standard components and was developed in a direct cooperation between industry and university.

2   THE HYDROSTATIC DRIVE

In the hydrostatic transmission technique the characteristics
   torque M
and
   speed n
of mechanical power P find their equivalent in the pressure p   and the flow Q:
$$P = 2\pi \times M \times n = \Delta p_{HD} \times Q \qquad (1)$$
On principle it is possible to manage the power-flow by affecting the pressure Δp_{HD}, the flow Q or both characteristics.

2.1   The conventional hydrostatic drive /4,5/

In the conventional drive, as shown in Fig.1a, the primary unit (pump) and the secondary unit (motor) are connected by the hydraulic flow Q, wherefore it is called the flow-coupled system. With an ideal efficiency the speed n_2 of the secondary unit follows by the pump-flow Q_1:
$$Q_2 \overset{!}{=} Q_1 \quad \longrightarrow \quad n_2 = n_1 \times \frac{V_1}{V_2} \qquad (2)$$
It is possible to change the speed n_2 by affecting the speed n_1 of the pump or by varying the volume V_1. In special cases - if the conversion rate isn't large enough - a change of the motor volume V_2 is additionally used.
If there is a resistance to acceleration or a load to be lifted, the reaction will be a rising pressure.
Because of the flow coupling it is necessary to have one primary unit for each secondary unit (motor or cylinder).
A reversed speed direction is only possible by changing the pressure sides of the primary or secondary unit.
Another problem is the influence of the hydraulic capacity c_h of the connecting pipes between primary and secondary unit (Volume V_l)
$$c_h = V_l / E_{\ddot{o}l} \qquad (3)$$
on the dynamic behaviour of the system /4/.

Another conventional concept is the open loop control of the secondary unit (motor or cylinder) by a servo valve on a constant pressure system. The speed n_2 of the secondary unit is related to the flow through the servo-valve /5/. The efficiency of the system is bad because of the throttle losses in the valve especially at partial load condition, whereby the installation of a large oil cooler becomes necessary.

2.2   Principle function of the secondary speed controlled system /6,7/

The system principally consists of a primary unit (pump), a hydraulic accumulator and the adjustable reversible secondary unit, as shown in Fig.1b.
The pump is pressure controlled and realizes, together with the hydraulic accumulator, the quasi-constant pressure system.
The adjustable reversible secondary unit gives a torque M_2 to its output drive shaft, which can have both directions:
$$M_2 = \frac{\Delta p_{HD} \times V_{2m}}{2\pi} \times \frac{\alpha_2}{\alpha_{2m}} \qquad (3)$$
The torque M_2 will induce an acceleration or deceleration $\dot{n}_2$ of the output drive shaft, when it won't be in equilibrium with the moment of load M_L and the moment of resistance M_R (friction). The gradient of acceleration or deceleration is given by the amount of the torque-difference on the output shaft and - at constant conditions - by the resulting moment of inertia θ_g of the secondary unit itself and the driven system:
$$\dot{n}_2 = \frac{\sum M_2}{2\pi \times \theta_g} = \frac{1}{2\pi \times \theta_g} \times (M_2 - M_L - M_R) \qquad (4)$$
To control the resulting speed n_2. it is necessary to affect the torque M_2 (means displacement α_2) as a function of the difference between the set value n_{2soll} and the actual value n_{2ist} of the speed, as shown in Fig.2.
If there is a resistance against acceleration or deceleration or a load to be lifted with a secondary speed controlled system, this will be followed by a flow reaction. which is similar to the current reaction of an electric drive on constant voltage.
The secondary speed controlled unit is working without any throttling losses on high efficiency compared to the conventional system with the servo valve.

On the other hand the hydraulic capacity doesn't have any influence on the dynamical behaviour because of the quasi-constant pressure system.

The speed control function can be installed with hydraulic (Fig.2a) or electro-hydraulic (Fig.2b) valve actuation.
When a hydraulic actuation is chosen, a small pump (1) is to be installed to give a constant flow Q_{Stp} into the signal circuit (Fig.2a).
With the flow control valve (2) the set value of the speed n_2 is set as a flow Q_{Srv}.
Because of the leakage in the signal circuit - shown by the throttle (3) - the pressure p_{St} will change and give a force against the constant counter pressure p_{Sto}, which is followed by a stroke x_v of the valve spool (4). This will cause a stroke x_k of the servo piston (5), which is rather proportional to the displacement α_2 of the secondary unit. The stroke x_k produces a mechanical feedback to the valve spool (4) as a force of the small spring (each stroke x_k is related to a force on the valve spool (4)).
It is important to mention, that with this mechanical force-feedback a torque-control (means displacement-controls) is realized.
Because of the rising displacement α_2 the secondary unit (7) changes its speed n_2 and the hydraulic 'speedometer' (6) gives a speed feedback as a flow Q_{TG}.
The displacement α_2 will be just as large as to hold the speed n_2 with a small influence of the load M_L, which is acting upon the drive shaft of the secondary unit.
The amount of that influence is related to the amplification of the closed loop speed control, which can be regulated with the throttle (3), but a changing throttle opening has an influence on the possible speed range, too.

On the other hand an electro-hydraulic signal circuit can also be realized (Fig.2b). Here the actual value of the speed n_2 measured by an tachogenerator (9), will be compared to a set value, amplified in the control unit (10) and changed into a electric current by the current amplifier (12), which will again - analogue to the hydraulic signal ciruit - induce a force upon the valve spool (4). The displacement of the secondary unit (7) follows to a definite value, which is related to the valve stroke force (mechanical displacement feedback).
The secondary unit (7) will change its speed n_2 till the set value will be reached. Then the displacement α_2 will be diminished onto exactly that value, which is needed to hold the speed.

As an alternative it is possible to use an electrical displacement-feedback instead of a mechanical force-feedback.

The main advantage of the electro-hydraulic version is a small power amount for the signal circuit and a great flexibility of installing different concepts into the control unit (10).
As an example any influence of disturbance can be eliminated by giving an integral behaviour to the control unit (10).
Normally the control unit (10) has standard algorithms like P-, PI- or PID-behaviour. In case of high claims on the dynamics of the whole loop it needs special developed algorithms, even digital control units are usual, especially if the speed controlled secondary unit is used as a torque amplifier in a closed loop rotation control system (robot drive).

The secondary controlled unit may be used in an open or closed hydraulic ciruit with remarkable advantages especially when
- brake or veering energy can be recovered (kinetic or potential energy in working- resp. driving machinery) /8,9/,
- several independent working units will be supplied by one primary unit,
- an energy exchange between both sides of the driven wheels of a vehicle with skid steering is possible /10/ (principle: Steering by speed differences on both sides, when the wheels themselves aren't steerable; examples: gear- or chain drives),
- a large output power is demanded only for a short time in a discontinous operation mode (examples: bus in city traffic, fork stacker).
Furthermore remarkable new concepts for the test facilities of the automotive industry can be realized. They have improved dynamical behaviour and - at the same time - a marvellous potential of reducing the energy amount by connecting several test beds for combustion engines /11/, gear-boxes and differentials (which in normal mode have to brake the test-piece) with extensive energy consumers (like vibration test beds).

The advantages and disadvantages of the introduced system are shown in Table 1:

Table 1: Advantages and disadvantages of secondary controlled hydrostatic units

+ four-quadrant-operation and regenerative braking and veering possible
+ central hydraulic primary unit with several secondary units can realize (with hydraulic accumulators) a circuit with quasi-constant operating pressure
+ remarkably improved efficiency
+ potential for optimized power-flow in vehicles with lateral steering (off-road vehicles and machinery in agriculture, earthwork, forestry and military)
+ lowered systems costs because of improved efficiency
- the dynamic behaviour can be critical, when stability criterions are ignored
- special emergency efforts are to be made in case of control system failure
- increasing system costs because of the reversible and adjustable secondary unit and the hydraulic accumulators

Fig.3 shows the block diagram of a linearized and simplified 2nd order model /7/, which gives us an impression of the system dynamics of the secondary speed controlled unit with electro hydraulic signal circuit.
The behaviour of the steering valve is describe as a system with proportional function. The servo piston is shown by a 1st order time function with a feedback by the main spring. The mechanical feedback of the servo piston stroke x_k is builded by a proportional function K_{Fk}.
The controlled process is described by a 1st order time function with a speed-proportional feedback K_n, which can be the model for a friction or a resistance.
In this simplified consideration several important influences are neglected:
- the non-linearities of the flow-pressure function of the steering valve ans
- the points of discontinuity in the friction characteristics of valve, servo piston and secondary unit itself.

Fig.4 shows the applied secondary axial piston unit in swash-plate design with the mechanical force feedback of the servo piston stroke.

Table 2 contains equations defining the natural frequency ω_o and the damping ratio d of complete speed control system. These have been derived from the linearized model. Additional to that an ideal no-load operation without friction was assumed ($K_n = 0$).
Because of these restrictions the equations of Table 2 are only to be used for principal considerations.
The stabilizing influence of the piston stroke feedback can be shown with the second term of the damping ratio d.
Also the effect of the velocity-amplification C_o of the displacement servo can be recognized: It increases the frequency ω_o and the damping ratio d.

3 INFLUENCE OF SYSTEM-PARAMETERS ON THE DYNAMICAL BEHAVIOUR

Based on simulation /12/ with a nonlinear and discontinous 7th order model for the dynamical behaviour /7/, the influence of varying the most important system parameters can be shown in Fig.5:
- A diminishing displacement time T_s (time the servo will need from neutral to maximum displacement),
- an increasing spring rate c_{Fv} of the spring in the steering valve,
- a diminishing volume V_2 of the secondary unit,
- the integration of the hydraulic-mechanical efficiency into the 7th order model,
- an increasing moment of inertia θ_g,
- a diminishing quasi-constant pressure Δp_{HD},
- and a stationary constant load M_L
have a stabilizing influence on system dynamics.

The same result can be recognized in the equations of Table 2.

4 QUANTITATIVE CRITERIONS FOR SYSTEM STABILITY

The dynamics of secondary speed controlled units are defined by the behaviour of
- the control unit itself
- the displacement servo
and
- the controlled process.
With the simplified 2nd order model it isn't possible to give any quantitative information about system behaviour because of the strong restrictions and assumptions.

The dynamics of the displacement servo can be described by the time-value T_s, the servo piston needs from neutral to maximum displacement.
This value depends on the volume V_k, which has to be displaced for this operation, and from the flow Q_{vm} through the steering valve /7/:

$$T_s = \frac{V_k}{Q_{vm}} = \frac{A_k \times x_k}{Q_{vm}} \quad (5)$$

The dynamics of the controlled process can be qualified by the coefficient T_R, which stands in dependence to the max. speed acceleration or deceleration /7/:

$$T_R = 2\pi \times \sqrt{\frac{\theta_g}{2 \times (\Delta p_{HD} \times V_{2m} - 2\pi \times (M_L + M_R))}} \quad (6)$$

The worst case (means the fastest behaviour) results, if the controlled process is in a no-load operation ($M_L = 0$ Nm) and the friction is neglected ($M_R = 0$ Nm).

With both these characteristics many simulations have been made, while the time T_s and the moment of inertia θ_g was varied and the type of control unit was constant.

The criterion, to qualify the solution to a step change of set value, was the complete missing of any overshooting (means a system damping ratio d = 1 in terms of a linearized or linear 2nd order model) and on the other hand the stability condition (phase lag $\approx 180°$).

The determined curve, which marks the displacement time T_s as a function of the time T_R (at a constant behaviour of control unit), gives us a global criterion to evaluate the presumable dynamics in stage of projecting the drive, Fig.6.

Besides, this curve was secured by measuring results with an experimental setup /7/, where the moment of inertia was changed by a gearbox between secondary unit and load. The influence of the volume V_{2m} of the secondary unit and the influence of the control unit have been examined.

The diagram is to be used as explained in the following part:
First of all the time T_s of displacement and the time T_R - it follows eq.(6) - must be determined. The necessary system parameters must be known anyway, when the drive should be projected. Then there are two possibilities:
If the point marked by the coordinates T_s/T_R is below the outlined curve, the behaviour of the secondary speed controlled unit will be free of overshooting. The distance to the curve gives us a kind of dynamic reserve.
If the point marked by the coordinates T_s/T_R is above the outlined curve, the behaviour will have some overshooting, the violence depending on the distance to the curve.
If the second case is true, perhaps it will improve the system dynamics, when instead of a control unit with P-behaviour one with PID-behaviour is used. If that won't suffice, control units with special algorithms must be applied.

The same diagram is also valid for a hydraulic signal circuit (only for closed throttle (3) (Fig.2a)). The band of curves in Fig.6 has its reason in the used signal circuits.
The influence of load and friction can be included by putting the proper values into eq.(6), whereby the time factor T_R is corrected.

As an extreme case the speed control isn't possible without any overshootings till now, when there is nothing coupled to the output-shaft of the secondary unit:
the amplification by the moment of inertia θ_e of the secondary unit (eq.(4)), which is between 50 and 100 times less than a comparable electric motor, is much larger than the complete control circuit will be able to manage, because of the time delay and the responsiveness of the displacement servo.
New and unconventional control units are in stage of development to handle this problem.

In normal applications the moment of inertia θ_g is much larger than the moment of inertia θ_e of the secondary unit, so that problems within normal operations aren't to be expected.

5 APPLICATIONS

5.1 Experimental vehicle of the German army

Fig.7 shows the principle hydraulic circuitry of the experimental vehicle before and after the change to secondary speed control /10,13/ with a hydraulic signal circuit; see above Fig.2a. The vehicle is steered by giving speed differences to the both sides (skid steering).

Because of the hydraulic accumulator and the reversible and adjustable secondary units the weight of vehicle increases from 3300 kg up to 4880 kg (+47,88%), in spite of removed power-dividing gear and the pump, which was eliminated.

A main advantage is the improved braking power, while it would have been possible to remove the mechanical brake-system completely. Additionally the steering-power flow is perfected and the efficiency of the whole system increased dramatically.
Table 3 shows a summary of the reduced fuel consumption of that experimental vehicle.

Table 3: Fuel consumption of the experimental vehicle in a special test cycle (transient/constant velocity) /13/		conventional primary controlled	secondary speed controlled
Vehicle weight	kg	3300	4880
- inconstant velocity fuel consumption	l	97,99	46,86
averaged velocity	km/h	18,08	21,76
averaged engine-power	kW	42	19
- constant velocity fuel consumption	l	45	38

The result: increasing efficiency at inconstant and constant speed by 52% together with increasing cycle-velocity   20%.

5.2 Combustion engine test bed

As already mentioned, the secondary speed controlled hydrostatic unit can realize remarkable new concepts for the test facilities of the car industry, which have improved dynamical behaviour and - at the same time - a great potential of reducing the energy amount by connecting the test beds, which in normal mode have to brake the test piece, with the intensive energy consumers like vibration test beds, or by giving the energy back to the electrical mains with a three-phase asynchronous generator /13/.
This last feature has been realized within the new combustion-engine test bed at the Daimler-Benz Test Centre in Stuttgart /11/, which was fitted with the principal of secondary speed controlled hydrostatic units.
Fig.8 shows the principal hydraulic circuitry.

The main technical data is shown in the following listing /11/:
maximum power : $P = \pm 290$ kW
maximum torque: $M = \pm 550$ Nm
speed range   :   600 1/min $\leq n \leq$ 7000 1/min
speed dynamics: $\Delta n = 6000$ 1/min   in $\Delta t \leq 1$ s

The advantages of the hydraulic system are /11/:
- extremely small moments of inertia θ_g allow high speed dynamics, when a relative small acceleration power is to be installed,

- at acceleration resp. deceleration modes an energy exchange with the hydraulic accumulators is realized. Therefore the feedback to the three-phase mains is missing completely
- the possibility of an energy recovery into the three-phase mains or into hydraulic central power circuits
- the design of the electric connection only for the nominal, not for the maximum power.
A detailed description of setup and function is to be found in /11/.
Fig.9 shows the speed dynamics. It is important to say, that the set-value of the speed was given by a triangle-function and that the necessary acceleration power was at about $P = 35$ kW because of the small moment of inertia of the secondary units (for that reason the measured torque was less than $M \leq \pm 10$ Nm).
Besides it is important to mention, that the cost of the complete system inclusive of connection the power supply, control, torque-measurement setting to work are similar to comparable electrical test beds.

6 SUMMARY

Summarizing the above arguments, we can state: The secondary speed controlled hydrostatic unit is a remarkable alternative to conventional hydrostatic and electric drives in several sectors of modern drive technology. The system stability of the complete control circuit can be checked up at the stage of projecting with one diagram which is easy to handle. Special control algorithms for critical applications are partly available, partly in development.

7 NOTATION

a_o lever arm in mech.feedback (stroke x_k)
A cross section
b_o lever arm in mech.feedback (stroke x_k)
c_o lever arm in mech.feedback (stroke x_k)
c_F spring rate
C_h hydraulic capacity
C_o velocity amplification of displacement servo
d attenuation constant
D differentiating
Δp differential pressure
ΔU difference voltage(set-value - actual-value)
E_o force amplification of displacement servo
$E_{öl}$ modulus of oil elasticity
F force
$I_{r,l}$ electric current
I integrating
K_{mess} electric speedometer constant
K_n constant (speed-linear load/friction moment)
K_{r2} current/voltage-coefficient
K_{r3} force/current-coefficient
K_{Fk} constant of the mech.feedback (stroke x_k)
K_{Fv} constant of the mech.feedback (stroke x_v)
K_{RE} constant of electric signal circuit
K_{RH} constant of hydraulic signal circuit
M torque, moment
n speed
$\dot{n}$ acceleration resp. deceleration (rotational)
p pressure
P power
Q flow
t time
T_s time coefficient of controlled process
T_R time from neutral to maximum displacement
U voltage
V volume

x   stroke
ẋ   velocity
ẍ   acceleration resp. deceleration

α   displacement
η_{hm} hydraulic-mechanical efficiency
θ_e moment of inertia (secondary unit)
θ_g moment of inertia (secondary unit + load)
ω_o natural frequency

1	primary unit	m	maximum
2	secondary unit	R	friction
B	acceleration	St	steering
Dr	throttle	Sto	steering (const.)
F	spring	Sv	displacement
HD	high pressure	Srv	flow control valve
ist	actual value	Stp	auxiliary pump
k	servo piston	TG	hydr.speedometer
L	load	v	steering valve

8 REFERENCES

/1/ Nikolaus, H.W.:
Antriebssystem mit hydrostatischer Kraft-
übertragung.
Patentanmeldung P2739968A vom 6.9.1977

/2/ Nikolaus, H.W.:
Hydrostatic mobile and winch drives with
energy reclamation.
IMechE Conference Publications 1981-8

/3/ Backé, W.; Murrenhoff, H.:
Regelung eines Verstellmotors an einem Kon-
stant-Drucknetz.
'Ölhydraulik und Pneumatik' 25 (1981) Nr.8

/4/ Hahmann, W.:
Das dynamische Verhalten hydrostatischer
Antriebe mit Servopumpen und ihr Einsatz in
Regelkreisen.
Dissertation, RWTH Aachen, Aachen 1973

/5/ Lee, K.-I.:
Dynamisches Verhalten der Steuerkette
Servoventil-Motor-Last.
Dissertation, RWTH Aachen, Aachen 1977

/6/ Murrenhoff, H.:
Regelung von verstellbaren Verdrängerein-
heiten am Konstant-Drucknetz.
Dissertation, RWTH Aachen, Aachen 1983

/7/ Metzner, F.:
Kennwerte der Dynamik sekundärdrehzahlgere-
gelter Axialkolbeneinheiten.
Dissertation, UniBw Hamburg, Hamburg 1985

/8/ Fahl, H.-J.; Metzner, F.:
Energiespeicherung in einem hydrostatischen
Fahrantrieb mit Serienaggregaten.
'Ölhydraulik und Pneumatik'28 (1984) Nr.7

/9/ Nikolaus, H.W.:
Hydrostatische Windenantriebe am eingepräg-
ten Druck.
Preprint der Tagung 'Transmatic', Universi-
tät Karlsruhe, Karlsruhe 1985

/10/ Fahl, H.-J.; Wassenberg, E.:
Vergleich zweier hydrostatischer Antriebs-
systeme in einem Fahrzeug mit Radseitenlen-
kung.
'Ölhydraulik und Pneumatik' 26 (1982) Nr.12

/11/ Kern, W; Reyer, K.; Schober, K.; Weiger, G.:
Hochdynamischer, hydraulischer Motorenprüf-
stand.
'Ölhydraulik und Pneumatik' 29 (1985) Nr.4

/12/ Mock, H.-W.; Metzner, F.:
Probleme der Simulation hydrostatischer
Systeme.
'Ölhydraulik und Pneumatik' 28 (1984) Nr.3
                                       Nr.4

/13/ Nikolaus, H.W.; Kordak, R.:
Hydrostatische Antriebe mit Sekundärrege-
lung und Energierückgewinnung.
Seminarumdruck, Fa.Mannesmann Rexroth GmbH,
Lohr 1983

/14/ Kordak, R.:
Sekundärgeregelte hydrostatische Antriebe.
'Ölhydraulik und Pneumatik' 29 (1985) Nr.9

Table 2 Characteristics of secondary speed control

Natural frequency ω_o:

$$\omega_0 = \frac{1}{2\pi} \cdot \sqrt{\frac{\Delta p_{HD} \cdot V_{2m}}{x_{km} \cdot \theta_g} \cdot K_{RH,E} \cdot \frac{c_0^2}{b_0^2 \cdot c_{Fv}} \cdot C_0}$$

Damping ratio d:

$$d = \pi \cdot \sqrt{\frac{x_{km} \cdot \theta_g}{\Delta p_{HD} \cdot V_{2m}} \cdot \frac{1}{K_{RH,E}} \cdot \frac{b_0^2 \cdot c_{Fv}}{c_0^2} \cdot C_0 \left(\frac{c_{Fk}}{E_0} + \frac{c_0}{a_0} \right)}$$

with the constant of

- hydraulic signal circuit K_{RH}:

$$K_{RH} = \frac{A_v \cdot V_{TG}}{K_{Drl}}$$

- electro-hydraulic signal circuit K_{RE}:

$$K_{RE} = K_{r1} \cdot K_{r2} \cdot K_{r3} \cdot K_{mess}$$

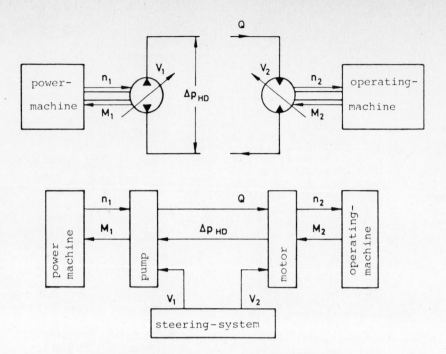

Fig 1a   Principle of a conventional hydrostatic drive

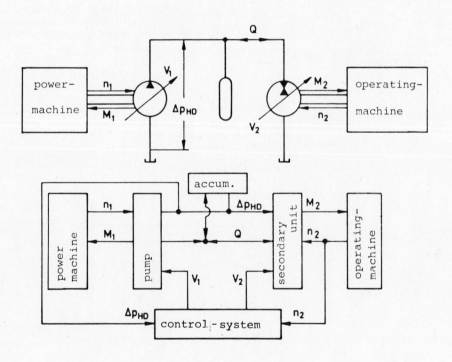

Fig 1b   Principle of a secondary speed controlled hydrostatic drive

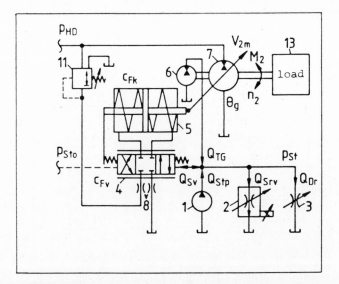

Fig 2a   Secondary speed controlled unit with hydraulic signal circuit

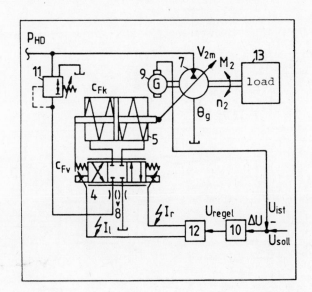

Fig 2b   Secondary speed controlled unit with electro-hydraulic signal circuit

Legend
======

1   auxiliary pump
2   flow control valve
3   throttle
4   steering valve
5   servo piston
6   hydraulic speedometer
7   secondary unit
8   throttles
9   electric speedometer
10 control unit
11 pressure control valve
12 current amplifier
13 load

soll : set value
ist   : actual value
regel : steering valve

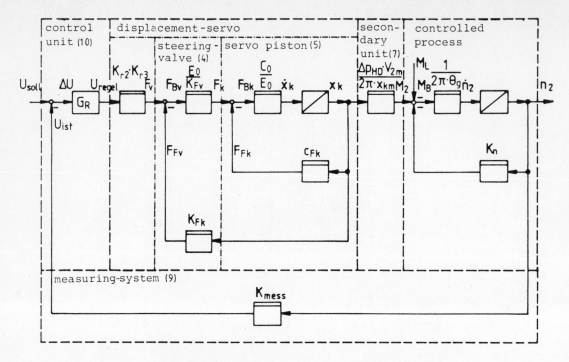

Fig 3   Block diagram of a secondary speed controlled unit (electro-
hydraulic signal circuit)

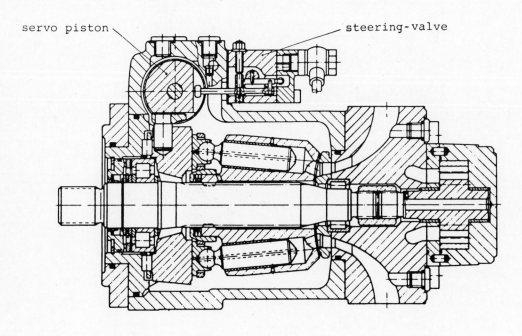

Fig 4   Axial piston unit

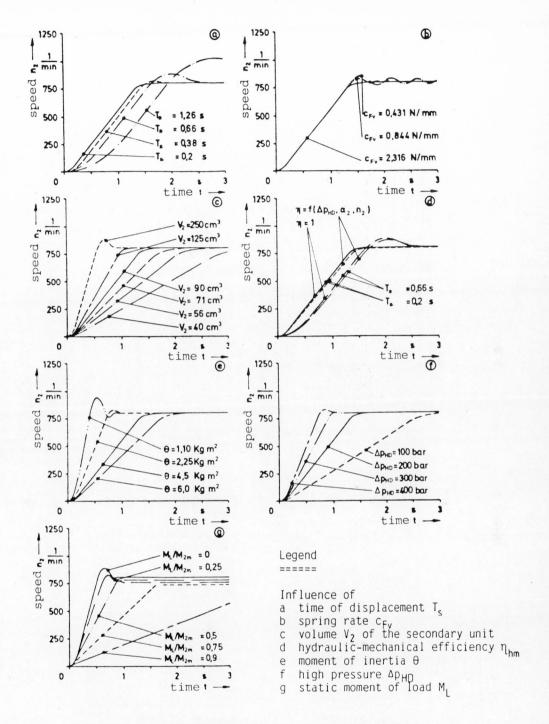

Legend
======

Influence of
a time of displacement T_s
b spring rate c_{Fv}
c volume V_2 of the secondary unit
d hydraulic-mechanical efficiency η_{hm}
e moment of inertia θ
f high pressure Δp_{HD}
g static moment of load M_L

Fig 5   Influence of important system parameters on the dynamics

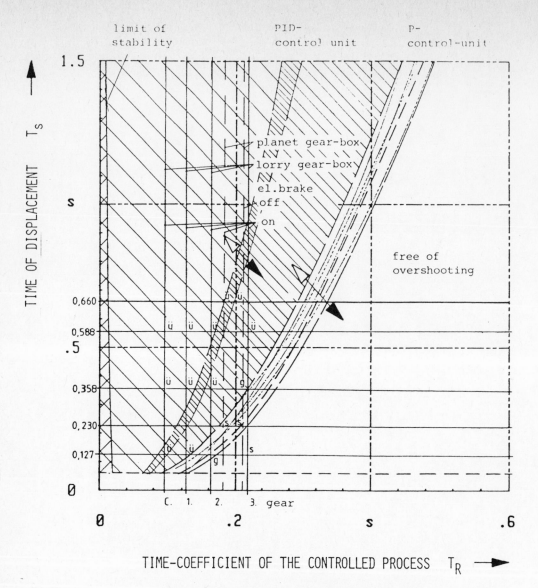

Fig 6   Diagram of stability of a secondary speed controlled unit
         on a quasi-constant pressure system (no-load operation)

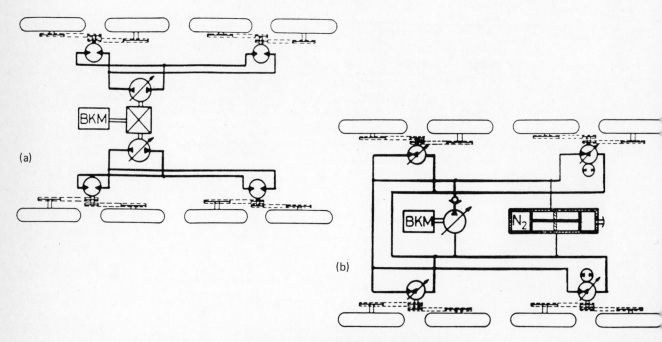

Fig 7   Principle circuitry of the experimental vehicle
         (BKM = combustion engine)

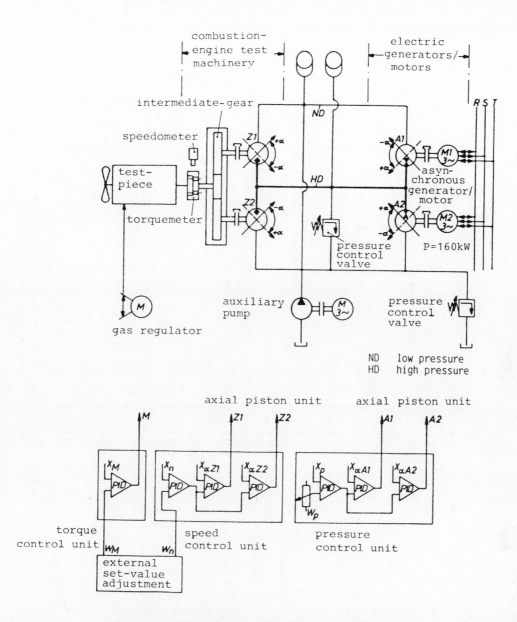

combustion-
engine test
machinery

electric
generators/-
motors

intermediate-gear

ND

speedometer

Z1   +α
      −α

−α A1
+α

M1
3~

asyn-
chronous
generator/
motor

test-
piece

HD

Z2   −α
      +α

+α A2
−α

M2
3~

R S T

torquemeter

pressure
control
valve

P=160kW

M

gas regulator

auxiliary
pump

M
3~

pressure
control
valve

ND   low pressure
HD   high pressure

M

axial piston unit

Z1   Z2

axial piston unit

A1   A2

x_M

PID

x_n

PID

$x_{\alpha Z1}$

PID

$x_{\alpha Z2}$

PID

x_p

PID

$x_{\alpha A1}$

PID

$x_{\alpha A2}$

PID

W_p

torque
control unit

W_M W_n

speed   control unit

pressure
control unit

external
set-value
adjustment

Fig 8   Principal circuitry of the combustion engine test bed

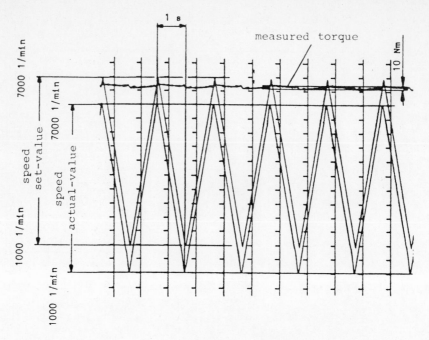

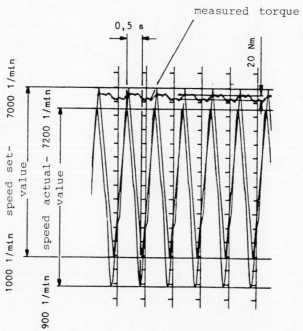

Fig 9   Measured speed curves of the combustion engine test bed

C202/86

Microprocessor control of a rail vehicle with hydrostatic transmission

K S PRESTON, BSc(Eng) and **P H SWIFT**, BSc(Eng)
British Railways Board, Railway Technical Centre, Derby

SYNOPSIS Last year British Rail Research concluded test running of a hydrostatically driven railcar. Each of the two engines drove a variable angle swash plate pump which passed oil to fixed angle motors mounted directly on the axle ends of one bogie. In order to optimise economic operation at a wide range of vehicle speeds, the engine, the transmission, the brakes and the engine auxiliaries were integrated under the control of a microprocessor based control system. The hydrostatic transmission proved not to have a sufficiently high efficiency to justify the cost of developing a production system and development will not be continued. However, the results of the tests were very encouraging and the principles of vehicle systems integration, under digital control, will be employed in future vehicles.

1 INTRODUCTION

A hydrostatic transmission is one in which the positive displacement of a fluid is used to transmit energy from an input to an output machine.

Hydrostatic transmissions are in common use on off-highway construction machines and, in rail use, on Civil Engineering track laying machines and cranes. In these applications a single prime mover is used to supply power both for moving the machine and for its other operations. Hydrostatic transmissions are also in common use for slow speed applications, such as mining locomotives, where space constraints preclude the use of conventional mechanical transmissions, the flexibility of installation of the hydrostatic drive system being of great advantage in such cases. The proven nature of more widely used mechanical, electrical or hydrodynamic systems, and the greater transmission efficiency of, in particular, mechanical transmission systems, has been considered more important that the advantage of flexibility of installation and potential low first cost of hydrostatic systems for use in passenger service rail vehicles, where constraints on equipment layout are not generally severe.

The advantages of a hydrostatic system are that, within the pressure limitations of the system, the full power of the prime mover can be transmitted continuously over the speed range of the vehicle. The mechanical systems currently in use operate at a number of discrete levels of transmission ratio and must accept a variable prime mover speed, with the corresponding variation in input power and efficiency, and periods, during gear changing, when no power is transmitted. A further advantage offered by hydrostatic systems is that as the hydrostatic machines are reversible, and can be used either as motors or as pumps, it is possible to use the drivemotors for vehicle braking duties. In its simplest form, the pressure produced by motor braking is destroyed by passing the fluid through a variable orifice transferring the kinetic energy of the vehicle into heat in the fluid, thus reducing wear on the vehicle's friction brakes. It would be feasible, however, to transfer the kinetic energy to some storage medium, such as a flywheel or pressure accumulator, for subsequent regeneration to traction energy when required. The potential for energy regeneration offered by a hydrostatic system could then offset its relatively low efficiency in its traction mode.

The high power-to-weight ratio of hydrostatic machines offers advantages of low unsprung mass on vehicles if an installation is used which eliminates the need for a conventional final drive gearbox. High unsprung mass is a major cause of track damage so its reduction is a considerable benefit. The use of standard production pumps and motors offers cost savings, compared with purpose built rail traction transmissions.

The main disadvantage of hydrostatic transmission systems against other mechanical systems is poor efficiency. Power losses occur due to internal fluid leakage past the moving components, pressure losses occur in the pipework and fittings between pumps and motors and energy is lost in compressing the fluid in the pump.

2 DEVELOPMENT OF "Hydra"

In 1979, following work by Volvo in Sweden, on the use of hydrostatic transmissions for high speed rail vehicles, a redundant double ended bogie railcar was converted by British Rail Research to form a test vehicle for the development of a hydrostatic transmission. Initially, only one of the two epicyclic gearbox transmissions was replaced by a hydrostatic system. This initial stage, together with the results of tests carried out, was reported in Ref 1. The results of this work had shown that, with a single 112 kW engine driving two 125 cc/rev pumps, feeding four 150 cc/rev motors mounted on the ends of the axles, rail speeds of 115 km/hr (72 mile/h) were possible. This was the speed at which the maximum fluid flow rate from the pump equated with the fluid flow of the motors and was considerably above the speed at which vehicle drag equated with the available tractive effort. Subsequent development work on the experimental vehicle "Hydra", and in laboratory tests, investigated various aspects of hydrostatic transmission systems, their control and total integration with other vehicle systems leading to the final development of the experimental vehicle as "Hydra 4".

3 "Hydra 4" - DESCRIPTION OF SYSTEMS

In its final form, "Hydra 4" (Fig 1) had two independant sets of power equipment. Each power system consisted of a 212 kW diesel engine driving a variable capacity swash plate pump of 250 cc/rev maximum capacity. On the same shaft were mounted one gear pump to provide boost pressure (to make up for internal leakage in the system) and to provide control pressure for the main traction pump, plus a second to provide a separate auxiliary supply of pressurised oil for operating the friction brakes and the engine and transmission cooling fans on the vehicle. All components which sense traction pressure were resiliently mounted from the vehicle to minimise noise transmission into the vehicle body. The transmission fluid passed through flexible pipes, to the adjacent bogie, where it drove four 150 cc/rev bent axis motors, mounted directly on the ends of the axles (Fig 2). Wheel diameter was 780 mm. Ignoring internal fluid leakage, an engine speed of 1900 rpm, at full pump displacement, equated to a vehicle speed of about 115 km/hr (72 mile/h) if all four motors were in use. Switching blocks on the bogies permitted individual motors to be switched out of circuit during traction and to freewheel whilst the remaining motors took the total pump flow, enabling the vehicle to run at higher speeds; up to a theoretical maximum of 227 km/hr (142 mile/h), vehicle drag permitting.

Fig 3 shows a simplified schematic arrangement of the traction system, the auxiliary system not being shown. For each direction of travel, one of the two freewheel valves was energised. This permitted oil pumped by the motors, during coasting or braking, to by-pass the pump. The freewheel arrangement also enabled the hydrostatic system to be used for braking. Passing the fluid through a variable orifice, thus building up a controlled pressure, applied a braking torque to the motors. During braking the kinetic energy of the vehicle raised the bulk temperature of the fluid, the heat then being dissipated to atmosphere either in the

transmission cooler or through heat loss from the pipework. To avoid its having to withstand the full traction pressure, the transmission cooler was placed in the leakage return line.

Conventional cast iron block brakes were also provided, applied by hydraulic brake actuators, on the bogies. The auxiliary pump on one of the two traction systems charged the brake pressure accumulators, from which a controlled pressure was passed to the actuators when braking was demanded. Either traction system could be selected manually for this purpose. In the case of an emergency application of the brakes a valve, by-passing the brake control valve, was opened and full brake accumulator pressure applied to the brake actuator. An automatic emergency application was also made if the brake accumulator pressure fell below the minimum pressure from which two full brake applications could be made.

4 CONTROL EQUIPMENT

4.1 Control Unit

Apart from emergency brake operation, all control of the vehicle in traction and braking was under the control of two microprocessor based control units, one for each traction system. These units were, effectively, independent, although sharing some input signals, with only a limited ability to communicate with each other during engine starting and braking. Each microprocessor unit received input signals from the driver, from its traction system and from some of the vehicle's other systems. Analogue input signals were preconditioned before conversion to digital signals in the control unit.

Output variables, from the control unit, were either digital signals which could be used directly or were analogue signals which had to be amplified before being passed to system control devices. The main analogue outputs were:-

demanded engine revs,
pump swash,
friction brake pressure, and
hydrostatic brake pressure,

For a vehicle designed to run in service, a microprocessor based control unit would be a totally closed unit, with all its control parameters and procedures fixed in the computer hardware. For an experimental vehicle, used for test and development purposes, it was necessary to try out different control parameters and procedures, to produce a record of the main transmission operating parameters and to interrogate the control computer in order to analyse problems. It was, therefore, necessary for the control unit to be a very much more open unit, with the control programs and parameters on EPROMs and with external connections to permit limited manual control of computer output signals.

4.2 Test Equipment

A micro-computer was used to interrogate the control microprocessors and to operate the data aquisition system. Fig 4 shows the equipment rack containing from top to bottom, No 1 microprocessor, the computer, No. 2 microprocessor, the disc drive unit for the computer and the data aquisition unit. Fig 5 shows the console, adjacent to the equipment rack, where test staff could observe operating parameters, on analogue gauges for clarity and rapid reading, and the state of digital signals by means of indicating lamps. Test buttons allowed some functions, such as engine starting, motor switching (over-riding the automatic control) and the emergency cancellation of all control functions to be operated from the same console from where test staff could keep in telephone contact with the driver.

4.3 Driver's Controls

The driving of "Hydra 4" was, primarily, by the operation of two levers, one on each side of the driver's control panel (Fig 6). The right hand lever selected the direction of travel, whilst the left hand selected the level of power or braking. No mechanical interlocks were provided, all such functions being undertaken by software in the control units. Operation of the direction selector whilst the vehicle was moving did not change the direction of travel but applied the brakes at a predetermined level; it was not possible to coast by selecting neutral. With the vehicle stationary, and the direction lever in neutral, pushing the power/braking lever forward simply increased engine speed without traction pressure.

By lifting the knob on top of the power/braking lever an emergency brake application could be made at any time. To permit starting on a gradient, a small friction brake demand was made, in parallel with the traction demand, until vehicle movement was detected.

5 CONTROL PROCEDURES

5.1 Power Control

The power control strategy on Hydra was to provide, for each combination of vehicle speed and driver's power demand, those values of engine speed and torque, pump swash angle, fluid system pressure and number of motors in circuit which were calculated to provide the best overall power train efficiency.

The level of traction power required was decoded by the control unit into 16 levels of demand. Vehicle speed was measured by timing pulses from toothed-wheel counters on the wheelsets and, for control purposes, converted to 32 equal steps from 0 to 160 kph. These two parameters were then used to find values from four look-up tables of the following variables:-

    demanded engine rpm,
    number of motors in circuit,
    system pressure, and
    initial pump swash angle.

The first three tables were read continuously whilst the fourth was only read on a change in power demand. The engine rpm demanded was sent directly to the engine governor, a separate analogue system to maintain engine rpm at the demanded level. The special software routine to undertake motor switching was only accessed if the number of motors read from the table had changed. The system pressure demand was used as the target figure by the main control loop in the software, whilst the initial swash value was only used following a change in demand or during switching. Pressure control was obtained by the control unit measuring the pressure in the traction system, calculating the rate of change of pressure and then, via a "fuzzy logic" control routine, an amended pump swash angle was determined and sent to the pump. In selecting which of its four motors to use at any instant, the control unit referred to a table, which it updated continually, of "motor damage". This contained factors relating to the theoretical level of damage each motor had received as a result of its operation. This selection routine was designed to equalise the wear suffered by each of the motors. The tables of parameters were calculated on a simulation computer to ensure that optimum efficiency was achieved over the whole operating range of the vehicle. It had been intended that the look-up tables would be amended by the control unit during operation in order to compensate for changes in component performance with time. In the event, however, it proved difficult to prevent the parameters becoming non-optimum and the project ended without this function performing satisfactorily.

5.2 Brake Control

As both friction and hydrostatic brakes were provided, the control unit had to co-ordinate their use so that maximum advantage was taken of the hydrostatic brake, to reduce wear on the friction brakes. Tests showed that, whereas the hydraulically operated friction brake was capable of stopping the vehicle within the BR specified distance (the "W-curve" of braking distance against initial speed) from any speed, the hydrostatic brake, although very effective at high speeds, only provided 60% of the required braking from 100 km/hr. In addition, the hydrostatic brake could only bring the vehicle to an absolute halt if reverse traction was applied because of fluid leakage. It was thus necessary to use a combination of both brakes for some or all of the stop. At all levels of braking, a minimum level of friction brake was applied, to ensure that slack in the linkage was taken up. The driver's brake demand was decoded into 26 levels of braking by the control unit. A look-up chart of three braking parameters was then accessed to determine the individual levels of friction and hydrostatic braking required. The three parameters were:-

    Friction brake level when operating alone,

    Hydrostatic brake level when combined with friction brake,

    Friction brake level when combined with hydrostatic brake.

Under normal circumstances, as the driver's brake demand increased to 60% of maximum, the hydrostatic brake pressure was increased proportionately up to the maximum value of 400 bar. If a higher demand was made an increasing friction brake pressure was applied, in addition to the hydrostatic brake. If the control unit detected, during the course of a brake application, that the required hydrostatic pressure had not been attained within a specified time, it automatically cancelled the hydrostatic brake and selected the value from the 'friction only' table. When vehicle speed fell to 30 km/hr braking was switched to the 'friction only' mode, for the final stop.

Fig 7 shows, graphically, the braking performance achievable, at full demand, with each of the three braking modes and compares this with the required "W-curve". Fig 8 shows the pressures at the friction brake actuators and in the hydrostatic brake for the various modes at different levels of demand.

5.3 Other Control Functions

The flexible nature of the microprocessor based control system was used to advantage by providing a number of control facilities which would have entailed considerable complexity and expense if applied to a conventional control system. An automated engine starting routine was incorporated. This was initiated by the driver inserting and turning his desk key, thereby switching on the vehicle control system and ensuring that the vehicle could only be driven from that cab. An engine cancel button was provided, for safety purposes, since otherwise the driver had no direct control of when the engine was running. Until the engine coolant temperature reached 25°C, the engine ran in "cold start" mode at an increased idling speed. Traction power could not be taken whilst the engine was in this mode.

Whenever the driver wished to maintain a steady speed, pressing a button on the control desk put the vehicle control into 'Speed Hold' mode. In this mode, the control unit held the vehicle speed, within limits to the speed at which the button was pressed. Any subsequent movement of the driver's controls automatically returned operations to normal.

The use of a digital microprocessor based control system brought wide ranging possibilities, not only in the provision of control and interlock functions within the software but also in the development of routines and hardware and adjustment of variables. Variations in timings, values of parameters at which actions should be initiated and to which they should be controlled, could be easily tried out by a few key strokes on the control panel.

6 OPERATING EXPERIENCE

6.1 General Experience

As "Hydra 4" was an experimental vehicle, containing data recording, laboratory and workshop facilities, and could only run as a single vehicle, there was no intention of operating it in commercial service. The aim of the project was to develop the system first and then to investigate its viability by running the maximum distance possible within the limits of the timescale allotted to the project. Delays in commissioning the vehicle, most of which related to neither the hydrostatic transmission nor to the microprocessor part of the control system, postponed the start of endurance running, reducing the total mileage below the 75 000 km (47 000 miles) that had been intended. In total, "Hydra 4" covered about 42 500 km (26 600 miles) of which 25 600 km (16 000 miles) represented main line running, at speeds up to 150 km/hr (94 mile/h), on the Derby to London main line between September 1984 and March 1985.

6.2 Performance

For the single 34 tonne railcar, a balancing speed on level track of 142 km/hr (88 mile/h) was obtained, this being close to calculated predictions. On the dedicated BR test track at Old Dalby, Nottinghamshire, a maximum speed of 163 km/hr (102 mile/h) was achieved. This is believed to be a world speed record for a hydrostatically propelled vehicle. Whilst running between London and Derby, on non stop runs at a scheduled average speed of 121 kph (75 mile/h), an overall fuel consumption of 1.5 litres/km (4.3 mpg) was obtained. Transmission efficiency on full power at about 130 kph (80 mile/h) was 78 to 80%.

Control of the vehicle was excellent, at all running speeds and levels of traction demand. There were occasional periods of pressure instability on one of the two traction systems, particularly at the start of a journey. This fault is believed to have been the result of damage to the pump swash plate, caused by overpressure, but there was insufficient time to explore and correct the fault. Some problems occurred due to erosion and wear on the port plates of the motors, causing increased internal fluid leakage in the motors. When the leakage rate of the four motors, at high system pressure, exceeded the capacity of the boost pump to make up the fluid loss, boost pressure fell and control of the pump swash plate was lost, also resulting in poor pressure stability.

Although the timescale available did not permit a full analysis and rectification of these two problems there is no reason to suppose that they could not have been cured. Occasional short term malfunctions of the control system occurred but these were overcome by resetting the controls and repeating the required control action. The open nature of a development microprocessor control system made it more vulnerable to external effects than a fully developed, totally sealed, production system. It is believed that most, if not all, of the unexplained random control faults were caused by electrical interference from systems within the vehicle.

Motor switching took place automatically, when required by the control program, with no noticeable surge of traction being sensed inside the vehicle. This was as expected since there was no change in engine rpm or traction thrust during switching. Braking performance and control was excellent, both when using the friction brake alone and when using the combined friction and hydrostatic brake. The hydrostatic brake was very smooth in operation and the automatic changeover to friction brake alone, at 30 km/hr, was only detectable by the momentary flick of the pressure gauges, with no noticeable change in the braking retardation. A temperature increase of 35°C had been predicted in the trasmission fluid during braking. The measured value was only 15°C when stopping from 140 km/hr. The discrepancy being caused by a very much greater heat dissipation from the system and a higher thermal capacity than had been predicted.

The simple layout of the driver's desk and automatic control functions, such as the speed hold function, were much appreciated by the drivers who operated the vehicle during its trials.

7 CONCLUSIONS

Development, testing and endurance running with the experimental vehicle 'Hydra 4" have shown clearly that a hydrostatic transmission system is fully feasible for a medium performance passenger railcar. However, the relatively poor transmission efficiency does not make the system an attractive option if installation constraints permit more efficient mechanical systems to be used. To make best use of the hydrostatic system, it was necessary to use a microprocessor based system to control the total engine and transmission package. The use of this system was extended to control vehicle braking and to provide a number of control functions which would have entailed additional expense and complication if a conventional control system had been used.

Operation of the vehicle showed clearly the advantages to be gained by the use of a total microprocessor control system; namely:-

flexibility of control system,

ability to control all components of the power train, for optimum efficiency,

simplicity of control system interlocking,

ability to add additional control functions, without additional control hardware,

ability, during development stage, to investigate varying control system parameters, by making alterations to the software.

REFERENCE

(1) TUNLEY, J.D. and Preston, K.E., A Hydrostatic Transmission for a Railway Passenger Vehicle. I Mech E 0155/81.

Fig 1   Hydra 4

Fig 2   Axle end motor arrangement

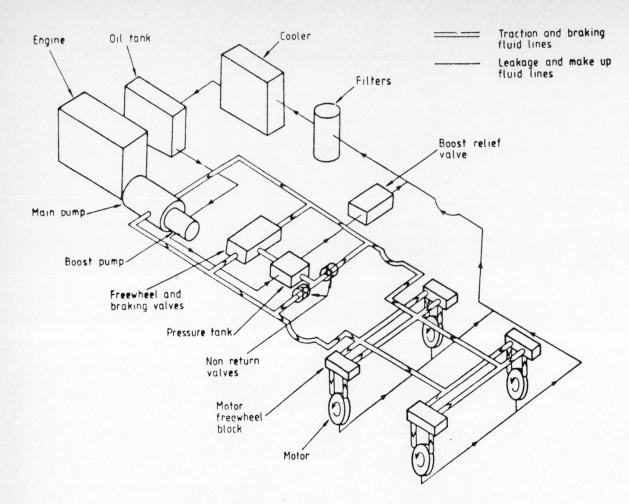

Fig 3   Simplified arrangement of power equipment (one end of vehicle)

Fig 4   Microprocessor computing and data acquisition
         equipment

Fig 5   Control console

Fig 6　Driver's controls

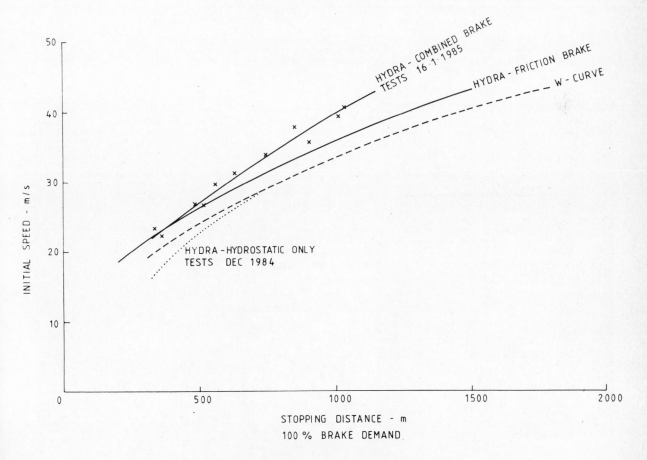

STOPPING DISTANCE – m

100 % BRAKE DEMAND

Fig 7　Hydra – brake performance

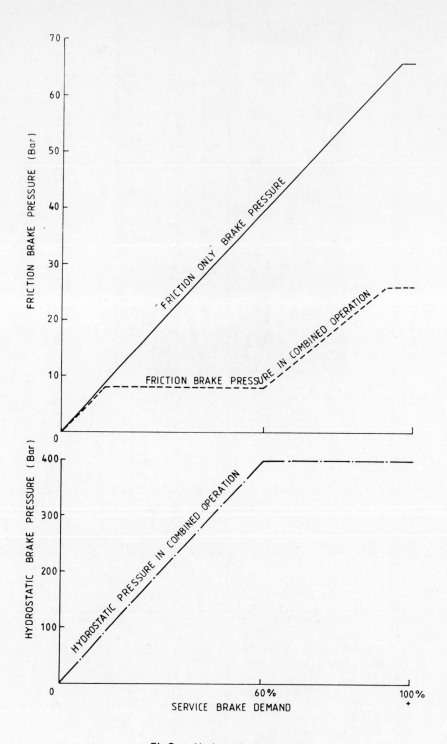

Fig 8   Hydra — brake pressures

32

C198/86

Interactive powertrain controls

J J MAIN, BTech
Ford Motor Company Limited, Basildon, Essex

SYNOPSIS   A combination of an advanced, highly controllable engine and an electronically controlled belt type CVT (Continuously Variable Transmission) formed the basis of a powertrain system for the Ford ELTEC (ELectronic TEChnology) vehicle.   A powerful automotive microprocessor was used to operate a comprehensive interactive control strategy intended to improve driveability and fuel economy within forthcoming emissions constraints.

A number of novel control features, such as comprehensive inlet port controls, ionisation feedback control, throttle control and transmission ratio and line pressure controls have been developed and their individual worth assessed.   Particular attention has been paid to the dynamic performance of the system.

A plan for future developments has been evolved to reduce hardware costs and further improve vehicle driveability and economy.

1.   INTRODUCTION

The critical current and future European requirements for a reduction in exhaust emissions whilst maintaining or improving current levels of fuel economy, vehicle performance and driveability have faced the powertrain designer with a difficult task.   The use of a lean burn engine operating with a continuously variable transmission under interactive microprocessor control is a way of meeting these conflicting requirements at an affordable cost.   The Ford ELTEC (ELectronic TEChnology) vehicle was built with such a powertrain and control system.

The Ford CTX belt type transmission was chosen and was matched with a unique all aluminium 1300cc engine which was designed to maximise the advantage of the continuously variable transmission.

Microprocessor control systems offer a more precise, reliable and comprehensive control of powertrains than their mechanical predecessors. By combining the control of both engine and transmission into the same microprocessor a reduction in hardware and software complexity is realised as duplication is avoided.   It also allows direct interaction between the two software strategies resulting in a further improvement in driveability and fuel economy.

The powertrain efficiency is enhanced by the inclusion of combustion feedback control and comprehensive management of the engine intake including an electronic throttle.

A schematic of the control system is shown in Figure 1.   The main control features are described later in the paper.

2.   POWERTRAIN DESCRIPTION

The 4 cylinder 1.3 litre all aluminium engine was specially designed to be as compact and light as possible, to have low engine friction, and to have high performance and low emissions throughout the engine speed range by the use of fast, lean burn combustion.   It develops 60kw DIN at 5000rpm and has a maximum torque of 125Nm.

As the engine has to operate at high loads and low speeds for good fuel economy, a rigid bedplate design was used with direct connection to the transmission to ensure maximum stiffness and so minimise noise and vibration.   Friction, noise and cost were reduced by the use of a 4-main bearing crankshaft and a single overhead chain driven camshaft operating within a lightweight valve train.   Twelve valves – 2 inlet and 1 exhaust per cylinder – were chosen for good gas flow characteristics for peak power and to allow an optimum spark plug position for good part load economy.   It also permits a comprehensive control of the intake charge which is described under 'Engine Intake'.

The potential of continuously variable transmissions (CVTs) to provide fuel economy and functional advantages over conventional stepped ratio transmissions (both automatic and manual selection) is well recognised (1), (2), (3), (4), (5), (6).   As the vehicle design dictated a front wheel drive layout the choice of transmission fell naturally to the Ford CTX (continuously variable transaxle) shown in Figure 2.   Apart from efficient packaging for fwd this belt type CVT offers high efficiencies (maximum of 92%) and a ratio range of 5.5:1 for the 125Nm torque capacity version used.   Pull away from rest is arranged by multi plate wet clutches and an epicyclic gearset provides reverse gear.

The CVT can be described in control terms as no more than an engine speed controller allowing any point in the engine operating map to be selected within the overall ratio constraints. The closed loop electronic control of ratio, described in detail later, is used to ensure that the most efficient parts of the operating map are always used and so the engine design has concentrated on further efficiency improvements in these specific areas. The more difficult to achieve control of torque is not necessary as the transmission does not have a geared neutral and the associated pullaway feel issues.

The CVT is also able to limit the maximum engine speed to that corresponding to maximum power output. There is no need to exceed this speed with a CVT and consequently greatly reduced valve spring loads are possible resulting in lower engine friction and improved specific fuel consumption (sfc).

3. MICROPROCESSOR SYSTEM

In recent years Ford Motor Company and the Intel Corporation have joined forces to develop a series of advanced powertrain controllers. This effort has culminated in the production of the highly sophisticated EEC IV system.

EEC IV is based on 16-bit architecture but it is able to operate in 8-bit mode for improved speed or 32-bit for arithmetic accuracy. A 15MHz clock permits high speed of program operation and precise resolution of timed events which can be measured to the nearest 2.4 microseconds. This translates, for example, to less than 0.1° crankshaft rotation at 6000 engine rpm.

The EEC IV is a two chip system with all the computing and input/output (I/O) being handled in the 8061 microprocessor chip whilst the software instruction (ROM) and calculation results (RAM) are held in the 8361 memory chip. An eleven line memory bus (8 data, 3 control) provides the interface between the two chips. A total of 41 I/O lines are available including 13 analogue inputs with 10 bit accuracy. 64K of memory is addressable but the system as described occupied less than 16K.

All software is written in machine code for maximum program efficiency in terms of total software size and operating speed. A mainframe software development system is employed which has been developed with particular attention to ease of program calibration.

Calibration is further eased by use of the in-vehicle Calibration Console which allows the engineer to alter the program data, in engineering units, whilst performing in-car tests - for example on emission rolls. Initial software strategy development was carried out in the laboratory using the target system which was connected to a vehicle simulator. This is monitored by an Engineering Console which allows real-time tracing of program logic and modifications to the programs without recourse to the mainframe assembler so allowing rapid and safe software development.

In car development of sophisticated multi variable control systems requires a rapid data logging facility to allow later analysis of actual parameters calculated in real time. To assist this a Tandy TRS80 Model 100 desk top computer was programmed to log eight variables (word or byte long) which were communicated via an RS232 link from the calibration console. At first the data logging program was written in Basic for speed of program writing but this resulted in sampling times of 500ms. This was too slow for some tasks as the EEC IV background loop time was typically 20ms for the complete ELTEC program. To improve this the data logging program was re-written in machine code giving vastly improved sampling times of typically 40ms.

To further aid and speed program development (in total it only took 18 months) an in car multi colour plotter was used so allowing the engineers to plot results immediately after a test and clearly identify the effect of their calibration changes. The plotter also acted as a printer to provide a hard copy of the data collected.

4. CONTROL FEATURES

4.1 General

All the basic engine controls - spark advance, fuel injection, exhaust gas recirculation and idle speed - are operated from the EEC IV microprocessor. The engine speed is measured by an eddy current sensor observing vanes fitted to the flywheel to minimise mechanical inaccuracies such as backlash and wind up typical in distributor drives. Intake air flow is measured to represent engine load and the temperatures of the incoming air and coolant water are also measured.

The ignition high tension is supplied by two coils to avoid the necessity of mechanical distribution - the timing being supplied by the EEC IV from a 3D-map.

Fuel supply is by multipoint injectors located close to the inlet valves to minimise delay, and wall wetting.

Exhaust gas recirculation is necessary to reduce NOx emissions while a fuel economy gain can be realised by accurate control of the engine idle speed.

4.2 Ionisation Feedback Control

The electronic control of fuel and spark have permitted a much tighter control over the in cylinder combustion. Developing with this accuracy of control has been computer derived calibration in the form of engine mapping (7), (8). This permits the very accurate calibration of a test engine running in a very carefully controlled environment. However, this does not allow for the variation of engine builds from a production line. Also it is not possible to test for optimum settings for various fuel qualities and ambient conditions that will be found while the engine is in service. Also as the engine wears it would require complete recalibration to be kept running at its optimum for emissions, driveability, performance and economy. Ionisation feedback control is intended to allow the on board microprocessor to adjust the open loop calibration to suit the engine and its environment at any point from just leaving the production line right through its working life.

© IMechE 1986 C198/86

The system relies on in-cylinder sensors which detect the ionisation front associated with the flame front. The sensor, which has to be positioned very carefully in relation to the spark plug, has a dc bias applied. As the flame propagates from the spark plug it causes the applied voltage to flow to the cylinder head. This instantaneous current is monitored and at set threshholds of current and rate of change of current a signal is sent to the microprocessor which calculates the current crankshaft angle. The angle is then used in two ways.

Firstly, an average is taken of successive arrival angles and is compared to a target arrival angle table which has been produced under ideal conditions. The error signal is then used to calculate a correction for the next open loop spark advance angle.

Secondly, the average scatter of the arrival angle is calculated for use in a similar manner to the arrival angle but in this case to control the fuel injection period.

The system is not intended to replace the normal open loop spark and fuel maps but effectively to change the datum by the application of modifiers. Because a number of cycles are necessary to determine the average arrival angle and a greater number for calculating the average scatter, transients cannot be handled. The values calculated during transients are ignored because of the effect of acceleration fuel enrichment, deceleration fuel cut off etc and only values calculated during steady state running are used. This is not a disadvantage of the system because transients will always be handled fastest with open loop control which is not error driven. It is only intended to use this system to allow for open loop calibration datum shift and hence allow the production engine, throughout its service life, to work as well as the test engine on its carefully controlled dynomometer.

4.3 Engine Intake

Lean burn engines require accurate control of both intake charge velocity and swirl to achieve optimum combustion with the EGR enleaned mixture - in particular at low engine speeds and loads.

This accurate control can be achieved by operating a swirl control vane in the inlet port so providing the optimum in-cylinder motion with the resultant reduction in emissions and fuel consumption. This system has the disadvantage of restricting intake flow at high engine speeds so limiting maximum engine power. As good vehicle performance will remain a priority in the market place it is not acceptable to achieve low speed efficiency at the expense of reduced maximum power so a dual characteristic must be achieved. This has been accomplished by having two inlet valves, each with its own inlet port whose flow characteristic is controlled from the EEC IV.

Figure 3 shows the layout of the system for one cylinder. The intake is shown dividing into two ports which are labelled 'primary' and 'secondary'. The secondary port is only opened during high power requirements and otherwise is closed off by the deactivation plate. The primary port flow is modulated by the swirl vane.

Vacuum motors, supplied by manifold vacuum which is controlled by variable force solenoids are used to operate the vanes. A single output from the EEC IV is used to signal both solenoids. A duty cycle (mark space ratio) output is varied between 5% and 75% for the proportional control of the swirl vanes. Switching from 75% to 95% opens the secondary port with the swirl vane remaining fully open.

Figure 4 shows the effect of these controls on specific fuel consumption. The contours have been both enlarged and moved towards the low torque, low speed region which is critical for urban driving. This ensures that a greater percentage of any journey can be conducted at or near to the most fuel efficient region for the engine.

Engine operating characteristics are further modified and optimised with a variable geometry intake manifold. It is well recognised that inlet tract length can be chosen to optimise the torque curve over a narrow engine speed range. By arranging a long intake length (for low rpm torque) with a break at a shorter length which can be opened or closed by sliding sleeves, a dual characteristic is achieved.

Figure 5 shows the system used in ELTEC. For low speed running the sliding sleeve shown in the rear plenum is held in the closed position so the effective intake length is the full 745mm to the forward plenum. At high engine speeds the sleeve, which is activated by a vacuum motor similar to that for the port deactivation and variable swirl blades, is released and so allowed to open giving an effective intake length of 460mm to the rear plenum. The vacuum motor is switched at 4100 rpm which is the point at which the torque curves for the two intake lengths crossover as shown in Figure 6, so giving a clear torque enhancement over a wide speed range without a torque step at switchover.

4.4 Transmission

The optimised engine characteristic described above is used to its full potential by the CTX transmission. The two shift schedules, which can be selected by the driver with a switch on the gear selector, are shown in Figure 7.

The Economy schedule passes through the minimum sfc contours giving optimum fuel economy for the performance demanded by the driver up to a set limit at 4200 rpm. The excess torque available for acceleration of powertrain inertia between the economy line and the maximum torque line is small. For rapid transients and peak performance a second schedule is defined which passes through points below the economy line on the engine torque map giving greater excess torque available for rapid response to driver requirements and ending at maximum engine speed for maximum power and so vehicle performance and speed.

Figure 8 shows the transmission ratio diagram for the CTX. The road load line is shown on the left hand side with clutch engagement at 1400 rpm and then vehicle and engine speed increasing along the low ratio line until the minimum control speed is reached. The ratio is then increased at constant engine speed until the high ratio line which is followed until the ratio has to be reduced to reach maximum speed. The two right hand lines are for full throttle performance for the Performance and Economy modes. Clutch engagement is completed at 2200 rpm and for Performance low ratio is held until 4800 rpm when ratio changing commences and then peak power speed is held to provide maximum performance. In Economy the performance is suppressed by commencing ratio changing at 3000 rpm and then allowing the engine speed to increase with vehicle speed to a maximum of 4200 rpm. This strategy gives the driver a good performance 'feel' but lower levels of performance and top speed. For emergency situations when the pedal is pushed quickly this suppression of performance is switched off and maximum power is made available.

A further refinement is necessary during vehicle decelerations where the driver feels that as he reduces pedal position in the economy mode the subsequent increasing transmission ratio and the engine inertia effect either accelerate the vehicle or reduce engine braking to negligible levels. Two actions are taken to reduce this feeling. Firstly with reducing throttle at speed the ratio is not immediately increased and secondly, if the brake pedal is touched the minimum engine speed is increased so providing increased engine braking. These actions do result in small increases in fuel consumption but they make the Economy schedule more acceptable to the driver and it is therefore more likely to be selected.

A second level of transmission control is used to set the line pressure which is used to provide the belt clamping force. It is essential for this type of transmission that the belt is not allowed to slip but conversely too high a clamping force results in higher friction and so reduced efficiency. With hydraulic logic the line pressure is controlled with a relatively wide safety margin due to the system of engine speed measurement (pitot tube) and torque vs throttle relationship (cable operated cam) which assumes a constant relationship across the speed range. A much finer control can be exerted from the EEC IV with subsequent benefits in efficiency and therefore fuel economy.

4.5 Electronic Throttle

Mechanical connection between the accelerator pedal and the engine throttle plate has been dispensed with. Instead the pedal now simply moves a potentiometer which indicates the drivers demand to the central processor (it also allows ideal pedal efforts to be chosen). An integrated throttle body and dc motor with feedback potentiometer was designed to give maximum speed and accuracy to allow a wide range of control strategies to be implemented without hardware constraints. A lower cost and more readily implemented approach would have been to use a conventional throttle body with an external link to a dc motor, but this was rejected as it has inherently lower resolution and speed due to the higher mechanical friction and return spring loads.

The two main purposes of the electronic throttle are described under 'Anti Spin Control' and 'Engine Transmission Control Interactions' but a number of secondary advantages can be realised.

In the conventional engine control it is normal to provide extra fuel during increasing throttle to provide for wall wetting - this is often known as acceleration enrichment. By damping small throttle movements it has been possible to reduce the amount of fuel used in this manner. Similarly it is used to prevent excessive powertrain movement caused by excessive rate of change of throttle at low speed (often called 'tip in' and 'back out').

Idle speed control is possible from the electronic throttle so allowing deletion of the idle by-pass valve.

The electronic throttle is also ideal for a sophisticated 'cruise control' which can provide an economical and accurate control of vehicle speed.

4.6 Engine Transmission Control Interactions

The mechanical design described above gives the basic characteristic of the powertrain, both components of which have been optimised to suit the other to give a truly integrated powertrain design. The gains reaped by having the control from a single microprocessor are reduced hardware complexity and deletion of software duplication. Associated with reduction of hardware must be improvement of reliability and cost reduction. Having a single software listing means that calculated values are immediately shared and do not have to be communicated between modules or recalculated. Also calibration changes are automatically shared for both engine and transmission controls. These advantages can be placed under the heading 'integrated powertrain controls'. Further gains are made if the engine and transmission control strategies interact.

A central part of the interactive strategy is the electronic throttle which allows the EEC IV to decide the best combination of throttle opening and engine speed (by means of ratio control) as well as all other engine parameters to satisfy this driver demand in the most efficient manner.

The Performance or Economy select switch, which conventionally only affects the transmission strategy, has been extended to affect the pedal angle vs throttle angle relationship so allowing the ideal relationship between pedal position and vehicle performance for both modes. This is particularly useful for the economy mode where the relationship between throttle angle and vehicle performance is very non-linear. It also allows the performance line to be defined much closer to the economy line.

The electronic throttle allows compensation for one of the problems that is encountered with a CVT during transients. Take the case when the vehicle has been operating at steady speed for a period with the optimum settings selected. The driver then decides to accelerate and indicates this by pressing the pedal further. The conventional system will proportionally open the throttle and decrease transmission ratio to allow greater engine power on the transmission schedule line. By decreasing the ratio it is necessary to accelerate the powertrain inertia which delays the acceleration of the vehicle. This is particularly noticeable with an economy schedule where the engine will be running at low speed and makes the car feel unresponsive and gives low customer acceptance.

The most obvious solution is to compromise the economy strategy by increasing the engine speed and throttling the engine more which improves driveability but worsens fuel consumption. The electronic throttle allows an alternative approach by imposing independent modulation of the throttle position to compensate for the powertrain inertia. This permits a true economy schedule to be used and fully acceptable to the driver at a small cost in fuel economy during transients.

This demonstrates the way in which a more optimum system is possible if the engine and transmission control interacts to take account of each others limitations. Another example is anti spin control.

4.7 Anti Spin Control

Much work has been performed on the application of control systems to brakes to avoid wheels locking and the consequent loss of steering control. There is an equivalent loss of control during wheel spin which occurs due to loss of adhesion during acceleration or on encountering low friction surfaces such as snow.

ELTEC has been designed with a comprehensive system for wheel spin control closely linked to, and using the wheel speed sensors for, the anti-lock braking system.

To maximise the use of the traction available the driven wheel speeds are equalised by applying brake pressure to the fastest spinning side - acting as an intelligent limited slip differential. In parallel to this the wheel torque is reduced by controlling a combination of spark angle, throttle angle and transmission ratio. At perception of wheelspin the spark angle is reduced to zero for a rapid reduction of torque, while the throttle angle is controlled by a PID closed loop on spin speed providing the majority of control, but with a delay associated mainly with the engine intake volume. The transmission ratio is the slowest to respond but is used to desensitise the throttle control on very low grip surfaces by selecting a higher ratio. An in depth computer simulation study was performed to optimise the anti spin control system resulting in wheel spin being controlled in less than 1.5 seconds even in the most severe circumstances.

5. FUTURE PLANS

Future work will concentrate on methods of cost reduction for the ELTEC system. For example recent testing has shown that the idle speed by-pass valve can be deleted as the electronic throttle has sufficient resolution to achieve idle speed control.

The worth of inlet port controls has been demonstrated but the gain which is achieved by port deactivation is much greater than that for variable swirl with the layout as shown. A production system would almost certainly have only one such control and for this engine it would be port deactivation - thus requiring a simple low speed logic output from the microprocessor and an on-off vacuum switch.

Ionisation sensing has been achieved in each cylinder - this allows the optimum system with rapid data update or individual cylinder corrections but naturally at a cost penalty. For production two cylinder sensing is likely so giving an averaged correction with medium rate of update.

The transmission control will be extended from ratio and line pressure to include clutch pressure control by the addition of a third variable force solenoid. This will be used to give modified engagement characteristic for the P and E modes so ensuring consistency of driveability 'feel' throughout the speed range. It will also be used to alter the clutch characteristic when the engine is cold to avoid excessive clutch drag and engine 'stumble'.

6. CONCLUSIONS

The ELTEC car and a standard Escort fitted with the ELTEC powertrain have been built and used for dyno roll and on-track testing and evaluation.

The powertrain and control system described have resulted in lower total exhaust emissions without treatment of the exhaust gas and very low NOx emissions making it possible to operate without a catalyst in most European countries and only requiring a low cost oxidation catalyst for the most stringent emission levels.

Fuel economy has not been compromised as is demonstrated by the 5.5l/100km achieved over a mixed city and highway route. The European motoring press have driven the cars on both the open road and test track achieving a top speed in excess of 160 kph and 0-100 kph in less than 13 seconds in a hand built car weighing 200kg more than the weight predicted for a production version.

This confirms that lean burn engines, and continuously variable transmissions working under interactive microprocessor control offer a more optimum balance between emissions, fuel economy, driveability and performance. Also the potential is created to integrate other features such as cruise control and anti spin control at a low incremental cost.

REFERENCES

(1) KRAUS, JH KRAUS, CE GRES, ME A continuously Variable Transmission for Automotive Fuel Economy.   SAE Paper 751180
(2) BAUDOIN, P Continuously Variable Transmission for Cars with High Ratio Coverage
          SAE Paper 790041
(3) CHAN, C et al System Design and Control Considerations of Automotive Continuously Variable Transmissions   SAE Paper 840048
(4) STUBBS, PWR The Development of a Perbury Traction Transmission for Motor Car Applications.   ASME Paper 80-C2/DET-59
          August 1980
(5) IRONSIDE, JM STUBBS PWR Continuously Variable Transmission Control. IEEE Paper
          80CH1601-4 (B-43) September 1980
(6) ADVISORY COUNCIL ON ENERGY CONSERVATION Department of Energy 1977   Paper No.18
(7) BAKER, RE DABY, E Engine Mapping Methodology   SAE Paper 770077
(8) GANESAN, V IVENS, J Engine Mapping - an Update for Europe   FISITA 1980

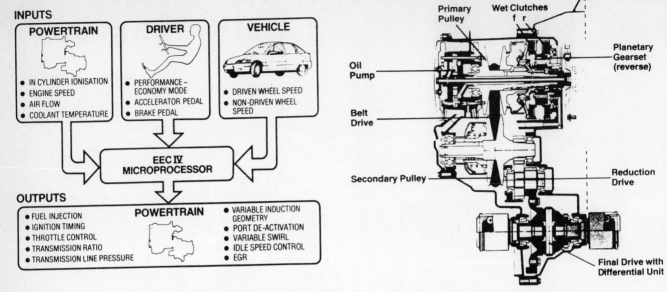

INPUTS

POWERTRAIN	DRIVER	VEHICLE
• IN CYLINDER IONISATION • ENGINE SPEED • AIR FLOW • COOLANT TEMPERATURE	• PERFORMANCE – ECONOMY MODE • ACCELERATOR PEDAL • BRAKE PEDAL	• DRIVEN WHEEL SPEED • NON-DRIVEN WHEEL SPEED

EEC IV MICROPROCESSOR

OUTPUTS

POWERTRAIN

• FUEL INJECTION
• IGNITION TIMING
• THROTTLE CONTROL
• TRANSMISSION RATIO
• TRANSMISSION LINE PRESSURE

• VARIABLE INDUCTION GEOMETRY
• PORT DE-ACTIVATION
• VARIABLE SWIRL
• IDLE SPEED CONTROL
• EGR

Fig 1   Schematic of control system

Fig 2   Ford CTX transmission

Primary Pulley — Wet Clutches f r — Planetary Gearset (reverse) — Oil Pump — Belt Drive — Secondary Pulley — Reduction Drive — Final Drive with Differential Unit

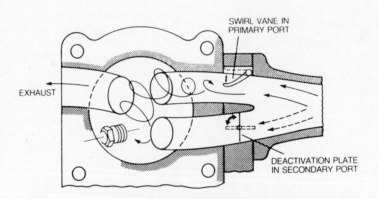

SWIRL VANE IN PRIMARY PORT

EXHAUST

DEACTIVATION PLATE IN SECONDARY PORT

Fig 3   Intake port controls

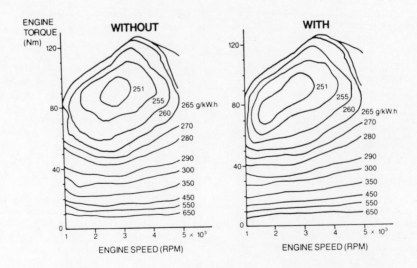

ENGINE TORQUE (Nm)

WITHOUT   WITH

251   255   260   265 g/kW.h
270   280   290   300   350   450   550   650

ENGINE SPEED (RPM)

Fig 4   Effect of port controls on specific fuel consumption

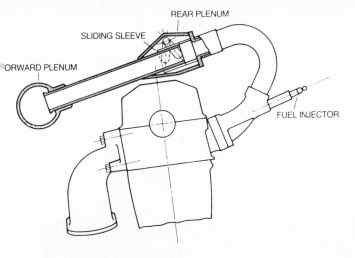

Fig 5   Variable geometry induction

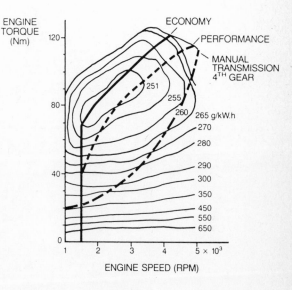

Fig 7   Transmission shift schedules

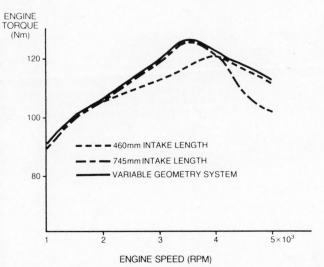

Fig 6   Effect of variable geometry induction on torque

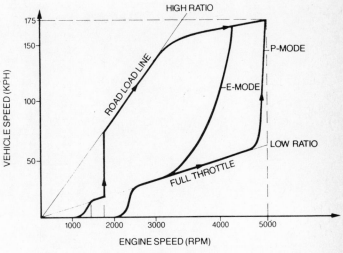

Fig 8   Transmission ratio diagram

C200/86

Modelling and simulation of an automotive powertrain incorporating a Perbury continuosly variable transmission

R P JONES, I F KURIGER and M T G HUGHES
Department of Engineering, University of Warwick
M J HOLT and J M IRONSIDE
Lucas Research Centre, Solihull, Warwickshire
P A LANGLEY
B L Technology, Lighthorne, Warwick

SYNOPSIS This paper is concerned with the development of a computer simulation model of an automotive powertrain incorporating a Perbury traction continuously variable transmission (CVT). The model has been developed for use in the design and evaluation of engine/transmission control strategies and the matching of control system and powertrain components. The paper discusses the conceptual and theoretical basis of the powertrain model together with the experimental work necessary to provide data for incorporation into the model. Consideration is given to the computer implementation of the simulation model, specifically, in relation to the use of the ACSL high level simulation language embedded within a special purpose computer aided modelling and simulation environment. Finally, the paper includes illustrative results derived from simulation studies and vehicle experiments.

NOTATION

ω_F engine flywheel speed (rad s^{-1})

T_q gross engine torque (Nm)

J_F effective inertia at engine flywheel (kg m^2)

T_c compliant torque in engine-transmission coupling (Nm)

ϕ throttle angle (deg)

ω_I transmission input shaft speed (s^{-1})

J_B effective inertia of engine block on mountings (kg m^2)

J_T effective inertia of transmission on mountings (kg m^2)

ω_B rotational velocity of engine block on mountings (rad s^{-1})

T_B compliant torque in engine-transmission mountings (Nm)

T_I torque at transmission input shaft (Nm)

T_V torque at transmission output shaft (Nm)

J_I effective inertia of transmission input components (kg m^2)

J_o effective inertia of transmission output components (kg m^2)

r_p Perbury transmission ratio

i_A ratio control signal current (A)

ω_o transmission output shaft speed (rad s^{-1})

v vehicle velocity (m s^{-1})

M vehicle mass (kg)

F_V tractive effort (N)

F_L road load (N)

F_B braking force (N)

θ aggregate angular deflection in drive-line (rad)

r_V effective driving radius (wheel radius/final drive) (m)

k, β aggregated stiffness and damping of vehicle model

a, b, c parameters of vehicle road load model

1. INTRODUCTION

The application of electronics in the management and control of automotive vehicle functions has become widespread within the past few years (1,2). Initial developments were, almost exclusively, concerned with electronic engine management systems but, lately, this initial emphasis has broadened to include the electronic control of transmissions, thereby facilitating the trend towards integrated control of the total powertrain. Examples include the microcomputer control of a CVT in an automobile (3) and, more recently, the microprocessor control of HGV transmissions (4,5).

The introduction of electronic transmission control into automotive vehicles has fundamental implications for the approach to powertrain development, due to the added scope for complex interactions between the engine, transmission and vehicle dynamics. With such advanced systems it is clearly important that the powertrain be considered as a whole, since separation of the design of engine management and transmission control systems is unlikely to yield controls that provide for optimum driveability; nor is it likely to exploit, fully, the potential for fuel economy and performance. This is true, both in the design and evaluation of engine and transmission control systems, and in the selection and matching of engine, transmission and vehicle components (6).

Advanced automotive powertrains (7), incorporating electronic transmission control and/or engine management, can be considered to consist of three basic interacting subsystems, viz. engine, transmission and vehicle, which are controlled by an electronic control system under the overall supervision of a driver. The general configuration consists of a three level hierarchy and is illustrated in figure 1. The individual powertrain subsystems are inherently complex, displaying characteristics which, in systems terms, are multivariable and/or nonlinear. Furthermore, the frequencies associated with the dynamics of individual subsystems, typically, vary from 0.1 Hz and below, to 300 Hz and above, and result in an overall system which, in systems terms, is described as stiff.

It is evident that the development of advanced powertrains requires the availability of design techniques which enable the whole powertrain to be addressed as a complete dynamic system. Furthermore, in view of the inherent complexity in automotive powertrains, there is a clear need for the availability of computational aids to facilitate the formulation and evaluation of powertrain control strategies and the subsequent optimisation of overall powertrain system performance (7). Computer based modelling and simulation is a useful tool which is widely used to address related problems in other applications areas, e.g. aerospace and process control, and which is finding increasing application in the development of automotive powertrains, and in the analysis and control of the interacting subsystems (6,8).

This paper discusses the application of computer based modelling and simulation to a road vehicle incorporating electronic control of a continuously variable transmission (CVT). It is specifically concerned with the construction of computer simulation models for use in control studies and fuel consumption prediction. The computer simulation is formulated on the basis of a disciplined and systematic approach to the modelling of complete automotive powertrains, involving concepts and theoretical ideas together with experimental work to provide data for incorporation into the model. In particular, the simulation model has been developed via an incremental, modular approach, resulting in a set of distinct powertrain modules, corresponding to the individual powertrain subsystems highlighted in figure 1, for exercising as an integrated powertrain simulation within a special purpose computer aided modelling and simulation environment (6,7,9).

2. CVT POWERTRAIN MODEL

2.1 Aim and Scope

This paper describes the application of computer based modelling and simulation to control and fuel consumption studies related to a vehicle equipped with a continuously variable transmission (7). The basis for the study was an experimental vehicle, incorporating a Perbury traction transmission (13) developed by BL Technology Ltd., and an electronic controller which was developed by Lucas Research Centre. The modelling and simulation work reported here was aimed at identifying the experimental and conceptual background required to support the construction and use of computer simulation models in the development of electronic control systems for CVT powertrains. In view of this, the scope of the simulation model was restricted, initially, to include powertrain phenomena in the frequency range 0 - 10 Hz.

Simulation models were developed to provide tools for:

(i) analysis of responses to control inputs, arising from the complex interactions within the powertrain;

(ii) prediction of the fuel consumption performance of the vehicle over specific driving schedules.

A schematic overview, providing a conceptual description of the CVT powertrain model, is given in figure 2. The model was constructed in an incremental, modular manner; whereby distinct modules, representing the individual powertrain subsystems highlighted in figure 1, were developed and tested independently, prior to being assembled into a complete powertrain simulation.

2.2 Engine

The engine module represents the dynamics of the engine block and flywheel in terms of the response in block movement and flywheel speed to variations in throttle position and driveline torque. The dynamics associated with the fuelling/combustion process and the cyclic nature of torque production are neglected, as their associated frequencies are beyond the initial range of interest.

The engine flywheel and mounting dynamics are represented by equations of the form

$$J_F \, \omega_F = T_G(\phi, \omega_F) - T_C(\omega_F, \omega_I) \qquad (1)$$

$$[J_B + J_T]\dot{\omega}_B = T_G(\phi, \omega_F) - T_B(\omega_B) \qquad (2)$$

where the engine gross torque T_G is based on analysis (using multiple regression analysis techniques) of steady state engine data measured on a test bed; and the inertias and the characteristics of the compliant elements, on measurements taken on an appropriate rig.

2.3 Transmission

The transmission module represents the input/output characteristics of the CVT in terms of the behaviour of the input and output shafts to control actuation signals. More specifically, the dynamics of the electro-hydraulic interface to the controller, the ratio change actuator and the power transmission elements are separately modelled. The main equations for the power transmission elements and the ratio change actuator, respectively, take the form

$$[J_1 + r_\rho^2 J_o]\dot{\omega}_1 = T_c - r_\rho T_v - r_\rho \dot{r}_\rho J_o \omega_1 \qquad (3)$$

and

$$\dot{r}_\rho = f(T_c, T_v, \omega_1, r_\rho, i_A) \qquad (4)$$

where the relationships are derived from physically based models, and experiments performed on specialised equipment such as fluid flow rigs.

In addition, the compliant coupling between the engine flywheel and the transmission input shaft is incorporated; though the major frequencies associated with the element are outside the intended scope of the model.

2.4 Vehicle

The vehicle module represents the linear movement of the vehicle, considered as an unsprung mass and incorporating the aggregate effects of driveline compliance downstream of the transmission. It is described conceptually in figure 3.

The vehicle velocity is represented as

$$M\dot{v} = F_v - F_L - F_B \qquad (5)$$

and the aggregate angular deflection in the driveline as

$$r_v \dot{\theta} = r_v \omega_o - v \qquad (6)$$

The tractive effort, including compliance effects, is incorporated as

$$F_v = k r_v \theta + \beta (r_v \omega_o - v) \qquad (7)$$

where

$$T_v = r_v F_v \qquad (8)$$

Finally, the road load is represented as

$$F_L = a + bv + cv^2 \qquad (9)$$

The parameters k and β define the aggregate driveline compliance in terms of a linear spring rate and equivalent viscous damping, respectively, and were chosen on the basis of the experiments discussed below. Note that this representation was adopted as a modelling convenience (7) and should not be interpreted, literally, in a physical sense. Finally, the parameters a, b and c define the vehicle rolling resistance and aerodynamic drag, and were derived from multiple linear regression analysis of experimental data.

2.5 Controller

The control system module is a representation of the hybrid electronic control unit developed by the Lucas Research Centre (3), and the model is based on information provided by the company.

The controller is complex, owing to the fact that it has to interpret the driver's demands correctly, and control throttle angle and transmission ratio in order to meet the driver's expectations of vehicle performance and driveability, while making efficient use of fuel.

In addition to this extensive model, it was necessary to develop simpler controller modules to enable the system to be exercised in an open-loop manner, using normal test signals; thus a range of modules were developed to permit driveability and fuel consumption considerations to be addressed.

2.6 Driver

A number of driver modules were developed to provide:

(i) the ability to 'drive' the simulation model over any given driving schedule, for fuel consumption work

(ii) simple test signals for investigating system interactions

(iii) the ability to use time series data, obtained from vehicle experiments, to exercise the simulation model

Simple test signals are easily incorporated using the built-in features of ACSL; for the driving schedule work, the driver algorithm was based on classical PID techniques, which proved extremely robust in this application owing to the complexity of the existing controller, which adequately tailors the response of the system to the expectations of a human driver.

3. EXPERIMENTAL WORK

This modelling and simulation study was supported by a set of experiments which were performed on the vehicle to establish the dynamic characteristics of elements of the powertrain for which adequate alternative information, e.g. a priori knowledge and design specifications, was unobtainable. These experiments were designed to obtain information specifically concerned with:-

(i)   vehicle road load,

(ii) inertia of powertrain components,

(iii) engine steady state fuel and torque characteristics,

(iv) driveline oscillations associated with the compliances: between the engine and transmission, between the transmission and road wheels, and the engine-transmission mountings,

(v) dynamic and static characteristics of the transmission actuators, ratio change mechanism, and power transmission components.

Experimental studies to obtain data such as moments of inertia, transient and steady state torque and speed relationships were pursued using facilities provided by the companies. This included the use of an engine test bed and a vehicle simulation rig at Lucas Research Centre, and a hydraulic flow rig, a chassis dynamometer and the experimental Perbury CVT Dolomite vehicle, suitably instrumented, at BL Technology. The vehicle was also used to provide transient and steady state data for validation purposes.

The engine test bed experiments were aimed at obtaining adequate models of the steady state fuel flow and gross torque characteristics of the engine. Other experiments in the vehicle, enabled a single degree of freedom model of the motion of the engine block and transmission on its mountings, to be developed.

The compliance characteristics for the model were obtained from static and dynamic experiments relating to the application of known torques to the respective compliant elements, e.g. the towing of a vehicle with its propshaft anchored at a suitable point. These experiments resulted in an empirical representation of the compliant elements in terms of stiffness and viscous damping. This representation was adopted for modelling convenience and, clearly, should not be interpreted in a physical sense.

Commercially available instrumentation was used for most of the engine dynamics experiments and driveline compliance experiments, and the measurements were recorded using a multichannel Racal Store-14 analogue tape recorder. The recorded measurements were subsequently transcribed to a Prime 550 computer for analysis using the IDA data analysis facility (10).

In addition to experiments for system characterisation, a number of other experiments were performed specifically to enable subsequent validation of the simulation models. Of note, in the context of fuel consumption performance, are driving schedule tests performed on a chassis dynamometer; and coupled with this, equivalent tests of the engine itself on a test bed dynamometer.

Figure 4 illustrates the configuration for a driving schedule test. Here, a human driver manipulates the accelerator and service brake, in order to minimise the error between schedule velocity and effective vehicle velocity; both of these velocities being displayed on the driver's aid. During the course of these experiments many system variables were logged, including fuel rate, throttle angle and engine speed. These latter two measurement variables were used to exercise the engine on a test bed (figure 5), as if it were still in the vehicle undergoing a driving schedule run.

4. COMPUTER AIDED MODELLING AND SIMULATION

The powertrain simulation model was developed on a modular basis (11) using the ACSL high level simulation language (12), embedded within the DAPS computer aided modelling and simulation environment (6,7,9). DAPS is an interactive, user friendly computer aided engineering (CAE) facility designed, specifically, for the creation and exercising of dynamic simulation models of automotive powertrains. It incorporates a menu driven, user interface, with a comprehensive on-line 'Help' capability, enabling full use of the facility without the need for knowledge of the computer operating system or file management system; thereby providing a CAE tool capable of being used by engineers with limited knowledge of computing.

The DAPS computer aided modelling and simulation environment (6,7,9) facilitates the creation and management of distinct modules representing the individual powertrain subsystems highlighted in figure 1; the assembly of a set of user chosen modules, resident within the system, into an integrated powertrain simulation; and the interactive exercising of such a powertrain simulation. Throughout the use of DAPS, all of these operations are highly automated and require a minimum of effort on behalf of the user. Within DAPS, the individual powertrain modules are developed independently, in the ACSL high level simulation language, via interactive dialogue with the DAPS user interface.

The ACSL simulation language (12) is a general purpose, high level computer language for the formulation of dynamic simulation models of continuous systems. It consists of two sections – a model definition section incorporating a translator which generates a FORTRAN program from high level ACSL code, together with a run-time executive which provides an interactive means of exercising a simulation model with a capacity for the graphical display of simulation results and on-line modification of data. An important feature of ACSL is its inbuilt integration algorithms which provide a transparent and automatic means of solving the nonlinear differential equations defining the dynamic simulation model. Of particular relevance in automotive applications are its inherent capabilities for handling stiff dynamic systems (7), i.e. systems with widely separate time constants, and systems incorporating nonlinear switching between states, such as occurs in the engagement and disengagement of a clutch. However, in its conventional, stand-alone mode, ACSL lacks the capability for a user friendly, modular approach to the development of computer simulation models, requiring the user to intervene manually with the computer operating system in the management and creation of the source code files and simulation results.

The DAPS computer aided modelling and simulation environment is implemented on a Prime 550 computer and, essentially, provides a high level user interface to the ACSL simulation language and the computer operating system and file management system. It represents a significant enhancement of the stand alone capabilities of ACSL, specifically, in respect of the capacity for a strictly modular approach to simulation model development, together with the inbuilt, automated file handling facility. DAPS represents the initial phase in the development of a comprehensive CAE environment for use in automotive powertrain control systems design. Further developments in this area should concentrate on the integration of a computer aided data management and analysis system, and computer aided control system design facility, within such a CAE environment (6,9,11).

5. SIMULATION EXPERIMENTS

The modularity and flexibility of the DAPS computer aided modelling and simulation environment enables the testing of individual modules prior to their assembly into a complete powertrain simulation. In particular, it allows for the rapid reconfiguration of a simulation model using alternative modules of the necessary complexity, in order to perform simulations which mimic experiments on the actual vehicle.

Open loop simulations were particularly useful in analysing complex powertrain interactions, in order to address the control and driveability of CVT-equipped vehicles - some of these experiments are referred to elsewhere (6,7). For the fuel consumption work, the development of an algorithm for the driver module permitted a model to be configured (figure 7), and closed loop simulations to be performed, which were analogous to the driving schedule experiments (figure 4). However, as an intermediate step the fuel model, in isolation, was exercised (figure 6), in a configuration which mirrored the experiments on the test bed (figure 5). These experiments combined to improve confidence in the validity of the simulation models; and aided in the development of a methodology for addressing similar or related problems in the future.

Figures 8-10 refer to a simulation of the first three cycles of an ECE 15 driving schedule, using a simulation model of the vehicle system as depicted in figure 7.

Simulated vehicle velocity, overlaid on a graph of the schedule velocity, is shown in figure 8a. Even with the simple driver model employed here (based on a PI controller), it is difficult to see the very small tracking error (figure 8b). The driver produces accelerator and brake settings (figure 9) to be received by the controller; which manipulates throttle angle and transmission ratio (figure 10) in a way which ensures that the engine is operated in a fuel efficient manner, while maintaining the necessary system responsiveness to driver inputs.

It should be noted that the transmission is a two regime device with a 'geared neutral' capability (13), and that the ratio depicted in figure 10 relates to the variator portion of the transmission.

7. CONCLUSIONS

This paper has described the application of computer based modelling and simulation to control and fuel consumption studies related to a vehicle equipped with a continuously variable transmission. The basis for the study was an experimental vehicle, incorporating a Perbury traction transmission developed by BL Technology Ltd., and an electronic controller which was developed by Lucas Research Centre. This vehicle, and a number of experimental facilities, were made available by both companies for the development and validation of models of the vehicle system.

Discussed in this paper are the conceptual and theoretical basis of the powertrain model, together with the experimental work necessary to provide information and data for incorporation into the model. The model was constructed in a modular, incremental manner in which individual models of the powertrain subsystems were developed and tested independently, prior to being assembled into a complete powertrain simulation. This development was based on the use of the ACSL simulation language, embedded within the DAPS computer aided modelling and simulation environment. The major portion of the simulation study reported here, relates to the fuel consumption work; simulations related to the analysis of powertrain interactions for driveability, and related issues, are referred to elsewhere (6,7).

The paper includes illustrations of simulation results relating to driving schedule tests. It was found that simulation results were in excellent agreement with identical experiments on the vehicle, both in terms of the behaviour of the powertrain, and in terms of the fuel consumption performance. Such results improve confidence in the models of the system, and provide the foundation for further simulations to explore the trade-offs between various aspects of driveability and fuel economy, by adjusting the many controller parameters, or sizing powertrain or vehicle components, for instance.

ACKNOWLEDGEMENTS

This work has been funded in part by the Science and Engineering Research Council and Department of Trade and Industry through the BL Technology Ltd./Lucas Research Centre/University of Warwick Teaching Company Programme.

The authors gratefully acknowledge the contributions of many co-workers in the collaborating companies and the University. In particular, we mention K.W. Bird (BL Technology Ltd.), C.R. Sainsbury (Lucas Research Centre), M.J. Fokinther, A.J. Hulme and S.J. Marson (University of Warwick).

REFERENCES

1. 'Electronic Engine Management and Driveline Controls', SAE Publication P-104, 1982.

2. 'Electronic Engine Management and Driveline Control Systems', SAE Publication SP-481, 1981.

3. Ironside, J.M. and Stubbs, P.W.R., 'Microcomputer control of an automotive Perbury transmission', in Proc. 3rd Int. Conf. on Automotive Electronics, Mechanical Engineering Publications, 1981.

4. Page, R.P., 'A microprocessor based controller for a dry plate clutch and constant mesh gearbox', SAE paper no.850563, 1985.

5. Crossley, P.R., Jones, R.P. and Howarth, S.I., 'Modelling and simulation of a HGV powertrain for transmission control studies', Proc. ISATA 85, vol. 2, paper 85047, September 1985.

6. Jones, R.P., Hughes, M.T.G. and Kuriger, I.F., 'Computer-aided modelling and simulation of automotive powertrains for control studies', in 'Computer Aided Engineering', IEE Conf. Pubn. 243, 1984.

7. Jones, R.P., Holt, M.J., Hughes, M.T.G., Kuriger, I.F. and Marson, S.J., 'The role of simulation modelling in the control analysis and design of advanced powertrains', Proc. Int. Symposium: Advanced and Hybrid Vehicles, Glasgow, September 1984.

8. Sweet, L.M., 'Control systems for automotive vehicle fuel economy: A literature review', ASME J. Dyn. Syst. Meas. and Control, 103, 173-180, 1981.

9. Jones, R.P., Hughes, M.T.G. and Kuriger, I.F., 'Facets involved in the development of a CAE facility for use in automotive powertrain control system design', Proc. SERC/Inst.M.C Workshop: Computer Aided Control System Design, Brighton, September 1984.

10. IDA User Manual, University of Warwick, Department of Engineering.

11. Jones, R.P. and Hughes, M.T.G., 'The role of dynamic vehicle data in the control analysis and design of advanced powertrains', Proc. IEE Colloquium: Vehicle Test Data Collection and Analysis, London, May 1985.

12. Mitchell, E.E. and Gauthier, J.S., 'ACSL: advanced continuous simulation language - user guide/reference manual', Mitchell and Gauthier Assoc., 1981.

13. Stubbs, P.W.R., 'The development of a Perbury traction transmission for motor car applications', Proc. ASME International Power & Gear Conference, August 1980.

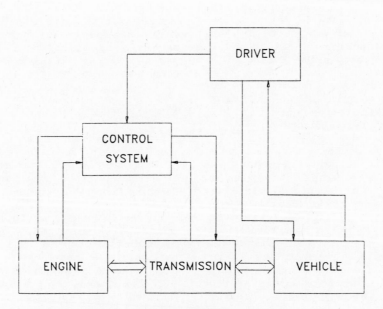

Fig 1 Advanced automotive powertrain

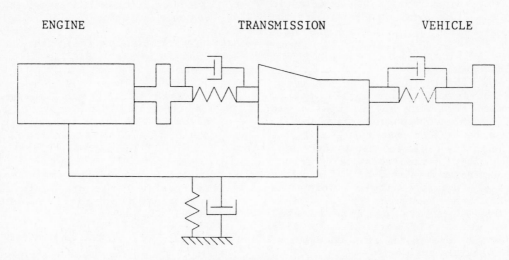

Fig 2 Conceptual model of powertrain

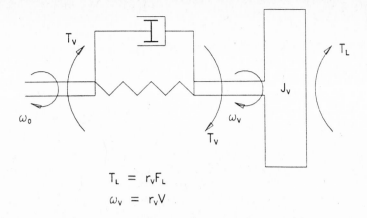

$$T_L = r_v F_L$$
$$\omega_v = r_v V$$

Fig 3   Vehicle module

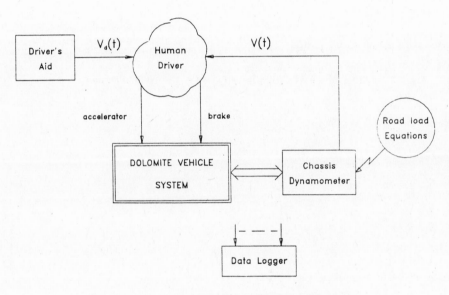

Fig 4   Configuration for driving schedule experiments

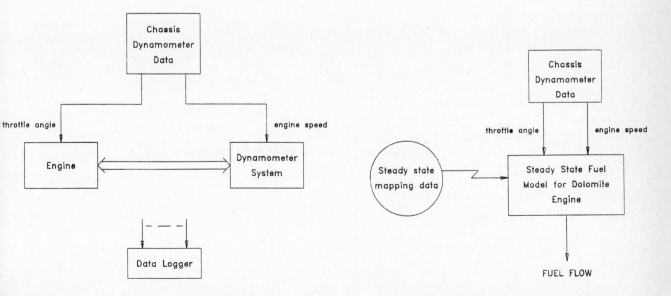

Fig 5   Configuration for engine test bed experiments

Fig 6   Fuel flow model validation simulation

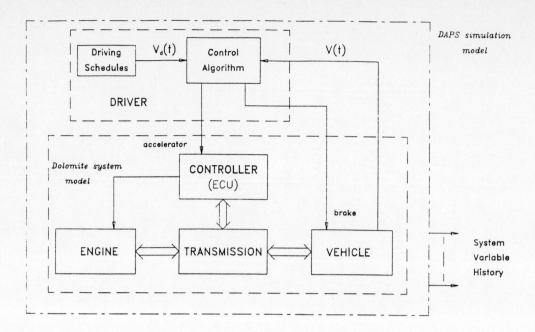

Fig 7   Model structure for simulation of driving schedules

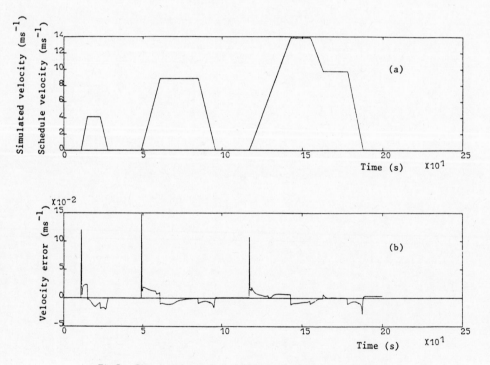

Fig 8   Simulation results — driving schedule control signals

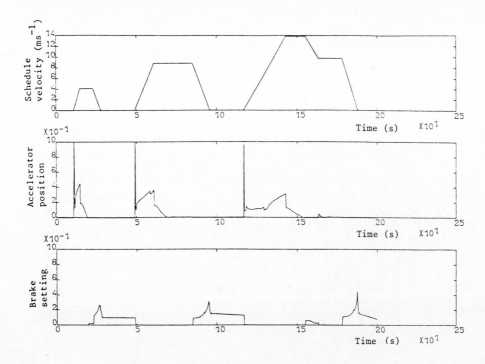

Fig 9   Simulation results — driver control signals

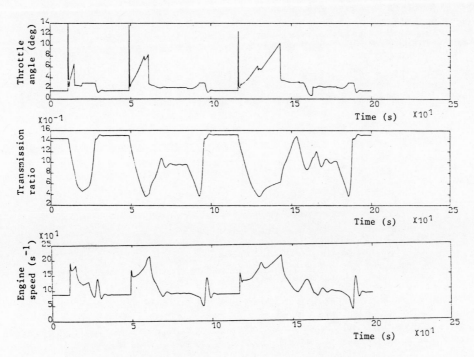

Fig 10 Simulation results — powertrain control signals (internal)

Increasing the operating economy of commercial vehicles by powertrain optimization

K SCHUBERT, Dr-Ing
MAN Nutzfahrzeuge GmbH, München, Germany

Increasing the Operating Economy of Commercial Vehicles by Power Train Optimization

1. Introduction

An important criterion in the evaluation of commercial vehicles is operating economy. In choosing vehicles for his fleet, which has to be considered as a major capital investment, the transport operator must pay particular attention to this aspect if he is to achieve a reasonable profit.

Factors affecting the operating economy of commercial vehicles include fuel consumption, achievable transport speeds, ease of maintenance and repair, reliability under severe operating conditions and the service lives of the vehicle and its components.

From these evaluation criteria fuel consumption and possibilities of reducing this cost factor have been selected for closer examination here.

2. The power train components

("Power train" is defined here as the combination of engine, clutch, transmission, propeller shaft and driven axle).

2.1 The engine

There is no substitute for the diesel engine as an economical commercial vehicle power unit. The gas turbine, which was for a long time regarded as an alternative to the diesel engine, has never been able to achieve equally good fuel consumption, particularly under part load. For a given power output, its costs are also many times higher than those of the diesel engine. Furthermore, certain other problems have still to be solved, for example slow response to throttle opening, inadequate operating life of the heat exchanger during short and medium-distance operation, poor efficiency in the necessary reduction gearing etc., before this power unit can be used in commercial vehicles.

The commercial vehicle diesel engine is today capable of operating at an efficiency distinctly above 40 per cent. This is reflected in specific fuel consumption figures below 200 grammes per kilowatt-hour, which scarcely twenty years ago were regarded as the best possible values obtainable from slow-revving marine diesel engines. M.A.N.'s contribution to the continuing development of the diesel engine is described below.

The first serviceable engine using the compression ignition principle was built by Rudolf Diesel at M.A.N. in 1897. These engines have retained the name of their inventor right up to the present day. More than twenty-five years were to elapse before the diesel engine was first installed in a motor vehicle.

Rudolf Diesel himself did not live long enough to see his engine used in a truck, in 1924.

But ever since its introduction to commercial vehicles, the diesel engine's outstanding economy, reliability and - if suitably designed and rated - long service life have made it increasingly the standard power plant for commercial vehicles, with no better alternative in sight to this day.

In the past ten years the diesel engine has reached an exceptionally advanced state of development, so that further reductions in fuel consumption compared with the best figures achieved at the moment are likely to occur only in relatively small increments. All M.A.N.'s development departments are of course working actively on this challenging task.

The standard power unit for heavy M.A.N. trucks is a 12-litre six-cylinder inline engine with a bore of 128 mm and a stroke of 155 mm. The individual development stages to which the engine has been subjected over the last eight years and the effects on the fuel consumption of M.A.N. commercial vehicles are described below.

Figure 1 shows three performance characteristics for this six-cylinder diesel engine in turbocharged form. The three graphs also represent stages in the past nine years of development work on this fundamentally unchanged basic engine.

The sector in which specific fuel consumption is below 215 g/kWh is shown shaded. The increase in the shaded area can be regarded as the outcome of the three development stages discussed here. The much larger shaded area resulting from the most recent development stage completed in 1983 means a considerable saving in fuel consumption for the commercial vehicle operator.

A further yardstick in evaluating the three engine versions with regard to fuel consumption during long-haul operation is their specific fuel consumption at a speed of 1600 revolutions per minute and a power output of 120 kilowatts. This is the average power output required by a heavy long-haul vehicle of 40 metric tons gross train weight, with a body height of 4 metres and an overall width of 2.50 metres at a road speed of 90 km/h on a level road. At this point on the graph, the engine consumed approximately 222 g/kWh following development stage II, but only 209 g/kWh after the completion of development stage III. This is equivalent to a 6 per cent reduction in fuel consumption. Engine development stage I cannot be taken into consideration as far as this fuel consumption comparison is concerned, because as a result of its much lower peak power output it had to be run at relatively higher load at this point on the graph, and for this reason proves to have a better specific fuel consumption, at 214 g/kWh, than the engine from development stage II, for which the primary objective was to increase both peak performance and power in reserve.

Assuming that in the travel conditions prevailing in Europe in particular a certain minimumum power reserve is necessary at the maximum legal road speed in order to cope with minor uphill gradients, headwinds or increased speeds when overtaking without the need to change down, the improvement in fuel consumption in development stage III becomes even more evident.

According to studies carried out at M.A.N., a power reserve of about 100 kW is desirable at a road speed of 80 - 90 km/h in order to ensure smooth, relaxed progress on European motorways and similar roads. Development stage I of the engine did not provide this power reserve at any operating point on the graph. In order to come anywhere near satisfying this justifiable requirement, a long-haul road train with engine I would have to have a final drive ratio yielding an engine speed of approximately 2000 rpm at 90 km/h and a power reserve of 80 kW.

The engine from development stage II would require a final drive ratio giving 90 km/h at an engine speed of 1600 rpm.

The D 2866 KF engine derived from development stage III could comply with the requirement for a power reserve of 100 kW with a final drive ratio capable of permitting a road speed of 90 km/h at 1400 rpm engine speed. The operating points plotted on the graphs for the three engines, that is to say development stages I, II and III, yield specific fuel consumptions of 227, 222 and 205 g/kWh at 90 km/h road speed. With the reservation that engine version I does not provide the required power reserve, this represents a relative reduction in fuel consumption of 11 % between development stages I and III and of 10.5 % between development stages II and III.

This improvement in fuel consumption, recorded in test bed operation, has been fully confirmed by road tests. I shall be dealing with this later in more detail.

Engine version I is equipped with conventional turbocharging, and has a nominal power output of 206 kW (280 hp). The change to engine version II was stimulated by the demand for higher power output together with increased torque. The engine's power rating was increased only modestly, from 206 to 235 kW, in other words by about 14 %. Maximum torque rose at the same time from 1040 to 1350 Nm, that is to say by almost 30 %. This outstanding good result was achieved by the application of combined turbocharging and charge air intercooling.

In the fairly high speed range this system supplies the engine with the necessary increased volume of air by means of a turbocharger, the compressed air from which is lowered in temperature by about 70°C in an intercooler. At lower engine speeds, the volume of air supplied by the turbocharger drops rapidly, and a tuned induction system is therefore used to make use of resonant vibration in the column of air and obtain a forced aspiration effect which results in a greater supply of air to the engine.

The intelligent combination of these two forced aspiration systems results in an impressive torque raise by more than 30 per cent in the case of the M.A.N. diesel engine under discussion, and an almost level torque curve between 1200 and 1600 rpm before the torque drops away at still lower speeds as a result of the principle adopted here.

Applied to heavy commercial vehicles, this engine characteristic offers previously unknown attributes such as relaxed driving with few gear changes at relatively low engine speeds, thus not only reducing fuel consumption but also environmental burden in general. The change from development stage II to development stage III and the improvements which resulted were obtained by further detail work on the engine's combustion and its fuel injection system.

In addition, it was considered desirable to increase the engine's displacement by slightly more than 7 % by enlarging the bore from 125 to 128 mm, in order to meet the current design specification. The outstanding results obtained with the M.A.N. turbocharging and charge air intercooling, have encouraged us to extend this system to smaller M.A.N. engines. At the German Motor Show in September 1983 we introduced a completely new range of medium-weight trucks powered by a 5.7 litre engine with combined turbocharging and intercooling, available in two power outputs: 170 and 192 hp.

The satisfactory results in terms of increased power and lower fuel consumption which M.A.N. has obtained from the engine in the last two years after increasing its displacement from 11.4 to 12 litres have now led to two further versions being introduced, with power outputs of 213 kW (290 hp) and 243 kW (330 hp) and torques of 1200 Nm and 1350 Nm respectively.

These engines have the same bore and stroke as the 265 kW (360 hp) version, and use the modified combustion principle with 4-hole injection nozzles. They are notable for their retention of the constant power output characteristic, for ample reserves of power in the main driving speed range, and for their high torque in the low engine speed range which is so important when moving the vehicle away from a standstill. The new engines supersede the former types which developed 10 hp less in both cases, and will enable vehicle operators to obtain better results at lower operating costs from their vehicles.

If the power train specification is the same as specified for development stage II (1600 rpm at 90 km/h), the two engines, that is to say the D 2566 MK dating from 1979 and the 2866 L of 1985, possess an identical power reserve of approximately 100 kW. However, the specific fuel consumption of 206 g/kWh at this operating point gives the new engine a fuel consumption reduction of approximately 7 %.

A potential saving currently being investigated intensively and which can actually be exploited in practice is represented by the engine's auxiliaries. For example, investigation of radiator and fan systems has shown that a number of individual measures can together have the effect of significantly reducing fan power consumption. These measures are primarily based on increasing the distance between the radiator and the front end of the engine and optimizing the fan. Together with aerodynamic improvements to the radiator fan shroud and a 9 per cent reduction in fan speed, the fan's power consumption on the 360 hp engine was reduced by 36 per cent, from 14 to 9 kW. If a permanently-driven fan is installed, the reduction in the power required to drive it is directly related to running speed, and therefore directly influences the improvement in fuel consumption obtainable during vehicle operation. In the case of the fans with a viscous drive coupling normally installed today, the reduction in fuel consumption depends on the length of time for which the fan cuts in, and is accordingly lower. If it is assumed that the viscous-drive fan runs for 45 per cent of vehicle operating time as an annual average, and that average speed is 60 km/h, there is a fuel saving of about 2 litres per 100 kilometres when changing from a permanently-driven to a viscous-drive fan and of 1 1/100 km when changing from a standard to an optimised viscous-drive fan.

Other potential savings involving engine auxiliaries are also possible, for instance if the air compressor were to be controlled in accordance with the vehicle's actual needs. Various systems are being investigated in this connection. The most radical way of reducing off-load-compressor-drive-losses is to shut down by means of a controllable clutch (Figure 2). This is an effective but comparatively expensive method of control, and therefore other methods are being investigated, such as increasing compression chamber volume, using it as a control parameter or installing a controlled induction-side throttle.

By way of examples, Figure 2 shows two possible methods of disengaging the compressor mechanically. The accompanying table shows that at a speed of 2000 rpm offload, the power consumption of a 300 cm^3 compressor can be reduced by from 0.4 to 1.9 kW, depending on the system used. On long runs by road trains and passenger coaches in particular, a measure of this nature would result in a significant drop in fuel consumption, the actual amount depending on the length of time the drive to the compressor is engaged.

2.2 Transmission and rear axles

Detail work on transmissions has shown that significant scope for increasing efficiency is almost exhausted. The main measures for reducing losses in the transmission are the use of rigid shafts and housings in order to minimise elastic deformation, ball or roller bearings for all loose gears, lowering the oil level to reduce splash losses, possibly the installation of baffle plates to shield individual gearwheels, optimisation of the inner contour of the housing, etc.

As far as rear axles are concerned, our own investigations have confirmed that, particularly in the part-load range, temperature as a function of running speed exerts a great influence on efficiency. Measurement revealed that at a transmitted power of 60 kW, an increase in temperature from 35 to 100°C and an oil of viscosity class 80, efficiency improves from 85.5 to 92.5 % at an input speed of 1500 rpm. With a transmitted output of 240 kW under the same conditions, it was still possible to increase efficiency from 94 to 96 %.

These are values which cannot be disregarded, particularly if there is reason to fear that in certain operating conditions, for example adverse weather conditions in the case of distributor trucks, the oil in the rear axle may fail to reach an adequate operating temperature.

By far the greater potential for reducing commercial vehicle fuel consumption, however, lies in the selection of the correct reduction gearing in the power train. In this connection, I would like to limit my remarks to the use of heavy commercial vehicles on European highways. For these vehicles, multi-ratio gearboxes with 12 to 16 speeds have become generally accepted. They create the right conditions for economical driving, since any tractive force as determined

by the vehicle's running resistance can be obtained at the vehicle's wheels within an engine speed range which results either in the lowest possible fuel consumption or in an increase in average journey speeds.

When selecting the final drive ratio, a compromise has to be arrived at between the available power reserve and optimisation of the fuel consumption at the road speeds most frequently used.

Figure 3 shows, in conjunction with the optimised engine from Figure 1 (development stage III), two extreme transmission ratio specifications. Assuming that the legal speed limit for the vehicle is 80 km/h, the change from a final drive ratio of 4.28 : 1 with a governed top speed of 102 km/h to a final drive ratio of 2.667 : 1 and a governed top speed of 164 km/h yields a fuel saving of 7.3 % at a constant speed (fig. 3 a). However, this high ratio means that the fully laden road train can climb a maximum gradient of no more than 0.55 per cent at 80 km/h (fig. 3 b). In addition, if severe increases in running resistances are encountered at speeds below 90 km/h, the engine is obliged to operate in a range in which torque drops off steeply - an undesirable state of operation.

On the other hand, the lower-ratio version can surmount a gradient as steep as 1.65 % at 80 km/h and exhibits increasing hill-climbing ability as engine speed falls, right down to a road speed of 60 km/h (fig. 3 c).

Our experience has shown that final drive ratios permitting a top speed in excess of 140 km/h are completely out of the question in European conditions for the reasons described above. The fully-laden vehicles create a more sluggish impression than the installed engine power of approximately 360 hp would suggest, and the driver is obliged to drop down by a gear or two in order to permit a more flexible driving approach, something which runs counter to the original transmission concept.

3. Effects of optimisation measures on long-haul road trains during the past ten years

The results of power train optimisation is shown in Figure 4, where we see the fuel consumption and average speeds of M.A.N. road trains between 1975 and 1985. The measurements were in each case obtained on the same routes by impartial test drivers from three different leading commercial vehicle periodicals. Test route I ("Truck", UK) presented the greatest and test route III ("Nutzfahrzeug", Germany) the least difficulty. Between 1975/76 and 1977/80, fuel consumption savings of up to 13 per cent were achieved on the various routes although the average speeds were almost unchanged. If the years 1975/76 and 1983/85 are compared, fuel consumption is as much as 30 per cent lower although average speeds were actually higher. Remembering that traffic density in Europe increased during the same period, it is probable that the actual fuel saving in genuinely identical conditions would have been even greater. These results illustrate the beneficial effects of optimization of engines and power trains, but a far from negligible proportion of the fuel saving is of course due to detail work on the reduction of drag and rolling resistance.

An interesting result was obtained from internal tests designed to establish the effects of the changeover from the D 2566 MK to the D 2866 K engine. Both engines were driven over the same route for two years, and their fuel consumptions recorded. Evaluation of these readings,

which are shown as dots in Figure 5, confirms
that the change from the D 2566 MK to the
D 2866 K engine brought about a reduction in
fuel consumption of approximately 8 - 10 per
cent on this route.

A further interesting finding, however, is
that the driver's influence can cancel out the
fuel saving made possible by technical improvements. To put this another way, the best driver
at the wheel of the vehicle with the engine
which would normally have the poorer fuel consumption can still save more fuel than the worst
of the drivers at the wheel of a vehicle with an
optimised engine. An untrained driver can in
practice negate the benefits of technical
optimisation work. M.A.N. therefore undertakes
intensive driver training with a view to making
the fuel saving potential inherent in the correct driving style available to its customers.

4. Future prospects

As already implied, motor vehicle diesel engines have already reached a state of development which permits only small further steps to
be made towards increased economy or efficiency,
with even these involving relatively high technical effort. The same applies to transmissions
and rear axles. Since the driver, whose driving
style is dictated by temperament or physical and
mental condition, remains the weakest link in
the chain, considerable potential for increasing
operating economy is evidently to be found by
eliminating the influence exerted by the driver.
Electronics are the answer here.

4.1 Electronics for diesel engine fuel injection systems

During the 1985 Frankfurt Motor Show, M.A.N. ex-
hibited its Electronic Diesel Control (EDC)
system for the first time on prototype vehicles.
EDC is a microprocessor-electrically controlled
injection system, which dispenses with the
hitherto customary mechanical injection pump
governor. A 360 hp six-cylinder turbocharged inline engine of type D 2866 KFZ was used to illustrate the potential of electronic control for
the Bosch inline-pattern fuel injection pump.

The control system takes into account accelerator pedal position, engine speed, boost pressure
and various other temperatures and limit values,
all of which are stored in the engine computer.
On a second, Series D 0226 MKF engine with
rotary injection pump, the advantages of electronic pump control in conjunction with electronic determination of fuel injection advance
were demonstrated.

In principle, Electronic Diesel Control (EDC)
offers the following benefits:
- the combined mechanical and pneumatic
  injection pump actuating linkage is no
  longer needed
- the fuel supply volume for starting can be
  easily programmed and varied according to
  temperature
- development costs can be reduced by means of
  an easily programmable full-load characteristic
- it becomes easier to keep stocks of injection
  pumps for a wide variety of models
- it becomes possible to provide additional regulating functions, for example exhaust gas
  recirculation and variable-geometry turbochargers
- operating data can be recorded as a means of
  early diagnosis of engine malfunctions
- the system can easily be integrated into the
  power train management system

In the case of the rotary (VE) injection pump

with control of fuel injection advance, further
electronic information can be utilised:
- simple programming of the start of injection
  according to temperatures and running speed
- unrestricted layout of injection start characteristic as a means of complying with exhaust
  emission limits

Operation of trucks with EDC will result in the
following advantages:
- improved starting and acceleration behaviour
- constant idle speed regardless of engine
  temperature
- option of alternative operation with different
  pump control characteristics (RQ, RQV), all
  speed + two speed
- highly stable running speeds
- no loss of performance if fuel temperature
  changes
- top speed can be programmed
- cruise control functions can be programmed

Electronic fuel injection control thus provides
a great many advantages both for the manufacturer and for the operator of commercial vehicles.

As the exigencies of environmental protection
and in particular the standards applied to
diesel engine exhaust emissions increase, an
electronically controlled exhaust gas recirculating system could also become of interest.

4.2 Electronics for the partial or full automation of multi-ratio manual-shift gearboxes

The most advanced current development aimed at
increasing the economy of commercial vehicles by
automating the manual-shift gearbox is the
Vehicle Management System (VMS) developed
jointly by M.A.N. and the transmission manufacturer ZF (Figure 6).

It permits optimum control of the vehicle power
train in terms of economy, refinement and
environmental acceptability. Existing part-
systems such as cruise control, speed governing
governing and electronic diesel engine fuel
injection can be incorporated into the VMS
vehicle management system.

The VMS concept comprises the following main
assemblies
- diesel engine
- automatic clutch
- vehicle management computer (Figure 7), the
  master computer which achieves optimum
  coordination of vehicle condition-indicating
  data
- electronic actuation of the injection pump
  in response to throttle movements, or
  Electronic Diesel Control (EDC)

The computer now controls the diesel engine
and the transmission rather than the driver
directly. The driver merely instructs the computer as to his wishes by moving the accelerator
pedal; the computer responds to
- accelerator pedal position
- kick-down
- speed of accelerator pedal movement

The vehicle management computer is a M.A.N.
development. It stores the complete engine
fuel maps and its running-speed and full-load
limits, as well as the individual gear ratios
and their efficiencies, and other vehicle data
such as final drive ratios and engine brake
and retarder operating strategies. To obtain
information on actual vehicle working conditions, the computer also receives a permanent
input of values such as vehicle load and acceleration.

The gearbox used with this system is a

© IMechE 1986 C189/86

ZF 16 S 130 Ecosplit unit with electropneumatic shift. Clutch operation has been rendered automatic, and the injection pump can be electronically controlled; furthermore, a simple electrically operated accelerator pedal system or a microprocessor controlled injection system (EDC) can also be used.

On the basis of desired driving data and stored engine, transmission and vehicle data, the vehicle management computer determines the desired values for injection pump control rod position and the most suitable gear ratio. It takes into account the load on the truck and the road gradient, as well as braking processes; for instance, when driving downhill it always selects the gear with the greatest engine braking effect.

Improved DRIVER CONVENIENCE
- automatic selection of the correct gear
- no risk of engine overspeeding
- the driver is able to concentrate fully on handling the vehicle and on the surrounding traffic

Improved WORKING CONDITIONS as a result of
- lower interior noise level
- fully-automatic starting and gear shifts, even on steep uphill gradients when the vehicle is fully loaded
  simplified manoeuvring

Improved ENVIRONMENTAL ACCEPTABILITY as a result of
- reduction in noise levels
- minimum-emission engine management (a subsequent vehicle management computer development)
- the ability to modify the computer program to permit different engines and gearboxes to be matched together and combined in the vehicle
- the engine and transmission management computer can be extended to act as a complete vehicle management computer, for example by the integration of operating data recording, an anti-theft system, antilock braking, anti-slip control and other individual functions.

A second approach to increasing the operating economy of commercial vehicles is partial automation of the gear shift action on the multi-ratio gearboxes installed on the vehicles in question. This simplifies the driver's workload and encourages greater concentration on selection of the most suitable gear ratio. The driver has more time to comply with recommendations regarding operation of the engine in its most economical speed range, the necessary information being conveyed to him by a large-diameter revolution counter bearing suitable markings.

SAMT is the abbreviation for a development now being undertaken together with the transmission manufacturer EATON, and based on a 12-speed twin splitter microcomputer-controlled gearbox for heavy trucks. The driver changes gear with the aid of a lever on the right of the steering column (Figure 8). If the lever is pressed down, the next-lower ratio is selected; if pulled up, the next-higher ratio. By moving the lever several times, one or more ratios can be omitted. The ratio which the driver intends to select is processed by an electronic control unit together with gearbox running speeds, accelerator pedal position and clutch pedal position, these items of information being obtained from sensors. The control unit compares these data with those stored in the microcomputer.

If a gear change is accepted as worthwhile, it is performed without the driver having to operate the clutch pedal, using electropneumatic shift valves and cylinders in the gearbox, and taking the engine speed limits in the gears into account.

The clutch is actuated automatically by compressed air. The driver is only required to operate the clutch when starting and stopping the vehicle. The selected gear is displayed to the driver on the instrument panel, together with the lower or higher ratios which the system would permit to be engaged. SAMT greatly simplifies the task of driving a heavy truck, in particular with regard to difficult situations such as steep downhill gradients or dense city traffic.

5. Summary

Optimisation work on the power train over the last ten years has made it possible to reduce the fuel consumption of commercial vehicles by a considerable degree. Further improvements can be achieved only in small stages and with a comparatively high technical effort. The one quantity that is still difficult to evaluate in any consideration of the fuel consumption of commercial vehicles in operation is the influence of the driver. Results of driver training programmes have shown that there is potential for saving a large amount of energy. The use of electronics for controlling the power train offers possibilities of reproducing this saving. In this connection M.A.N. has in the meantime begun to test a fully automatic mechanical gearbox, which is controlled by a power-train management computer, and an electronically controlled semi-automatic gearbox. The first results of these tests show that these developments are worth pursuing.

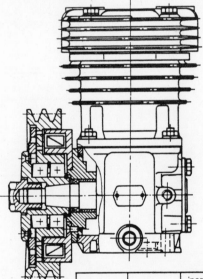

	series	clutch	increase of compression-chamber	intake throttle
flow at 8 bar [1/min]	370	370	349	370
power input at 8 bar [kW]	3,3	3,3	3,1	3,3
power input at idling [kW]	1,9	0	0,4	1,5

Fig 2   Air compressor with disengageable drive

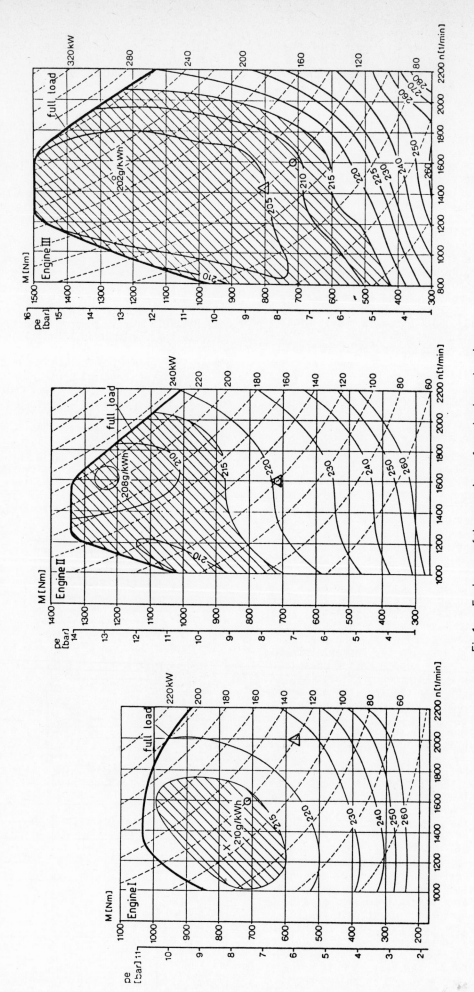

Fig 1   Fuel maps of three versions of a turbocharged engine

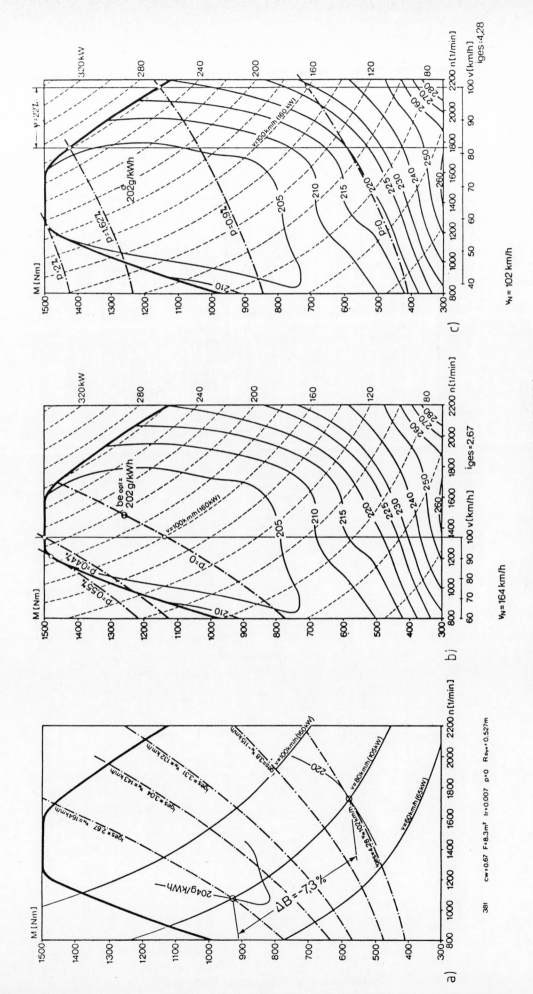

Fig 3   Two rear axle ratios for commercial vehicles

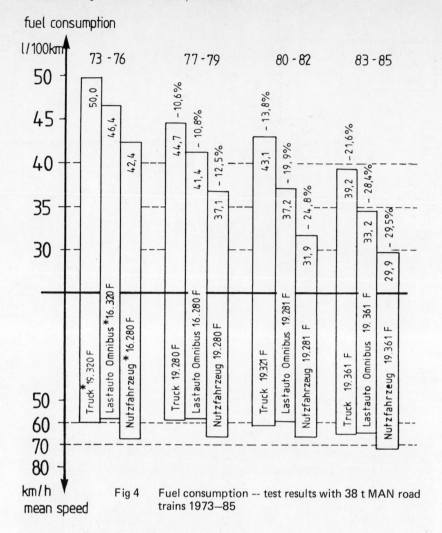

fuel consumption
l/100km

73 - 76   77 - 79   80 - 82   83 - 85

50,0
46,4
42,4
44,7 −10,6%
41,4 −10,8%
37,1 −12,5%
43,1 −13,8%
37,2 −19,9%
31,9 −24,8%
39,2 −21,6%
33,2 −28,4%
29,9 −29,5%

Truck *16.320 F
Lastauto Omnibus *16.320 F
Nutzfahrzeug *16.280 F
Truck 19.280 F
Lastauto Omnibus 16.280 F
Nutzfahrzeug 19.280 F
Truck 19.321 F
Lastauto Omnibus 19.281 F
Nutzfahrzeug 19.281 F
Truck 19.361 F
Lastauto Omnibus 19.361 F
Nutzfahrzeug 19.361 F

km/h
mean speed

Fig 4   Fuel consumption -- test results with 38 t MAN road
trains 1973—85

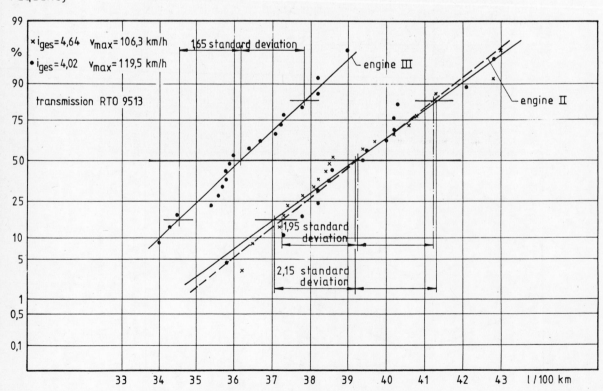

frequency

×i_{ges}=4,64 v_{max}= 106,3 km/h
•i_{ges}=4,02 v_{max}= 119,5 km/h

transmission RTO 9513

1,65 standard deviation

engine III

engine II

1,95 standard deviation

2,15 standard deviation

Fig 5   Fuel consumption test results for road trains in shift
operation

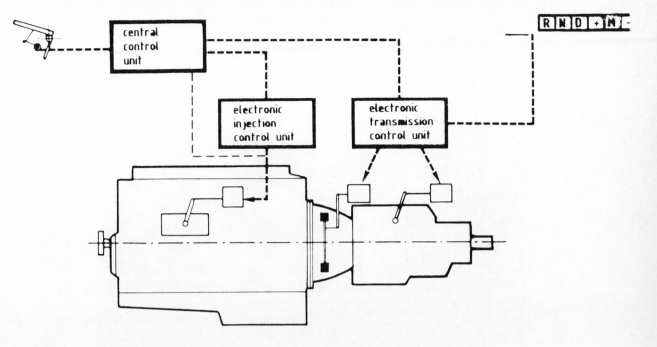

Fig 6   Vehicle management system

Fig 7   Vehicle management computer

Fig 8   SAMT control and display

C188/86

One approach to engine transmission matching

J H SPENCE, BTech, CEng, MIMechE
Self Changing Gears Limited, Coventry

SYNOPSIS   In the field of matching diesel engines to automatic transmissions with epicyclic gears the type of coupling is of primary importance.   The effect of coupling choice on tractive effort is explained and the calculations involved reviewed.   A new development in couplings is also presented. The use of computer programmes to predict full load performance and to simulate performance along a route is described with an outline of future developments.

1   INTRODUCTION

From a transmission manufacturer's point of view the phrase engine transmission matching does not describe the process fully.   It is more accurate to think of the transmission being used to match the engine to the vehicle.   Each component in the driveline, the engine, the engine to gearbox coupling, the final drive and the vehicle all serve to influence the choice of gearbox speed ratios.   It is the task of the driveline engineer to integrate those components so that the vehicle's performance specification will be met. Traditionally this has been confined to ensuring that the gearbox speed ratios could supply sufficient tractive effort to meet the hill start and maximum speed requirements from the engine power available.   Spot tractive effort calculations are relatively simple but to assess vehicle performance they must be repeated several times in each gear, a task for which the computer is most suited.   However full load performance is only one mode of vehicle operation and in recent years further developments of computer programmes have led to more accurate simulation programmes which allow part load performance and durability factors to be assessed.   In this paper the well known matching techniques are reviewed and current computational methods explained in the context of vehicle applications.   Three vehicle types have been compared, each of which requires a different aspect of performance; a road bus, a rail bus and a tracked military vehicle.   These vehicles use transmissions with compound epicyclic trains controlled in automatic or semiautomatic form.

2   NOTATION

A	frontal area (m²)
a	acceleration (m/s²)
d	distance travelled (m)
N_{rc}	speed ratio of coupling
R	resistance to motion (N)
r_a	ratio of final drive
r_g	ratio of gearbox
T	engine torque (Nm)
TE	tractive effort
T_{rc}	torque ratio of coupling
t	time (s)
v	road speed (m/s)
w	wheel radius (m)
ζ_a	efficiency of final drive
ζ_g	efficiency of gearbox
ω_e	engine speed (rad/s)

3   COUPLINGS

Fully automatic or semi-automatic transmissions require an engine to transmission coupling which also can be engaged and disengaged automatically. On road buses and on rail diesel multiple units the chosen coupling has been the fluid flywheel or torque converter.   These hydro-kinetic devices have the ability to take up drive from the engine in a gradual fashion yet be physically disconnected so that engine torsional vibrations or gear change speed discrepencies can be absorbed. These advantages are counterbalanced by the disadvantages of never achieving a 100 per cent speed ratio across the coupling.

The need for more efficient vehicles has led to the constant slip of hydro-kinetic devices becoming un-acceptable.   To overcome the problem such couplings are now equipped with a plate clutch which can be engaged under fully automatic control and so 'lock-up' the coupling.   With a fluid flywheel and a stepped transmission the lowest transmission ratio would have been used only for starting the vehicle but with additional torque developed from a torque converter a higher starting gear is permitted.   Thus fewer gear ratios are necessary. Fig 1.

On a military vehicle where performance outweighs ride comfort a centrifugal clutch is often employed.   This has the advantage of gradual automatic take-up of speed without slip across the coupling.   However all gear change energy must then be dissipated by the ratio selecting friction elements within the transmission.   The major problem with an automatic coupling device is establishing the correct match point with the engine torque curve.   With the steep torque rise curve of the modern diesel engine and the natural tendency of a centrifugal clutch torque curve to follow a square law the matching of centrifugal clutches has become increasingly difficult.

In an attempt to overcome such matching problems of self-engaging couplings a new type of clutch is being developed for automatic transmissions. This is a multiplate clutch where application pressure is controlled by the speed ratio selecting microprocessor. The clutch being engaged at maximum torque speed of the engine at a rate dependent upon load and the driver's demand. Fig 2.

When the driver initiates a start from rest sequence by moving the gear selector lever to the 'drive' position at a time, t_0, the engine speed control is taken away from the driver. The microprocessor will set the engine to run at that speed at which the engine would develop maximum torque. Operation of the driver's accelerator lever will not change engine speed but its position is detected by transducers and communicated to the microprocessor.

A speed sensor on the driving side of the clutch will detect when maximum torque speed has been achieved. At that time, t_1, the clutch engagement process is begun. The position of the driver's accelerator lever is an indication of the rate at which the driver wishes to move off. Full travel of the lever indicates maximum acceleration and a pressure rise ramp is chosen which would achieve full pressure in a minimum time, t_2. Alternatively small accelerator movement would select a pressure rise ramp which would give a maximum slip time, t_3.

Actual engagement is also dependent upon load on the vehicle. With a low tractive resistance, coupling of the clutch may be achieved before full pressure has been generated or where tractive resistances are high there may be a tendency to lug the engine down. A second speed sensor on the driven side of the clutch compares its speed with that on the driving side of the clutch. As soon as a 100 per cent speed ratio across the clutch has been achieved the pressure rise ramp is abandoned, full pressure is applied and engine speed control is returned to the driver. Should engine speed begin to slow, clutch pressure is eased to allow engine speed to rise before increasing clutch pressure is resumed. If full pressure has been reached yet the clutch continues to slip and the driven side of the clutch is not accelerating then the clutch is shut down and cooled before another attempt is permitted.

4 TRACTIVE EFFORT

Having chosen a coupling a first step in transmission matching is calculation of full load performance and curves of tractive effort plotted against vehicle road speed are well known. Fig 1. 3 & 4. These particular curves were plotted using a suite of computer programmes developed to run on a desk top computer. Input and edit programmes are used to create data files of vehicle weight, resistances to motion, final drive ratio and wheel radius. An engine torque curve is entered in digital form with associated coupling slip ratio, torque ratio and lock-up clutch point where appropriate. Gearbox speed ratios and associated efficiencies are also entered. Thus tractive effort available at the wheels with corresponding road speed can be calculated for each speed step of the digitised torque curve. A typical data set, used to calculate the data

for Fig 3, is shown as Table 1.

$$TE = T \times T_{rc} \times r_g \times \zeta_g \times r_a \times \zeta_a \times 1/w_r$$

$$v = \omega_e \times N_{rc} \times 1/r_g \times 1/r_a \times w_r$$

The gross tractive effort, TE, is reduced by the amount of effort required to overcome the resistances to motion to give the tractive effort available for acceleration. That tractive effort can be plotted against road speed for each gear. Acceleration can be found directly from Newton's second law hence distance travelled and elapsed time between engine speed points can be calculated

$$d = \frac{v_1 - v_2}{2\,a}$$

$$t = \frac{2\,(v^2 - v^2)}{a}$$

thus curves of road speed against time and distance travelled against time can be plotted. Further calculations are made to establish the maximum gradient on which the vehicle would be able to start from rest. The user is also able to select the maximum gradient for which resistances to motion are to be plotted and the gradient interval thus showing at which gradients down changes will be required.

As with any prediction programme the most important factor is to employ accurate data. This is particularly difficult with estimates of resistances to motion. With road and tracked military vehicles the use of a fixed percentage of vehicle mass added to the well known aerodynamic expression of

$$R = k\,A\,v^2$$

has proved to be an acceptable approximation. However a problem does occur with tracked military vehicles in that they operate over various types of surfaces. Therefore, for example, resistances to motion to establish maximum speed on a metalled road would be quite different from those to establish maximum starting capability on an off road gradient. Thus the programme needs to be used more than once for each application.

With rail vehicles more information exists to predict resistances to motion and a quadratic expression is built up depending upon the weight of the train, the number of vehicles in the train and a speed dependent factor.

A range of vehicle performance specifications can be seen by comparing Fig 3 & 4. Maximum speed of a 64 tonne rail bus is twice that of a 55 tonne tank yet requires only one tenth of the tractive effort to meet its gradient restart requirement. The power units of both vehicles are quite different; two 150 kW engines for the rail bus and a single 750 kW engine for the main battle tank. All of which ensures that the transmission ratios are also quite different. The ratio of maximum power speed to maximum torque speed of the high performance military engine is smaller than that ratio of the rail bus engine which means that to permit the engine to run in the optimum speed range a greater number of gearbox ratios is required in the military transmission.

When similar engines are used in different vehicles it would still not be accurate to match the gearbox solely to the engine although that is apparently true when comparing the road bus tractive effort curve, Fig 1. and the rail bus tractive effort curve, Fig 3. Both vehicles use engines in the 150 - 165 kW class and the top four gearbox ratios of the road bus are similar to those in the rail bus. Although it must be noted that the rail bus has two engines and therefore tractive effort for the train is shown as double that from one engine. However, the road bus has a lower final drive ratio and either a torque converter or an additional lower first gear. Thus the overall transmission ratios are different and ensure that the rail bus, which has twice the mass (per engine) of the road bus, has the greater speed whilst the road bus can climb the steeper gradient.

The 'ideal' curve shown is that tractive effort required to maintain the speed of the vehicle with maximum power from the engine and assuming a constantly variable transmission of 100 per cent efficiency. Thus the closeness of the calculated tractive effort curves to the ideal curve gives a comparative efficiency. Fig 1. shows a single deck city bus having a 165 kW engine with a 4-speed torque converter transmission and lock-up clutch. It also shows the same vehicle and engine with a 5-speed transmission and fluid flywheel (no lock-up clutch). They are both capable of the start on a 20 per cent gradient; the torque converter transmission working in the torque multiplication mode and therefore less efficient than the 5-speed transmission. The efficiency benefit alternates in the higher gears where the fluid flywheel is less efficient because the lock-up clutch in the torque converter becomes engaged, although the differences in tractive effort decrease with speed as the torque multiplication effect of the transmission is reduced.

5   PERFORMANCE SIMULATION

The full power performance of the vehicle cannot be used to choose the most appropriate number of speed ratios nor to make real efficiency comparisons. These factors are more readily assessed from a simulation programme. One such computer programme, 'Route Simulation and Vehicle Performance' (RSVP) has been developed by Leyland Truck Ltd. The programme is based on several data files defining route, vehicle, engine and transmission.

The route data defines gradients, speed limits, stopping points and lengths of stop. Vehicle data comprises weight, inertia, rolling resistance, air resistance and braking performance. The engine data is a detailed full and part load fuel consumption map. Transmission data describes the number of gear ratios, type of coupling, slip ratios and lock-up points.

In order to run the programme a variety of types of 'driver' are available; for example 'racing' where up-changes are made at maximum engine speed or 'economy' where up-changes are made at maximum torque speed. The vehicle is then 'driven' along the route in a time based stepwise fashion with calculations made for distance travelled, fuel consumed and total time taken. The 'driver' is able to 'look ahead' at the route data to make decisions about gear selection and braking. Calculated data is usually printed out at a less frequent rate than calcula-

tions are made within the programme. Summary data which is made available at the conclusion of a route can be used to make decisions about gear ratio selection.

This summary data will describe the total number of gear changes made, the percentage time spent in each gear, the total number of engine revolutions, the time to complete the route and fuel consumption. Thus performance and economy can be compared for different transmission with information which will help to give a comparison of potential durability.

A recent study of transmissions for a rail bus application showed some interesting results. From the tractive effort curves it was thought that maximum efficiency would be gained by having a multi-ratio transmission, that is the cascading curves of tractive effort would be close to the ideal line (compare Fig 3 & 4). In order to test the point three transmissions were devised for analysis using RSVP. These were all using the same torque converter with lock-up clutch and having 3, 4 & 8 speeds. Three different routes were used for the study; a rural route, a route between medium sized towns and a suburban route. The data shown here was taken from the results obtained using the suburban stopping route of some 26 km. The 8-speed transmission was shown to have an efficiency advantage, but only in the sense of total journey time. The transmission which was potentially the most durable was the 3-speed and because durability and reliability were the most important factors on which selection were to be made, Fig 5 & 6 show the comparison with the three speed transmission as the base. Assessment of durability was made by comparing the total number of engine revolutions for the journey and the total number of gear shifts made. An indication of reliability can also be gauged if one is prepared to equate maximum reliabilty with minimum changes of state. The 8-speed transmission has four times as many gear shifts with only a 4 per cent reduction in journey time and a $4\frac{1}{2}$ per cent decrease in fuel consumption. There was also a 5 per cent increase in the total number of engine revolutions. The other routes studied were longer with less frequent stops and under those conditions the journey times, fuel consumption figures and total number of gearshifts of the three transmissions tended to show a reduced difference whereas the differences in the total number of engine revolutions continued to grow.

For all routes the 4-speed transmission gave the best fuel economy with only a minor increase in engine revolutions and small (compared with the 8-speed transmission) increase in the number of gearshifts. Thus should the criterion for selection be cost effectiveness in a fixed journey time the recommendation would change to a 4-speed transmission.

6   FUTURE WORK

It has been shown that the basic expressions for performance calculations are relatively straight forward but it must be understood that they are only valid for constant acceleration. Therefore calculation intervals must be kept small, which means small speed steps to describe the engine torque curve for the full load performance prediction programme and small time steps for the simulation programme. Thus accuracy of results will be improved by a change from a digitised engine torque curve, as Table 1, to a third order polynomial approximation and more frequent calculation steps.

A second area of development is the prediction of more realistic gear change times. This is particularly relevent for military vehicles where resistances to motion are high and also with rail vehicles where gearchange times are long. A comprehensive analysis of the interaction of engine and vehicle inertias on the gear change friction elements relative to the rate of application pressure rise will enable such predictions to be made.

As well as the vehicle performance aspect of engine transmission matching there are other areas of increased study. Adoption of lock-up clutches in hydro-kinetic couplings implies that the driveline needs to be considered as a continuous shaft and tuned for an acceptable response to torsional vibration excitations from both engine and suspension. A computer programme to carry out such analysis is now undergoing development.

7   CONCLUSION

Practical engine transmission matching is selecting from those gear ratios available the number and spread to ensure that the vehicle's complete performance specification is met and not just its full load performance. Computer programmes are an essential aid in making the final choice especially when performance, fuel economy and durability factors need to be balanced.

Table 1 Data for performance prediction programme

Vehicle description	:	Typical rail bus		
Final drive ratio	:	2.33:1	Wheel radius (mm) :	400
Number of vehicles	:	2	Weight/vehicle (tonnes) :	32
Surface condition (wet/dry)	:	Wet	Weight on driving wheels: (tonnes)	16
Gearbox description	:	Self-Changing Gears R500.		

Gear Ratio	Efficiency (%)
4.25:1	96.7
2.41:1	95.9
1.59:1	93.8
1:1	94.3

Time to change gear (secs) : 3   Starting gear : 1   Coupling type : Fluid flywheel

Engine description   : Typical 150 kW (gross)

Maximum nett power to transmission : 142 kW at 1950 (r/min)

Maximum nett torque to transmission : 800 Nm at 1200 (r/min)

Engine Speed (r/min)	Torque (Nm)	Speed Ration	Torque Ratio
1080	793	0.1:1	1:1
1080	793	0.3:1	1:1
1080	793	0.5:1	1:1
1000	780	0.75:1	1:1
1100	797	0.8:1	1:1
1180	800	0.85:1	1:1
1260	800	0.9:1	1:1
1400	793	0.925:1	1:1
1540	784	0.95:1	1:1
1680	759	0.96:1	1:1
1800	739	0.965:1	1:1
1850	725	0.968:1	1:1
1900	712	0.97:1	1:1
1950	700	0.972:1	1:1

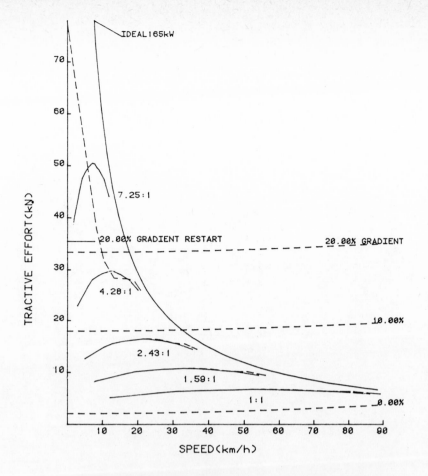

Fig 1   Tractive effort versus road speed for a 16 tonne single deck bus
          with 165 kW diesel engine and 4.78:1 final drive

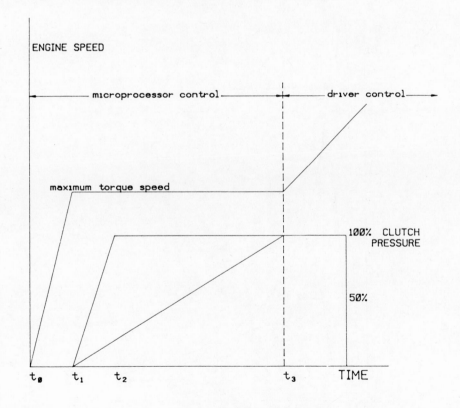

Fig 2   Controllable clutch operation

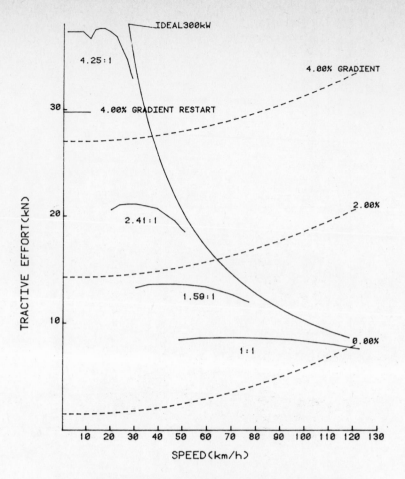

Fig 3   Tractive effort versus road speed for a 64 tonne rail bus
with 2 x 150 kW diesel engines and 2.33:1 final drive

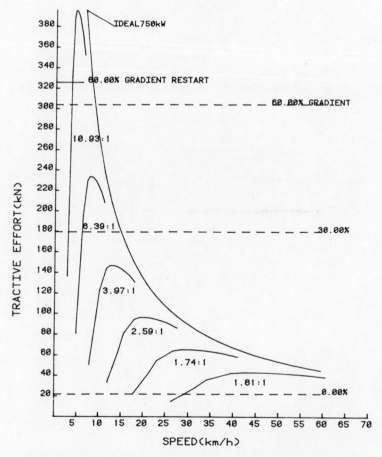

Fig 4   Tractive effort versus road speed for a 55 tonne main battle
tank with 750 kW diesel engine and 4:1 final drive

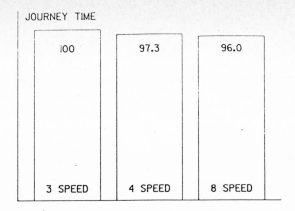

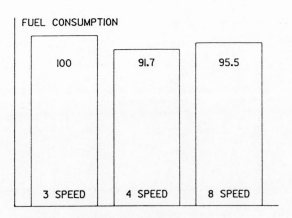

Fig 5   Performance and economy factors

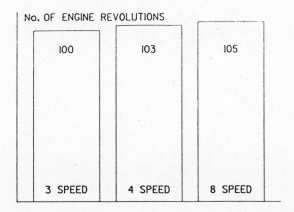

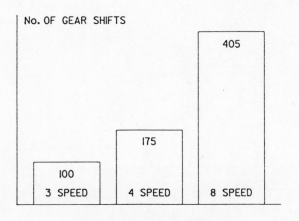

Fig 6   Durability factors

C190/86

The modelling of losses in mechanical gear trains for the computer simulation of heavy vehicle transmission systems

R E DOREY, BSc, PhD and **D McCANDLISH**, MSc, CEng, MIMechE
School of Engineering, University of Bath, Avon

SYNOPSIS This paper reviews the nature of the losses that occur in mechanical gear trains and compares analytical and empirical models proposed to represent the loss mechanisms. An examination of the efficiency characteristics of a simple gearbox shows that the models do not adequately account for speed dependent effects. A simple model is proposed which attempts to overcome this difficulty. The model is then applied to the performance simulation of a commercial compound epicyclic gearbox. The paper discusses the effect of the transmission losses upon vehicle driveline operation.

1 INTRODUCTION

In work concerned with the simulation of vehicle transmission systems efficiency is a most important consideration and should consequently receive very careful attention. Although a preliminary estimate of performance can be made using fairly gross assumptions more accurate work requires an improvement in the efficiency description. Simulation models may be constructed to use measured efficiency data directly or to interpret observed character- istics in some mathematical way. Usually, the generality and greater flexibility of the latter approach is preferred, but in either case the basic problem often facing the modeller is the complexity of the system to which test information refers and the limited nature of such information. The problem is particularly acute in the simulation of new designs and arrangements of transmission system. In such work the efficiency characteristics of individual components are important in shaping the overall behaviour of the system and interest often lies with performance over a wide range of operating conditions.

In this paper the loss mechanisms associated with geared transmission systems are discussed. Previous work in the field is reviewed and is assessed for its suitability in describing measured performance characteristics that have been obtained. Proposals are made to extend the theory to cover a wider range of performance conditions.

Initially the paper considers the losses in conjunction with a straightforward industrial mechanical gearbox. The modelling techniques met in this work are then taken forward to consider the losses in a commercial compound epicyclic gearbox and the effect that these have upon vehicle driveline performance. In particular consideration is given to the effect upon vehicle fuel consumption, speed and gradeability.

2 NATURE OF LOSSES IN MECHANICAL GEAR TRAINS

Mechanical gear trains are commonly recognised as an efficient method of power transmission in vehicle applications. The power losses associated with such systems are often quite small but are nonetheless important; in absolute terms because the losses though small do affect transmission performance, and in relative terms because it is important to be able to assess the effects of changes in transmission design.

The losses observed in geared transmissions arise from friction between the meshing gear teeth, friction in the bearings and losses due to oil churning in the casing. Since there can be no kinematic loss, these frictional effects appear as a reduction in the transmitted torque.

2.1 Gear tooth friction

Gear tooth friction may be considered as a function of the tooth geometry and the mechanism of lubrication between meshing teeth. At the point of contact between two gears there will be a force F_N, normal to the teeth flanks, which transmits the torque, and a frictional force F_F, tangential to the teeth flanks, opposing the motion. The ratio of these forces may be defined in terms of an instantaneous coefficient of friction

$$\mu_i = \frac{F_F}{F_N} \qquad 1$$

Alternatively, the work done in overcoming friction for a small displacement of the gears can be considered and this may also be expressed in terms of a frictional force and a coefficient of friction. In either case the coefficient of friction will depend not only on the tooth profile, surface finish and gear material, but also on the loading, the speed and the lubricant properties.

A more detailed consideration of the problem reveals two types of relative motion and two associated mechanisms of lubrication. In the small, high-pressure, hertzian contact zone, the meshing teeth are separated by a thin elasto-hydrodynamic lubricant film. The teeth slide under load and the friction is due to the shearing of the fluid film. In the approach to the contact zone, there is a larger region of hydrodynamic lubrication. The motion of the teeth is essentially a rolling action, oil is pumped into a convergent clearance and the friction is dependent on tooth velocity and lubricant viscosity. Although once popular, earlier theories of 'mixed-film' lubrication have now been discarded as a result of increased understanding of elastohydrodynamic effects.

2.2 Bearing friction

Friction in journal bearings is due to the viscous shearing of the hydrodynamic oil film and to the pumping action caused by journal eccentricity. The first of these effects predominates and a close approximation to the measured friction can be obtained by ignoring the eccentricity. In this case, the friction is dependent on bearing velocity and lubricant viscosity.

Friction in ball and roller bearings is similar to friction between meshing gear teeth and may be approached by the alternative methods already referred to. A suitable coefficient of friction may be determined empirically, but it is important to realise that it will vary with the operating conditions. Hence it may be better to define the loss in terms of a load dependent component and a speed dependent component.

A more rigorous analysis proves to be very complex. It has been shown that for loaded roller bearings, micro-slip and sliding effects make a negligible contribution to the frictional loss and that pure rolling motion may be assumed. One important frictional loss is associated with the hysterisis effect in the deformation of the bearing rollers and track, and this loss increases rapidly with load.

The second important loss is associated with elasto-hydrodynamic lubrication between the rolling surfaces. Since the film is very thin, often only slightly greater than the sum of the surface roughnesses, it is necessary to involve concepts of surface topology in any study. This loss is also a function of the fluid viscosity in the contact zone, which is dependent on local pressure and temperature conditions.

2.3 Oil churning loss

The losses associated with the movement of oil in the gearbox casing are difficult to predict. Oil churning losses are dependent on the gearbox size and shape; the type of gear and its operating speed; the viscosity of the lubricant and the method of lubrication. Under normal operating conditions these losses should be small, becoming important only at high speeds and low torques and practically they cannot be dissociated from the windage losses of the mechanical gears. Careful measurements show that these losses are proportional to speed at relatively low speeds, whilst they increase towards

a square law at very high speeds. Normal practice, however, is to assume a linear relationship.

3 THEORETICAL AND EMPIRICAL MODELS

3.1 Gear tooth friction

Merritt's analysis. Merritt (1) determined the frictional force opposing motion by considering a small displacement of the meshing gear teeth along the contact path. The work done in overcoming friction, δJ_F, expressed in terms of the instantaneous coefficient of friction, μ_i, is given by

$$\delta J_F = \mu_i F_N (\frac{2}{d_1} + \frac{2}{d_2}) \frac{x \delta x}{\cos \theta} \qquad 2$$

where d_1 and d_2 are the pitch circle diameters of the two gears
δx is a small displacement of the contact point along the contact path at a distance x from the pitch point
and θ is the pressure angle.

The work done in overcoming friction along the whole length of the contact path may be found by assuming an average value for the coefficient of friction, μ, and integrating equation 2 over the length of the approach path to the pitch point, ℓ_a, and the length of the recession path, ℓ_r

$$J_F = \frac{\mu F_N}{\cos \theta} (\frac{1}{d_1} + \frac{1}{d_2})(\ell_a^2 + \ell_r^2) \qquad 3$$

Since the ideal work over the same path, J_o, is given by

$$J_o = F_N (\ell_a + \ell_r) \qquad 4$$

the efficiency of the mesh may be expressed as

$$\eta = 1 - \frac{\mu}{\cos \theta}(\frac{1}{d_1} + \frac{1}{d_2})(\frac{\ell_a^2 + \ell_r^2}{\ell_a + \ell_r}) \qquad 5$$

Most estimates of coefficient of friction are based on empirical results, derived from disc tests or tests on gears. A form proposed by Shell International Petroleum (2) for spur gears is

$$\mu = \frac{.04}{\nu^{.25} \sin \theta (\frac{d_1 d_2}{d_1 + d_2})^{.5} V_o^{.5}} \qquad 6$$

where V_o is the pitch line velocity of the gears
and ν is the kinematic viscosity of the lubricant at the bulk temperature of the gears

Buckingham's analysis. A similar analysis by Buckingham (3) yields results which may be expressed in the same form as equation 5. His tests showed that the coefficient of friction varied with the sliding velocity of the meshing gears. At very low sliding speeds, the values of μ were high, reducing rapidly to a minimum of approximately 0.01 at speeds of the order of 0.15 m/s and then rising slowly for further increases in speed. For hardened spur gears, with sliding velocities greater than 0.15 m/s, Buckingham gave the empirical relationship

70

$$\mu = .019 \ V_s^{.5} \qquad\qquad 7$$

where V_s is the average sliding velocity of the gears in mesh.

Clearly there is some conflict between equations 6 and 7 since the coefficient of friction decreases with speed in the former but increases with speed in the latter.

Chiu's analysis. More recent authors, such as Chiu (4) have incorporated analytical and experimental work on elasto-hydrodynamic lubrication into their models. Chiu considered the two lubrication zones described in section 2.1. In the contact zone, the frictional force due to sliding, f_s, was expressed in terms of an instantaneous coefficient of friction μ_i

$$f_s = \mu_i \ F_N \qquad\qquad 8$$

where μ_i was evaluated from an empirical relationship proposed by O'Donohue and Cameron (5)

$$\mu_i = \frac{.0173 \ (\sigma + .55)}{\eta_a^{.125} V_r^{.167} V_s^{.333} \rho_r^{.5}} \qquad\qquad 9$$

where σ is the combined surface roughness of the gears in mesh
η_a is the absolute viscosity of the lubricant at atmospheric pressure and bulk temperature
V_r is the rolling velocity at the gear teeth, given by the sum of the tooth flank velocities
V_s is the sliding velocity of the gear teeth, given by the difference of the tooth flank velocities
ρ_r is the effective radius of curvature at the point of contact.

The associated power loss P_s may be determined by integrating the product $f_s V_s$ over the length of the gear tooth contact path.

In the approach zone, the frictional force due to pumping, f_p, was evaluated by the Dowson and Higginson relationship (6)

$$f_p = .715 \ E\rho_r \left(\frac{\eta_a V_r}{E\rho_r}\right)^{.71} \ell_w \qquad\qquad 10$$

where E is Young's Modulus for the gear material
and ℓ_w is the face width of the gear mesh.

The associated power loss P_p may be determined by integrating the product $2 \ f_p V_r$ over the length of the gear tooth contact path.

The efficiency of the gear mesh was then described in terms of the two power losses as:

$$\eta = 1 - \frac{P_s + P_p}{F_N V_o \cos\theta} \qquad\qquad 11$$

A series of experiments on the lubrication of rollers reported to the Royal Society by Crook (7) and quoted by Dowson and Higginson (6) give some support to the relationship expressed as equation 9. Values of the coefficient of friction for heavily loaded contacts lay chiefly in the range 0.02 to 0.03. As a function of sliding speed the friction was initially low, rising sharply to a maximum at sliding speeds of

about 0.5 m/s and then falling slowly to a steady value at speeds of about 4 m/s. As a function of rolling speed, the coefficient of friction fell slightly as the speed was increased; whilst as a function of load, the coefficient of friction increased significantly. Higher viscosity lubricant resulted in a greater film thickness, which led to higher friction under rolling conditions but reduced friction at high sliding speeds.

Simplified models. By considering mean values for the two forces at the point of gear tooth contact F_N and F_F, Magi (8) showed that the ratio of output torque, T_2, to input torque, T_1, could be represented by

$$\frac{T_2}{T_1} = \frac{d_2 \ (1-C_1)}{d_1 \ (1+C_2)} \qquad\qquad 12$$

where C_1 and C_2 are coefficients which are small compared with unity.

Edge (9) and Huckvale (10) have used this model, rewriting it as:

$$\frac{T_2}{T_1} = \frac{d_2}{d_1} (1-C_1-C_2)$$

or $$\frac{T_2}{T_1} = \frac{d_2}{d_1} (1-C_{12}) \qquad\qquad 13$$

where C_{12} is the torque loss coefficient for the mesh. The value of this coefficient should vary with the gear size, but is often taken as 0.01.

Tuplin (11) has proposed another simple empirical model for well-finished and well-lubricated spur or helical gears. Expressed in terms of mesh efficiency

$$\eta = 1 - .2 \left(\frac{1}{t_1} + \frac{1}{t_2}\right) \qquad\qquad 14$$

where t_1 and t_2 are the number of teeth on the driving and driven gears (a negative value of t should be used for an internal gear). This may be regarded as a simplified version of equation 5.

3.2 Journal bearing friction

Cameron's analysis. Cameron (12) gives an excellent discussion of friction in journal bearings and develops an expression for the frictional drag F_D at an angular velocity ω.

$$F_D = \frac{\pi \eta_a d \ell \omega}{C_D (1-\varepsilon^2)^{.5}} + \frac{We}{d} \sin \psi \qquad\qquad 15$$

where d is the journal diameter
C_D is the diametrical clearance ratio
ℓ is the bearing length
and for a load W
e is the bearing eccentricity
ε is the eccentricity ratio
and ψ is the bearing attitude angle

Simplified models. The first analysis, published by Petroff in 1883, ignored the effects of journal eccentricity. If the frictional drag force is due only to viscous shearing of the hydrodynamic oil film, then equation 15 reduces to

$$F_D = \pi \eta_a \frac{d\ell\omega}{C_D} \qquad 16$$

This simplified version is usually adopted, since the eccentricity is rarely known and its effect is relatively small. In fact the Petroff equation often gives a better approximation to experimental values than Cameron's equation. Ignoring the effect of eccentricity tends to compensate for the effects of aeration and cavitation in the low pressure regions of the lubricant film.

It is possible to simplify the model still further, since its function is simply to describe a viscous friction effect. The friction torque T_d may be expressed as the product of the speed and a loss coefficient f

$$T_d = f. \omega \qquad 17$$

For journal bearings the numerical values of the coefficient of friction are normally in the range 0.001 to 0.005, hence the bearing losses are an order of magnitude less than the gear tooth losses.

3.3 Ball and roller bearing friction

The frictional losses in ball and roller bearings may be even lower than those in journal bearings; coefficients of friction in the range 0.0003 to 0.003 are quoted in many texts.

For pure rolling motion the frictional loss is associated with the hysterisis effect in the deformation of the boundaries. Tabor (13) has shown that for elastic deformation, the coefficient of friction is proportional to the semi-contact width under Hertzian stress and to a hysterisis loss factor which must be determined empirically. It is inversely proportional to the roller diameter.

Johnson (14) extended this work into the plastic deformation region, showing that if the plastic deformation zone is small and contained within material subject to elastic deformation, the frictional loss is a function of the ratio of the Hertzian contact pressure to the material yield stress in simple shear. For plastic deformation the coefficient of friction is roughly proportional to the square of the load.

In practice, the frictional resistance of ball and roller bearings is a function of both load and speed. Palmgren (15) has published empirical data on bearing losses and life, derived from a careful programme of testing over many years.

The load dependent frictional torque loss T_{DL} may be expressed as

$$T_{DL} = f_1 F_r d_e \qquad 18$$

where f_1 is a loss coefficient dependent on the type of bearing, empirical values being given in Table 1
F_r is the radial bearing load
and d_e is the pitch diameter of the rolling element.

Equation 18 neglects axial loads, but an additional term may be added if these are significant.

The speed dependent frictional torque loss T_{DS} may be expressed as

$$T_{DS} = f_o P_v^{.33} d_e^3 (\eta_a \omega)^{.67} \qquad 19$$

where f_o is a loss coefficient, dependent on the type of bearing, empirical values being given in Table 1
P_v is the difference between the vapour pressure of the lubricant and atmospheric pressure
and ω is the angular velocity of the bearing ring

4   EXPERIMENTAL RESULTS

Figure 1 shows an industrial mechanical gearbox consisting of a fully floating epicyclic gear set and associated transfer gears. Detail of the gears and the bearings used in the gearbox are given Table 2. In this paper this data was used to assess the gear and bearing loss models.

Previously (10) the gearbox has been considered for use in a split power heavy vehicle transmission system. In the experimental work undertaken for this paper the arrangement was examined under two conditions. First shaft B was clamped with power transmitted from the input to shaft A, and then shaft A clamped and power transmitted from the input to shaft B. Power to drive the gearbox was provided by a 180 kw Perkins V8-605 turbocharged diesel engine. Power absorption was provided by a simple hydrostatic dynamometer. For each test condition measurements were taken of the input torque and speed and of the output torque at either shaft A or shaft B.

Figure 2 shows the experimental efficiency characteristics that were obtained in each case; the efficiency plotted against input torque for various values of input speed. At low torque levels the losses are predominantly speed dependent and there is a relatively wide spread to the curves, the efficiency reducing as speed increases. With higher torques the effect of speed reduces and the efficiency curves begin to merge indicating that the losses then become primarily dependent upon the transmission loading.

5   COMPARATIVE ASSESSMENT OF MODELS

From the previous discussion it is apparent that the mechanics of the loss mechanisms in gears and bearings are complex. The models that have been discussed range in their quantification of the losses from a simple dependency upon torque and speed, with minimal considerations of geometry and lubricant properties, to complex relations requiring great detail of the operating conditions. These models are each assessed for their ability to predict the foregoing gearbox efficiencies.

Figures 3 and 4 show the simulated efficiency characteristics obtained with shaft A and shaft B clamped. The effect of using the minimum and maximum bearing loss coefficients proposed by Palmgren was investigated and the better results found to lie in using the maximum values. Figures 3 and 4 both assume the use of the maximum values.

An examination of the figures shows firstly that there is a wide variation in the predicted losses and secondly that there is an underestimation of their speed dependency.

The analytical models proposed by Merritt and Buckingham to represent gear meshing losses rely upon determination of an average coefficient of friction. The relationships 6 and 7 were each investigated for this purpose and these gave rise to the results shown in Figure 3. It may be seen that neither gives good correlation with the experimental characteristics. The first produces efficiencies which increase with speed and which diverge with increasing torque, both of which are contrary to the experimental findings. The second produces results which exhibit the correct trends but with efficiency values that are too high.

The problem of efficiency increasing with speed is again present with the simulation results shown in Figure 4 for Chiu's model, which uses O'Donahue and Cameron's empirical relationship, 9, to evaluate friction in the contact zone of the gear mesh and the Dowson and Higginson relationship, 10, for friction in the approach zone. The results obtained with Tuplin's model are also shown in Figure 4. The model uses a constant value for gear mesh efficiency which considering its simplicity gives remarkably close agreement to the experimental characteristics, at least for medium to high torques.

The difficulty of using such models to adequately represent gearbox losses over a wide operating range has been recognised by Edge (9) and Huckvale (10). In their work they examined the effect of global changes in loss parameters, assuming constant values for mesh efficiencies and bearing losses linearly dependent upon speed. With a reasonable number of gears and bearings in a gearbox this gives enormous scope in selecting loss parameters to fit the experimental results, and Huckvale in his modelling of the gearbox described here achieved a fit of better than 0.2% over the range of the experimental characteristics.

6 MODEL SELECTION

Provided appropriate test data is available, it is possible to adopt the above approach and model the efficiency of a particular gearbox with considerable accuracy by determing coefficients for the load-dependent and speed-dependent losses. However, such a model lacks generality and it would be unreasonable to use the same coefficients in modelling another gearbox, particularly one of a different design.

Theoretical models, such as that of Chiu, take account of the gear geometry, lubricant properties and operating conditions and are therefore complex. But since they fail to recognise the importance of the speed-dependent losses, they are unlikely to be used generally in design or performance evaluation. The simple Tuplin model, which shows a slightly better agreement with experimental results, is to be preferred. Its disadvantage is that it predicts a constant mesh efficiency for a given pair of gears at all loads and speeds. Even when combined with Palmgren's equations for bearing losses, the predicted efficiency is far too close to a constant value.

A better model may be obtained by modifying Tuplin's equation so that it contains both a load-dependent and a speed-dependent loss. Examination of the test data used in this paper suggests that at maximum torque and speed it is possible to assume that two thirds of the torque loss, T_d, is load-dependent and one third is speed dependent.

With $T_d = C_1 T + C_2 \omega$

$\omega = \omega_{max}$ and $T = T_{max}$

then $C_1 T_{max} = 2 C_2 \omega_{max}$

Giving $T_d = C_1 T (1 + .5 (\frac{\omega}{\omega_{max}})(\frac{T_{max}}{T}))$ (20)

Taking C_1 as 0.133 the modified form of Tuplin's equation for mesh efficiency may be written as

$\eta = 1 - .133 (\frac{1}{t_1} + \frac{1}{t_2})(1 + .5 (\frac{\omega}{\omega_{max}})(\frac{T_{max}}{T}))$ (21)

The losses in ball and roller bearings might be expressed in a similar form, since they consist of load-dependent and speed-dependent components. This is attractive, since Palmgren's equation for the load dependent loss is simple, while the speed dependent loss is relatively complex. Any errors are unlikely to be serious, since the bearing losses are an order of magnitude less than the mesh losses.

The model could be further improved by raising the speed ratio to an index of 0.7. This corresponds to the index of 0.71 proposed by Dowson and Higginson, equation 10, and the index of 0.67 proposed by Palmgren, equation 19. The predicted efficiency of the gearbox may then be obtained by summing the mesh losses and the bearing losses for each rotating shaft.

$\eta = 1 - \left(\Sigma .133 (\frac{1}{t_1} + \frac{1}{t_2}) + \Sigma f_1 \right) \left(1 + .5 (\frac{\omega}{\omega_{max}})^{.7} (\frac{T_{max}}{T}) \right)$ (22)

The predicted efficiency characteristics for the gearbox, based on equation 22, are shown in Figure 5. These are based on the component loss values given in Table 3. Clearly there is a much better correlation between the predicted and experimental characteristics over the full torque range, with maximum errors of less than one percent. Although the matching cannot be exact with such a simple model, it does result in a significant improvement in performance prediction. Importantly it is also a model which lends itself to straightforward interpretation and use.

7 DRIVE SYSTEM APPLICATION

Subsequently the modelling technique was applied to an estimation of the losses in a commercial 5 speed semi-automatic compound epicyclic transmission, and the study broadened to examine driveline performance in a typical city bus duty. Figure 6 shows in schematic form the gearbox arrangement that was studied, and Figure 7 a comparison between the measured gearbox efficiencies and those predicted by the simple model. Considering the complexity of the gearbox, the match between the experimental and predicted results is quite reasonable. It is again of the order of one percent or better.

As well as detailed considerations concerned with the selection of gears and bearings at the component level, the transmission losses also contribute to overall vehicle performance; affecting vehicle fuel consumption, speed and gradeability. These issues were examined using a full driveline model of the vehicle, engine, fluid coupling and transmission system together with measured performance data collected from a bus operating in typical service conditions (16). Illustration of these data is given in Figure 8 which shows two velocity-time profiles for the bus operating over a city route. This was supplemented with information concerned with the vehicle loading and route gradient and used with the computer simulation model to estimate vehicle performance.

7.1 Fuel consumption.

Six separate recordings were made of bus operation and Table 4 shows the fuel consumption predicted by the simulation model for each journey made over the route. The previous velocity profiles shown in Figure 8 correspond to runs 4 and 6, respectively the most and least economical of the journeys. Examination of these profiles shows that the effect of the protracted stop-start driving sequences in run 6 is to significantly increase fuel consumption. Reduced economy in engine operation is a major factor contributing to this, but the increase is also a reflection upon the high utilisation of the less efficient mid-range gearbox ratios. Particular fuel consumption figures that may be identified for comment in Table 4 are those associated with the fare stages near the start of the route and those towards the end. Associated with these stages there is significant use of the mid-range gear ratios; the early stages represent heavy vehicle loading through city centre traffic, and the final stages operation with appreciable upward gradients.

7.2 Speed and gradeability

A more comprehensive insight into the operation of the driveline is obtained by considering the performance of the gearbox combined with that of the transmission fluid coupling. The effect that they have upon vehicle speed and gradeability is illustrated in Figure 9. The figure shows the variation of driveline efficiency with vehicle speed and route gradient, and the effect upon engine steady-state fuel consumption. It can be seen that a moderate gradient condition at a particular speed results in maximum driveline efficiency. The extremes of gradient result in a degradation of performance; at a low gradient condition the transmission loading is light and gearbox efficiency is low, whilst at a high gradient condition the appreciable transmission loading results in significant slip of the fluid coupling.

8 CONCLUSIONS

In the design or performance evaluation of a gearbox difficulty lies in an accurate assessment of the losses that may be expected to occur. Simple estimates may be based upon previous experience, but these lack the generality to be applied to different gearbox configurations.

Where experimental results already exist it is possible to construct an accurate model of the efficiency characteristics by determining coefficients for the load dependent and the speed dependent losses. A model of this type may be used where there is no necessity to consider different designs or arrangements of gearbox, but is of limited value where this is required.

Various analytical and empirical models of gear and bearing friction were assessed for their accuracy in predicting the efficiency characteristics of an industrial mechanical gearbox and all resulted in an underestimation of the speed dependent losses. It was shown however that a simple extension to Tuplin's relationship for gear meshing losses produced a significant improvement in performance prediction. The extension to the relationship also enabled the straightforward summation of the bearing losses for each rotating shaft to allow simple calculation of overall gearbox efficiency.

Application of the modelling technique to a commercial compound epicyclic gearbox and its use in a full driveline simulation has enabled an illustration of the effect of the transmission losses upon overall vehicle performance. Here, particular consideration was given to vehicle fuel consumption, speed and gradeability.

REFERENCES

(1) MERRITT, H.E. Gears. Pitman, 1946.

(2) ANON. The lubrication of industrial gears. Shell Int. Petroleum Co. Ltd. 1964.

(3) BUCKINGHAM, E. Analytical mechanics of gears. McGraw-Hill, 1949.

(4) CHIU, Y.P. Approximate calculation of power loss in involute gears. Joint ASLE-ASME Lubrication Conf., Florida, 1975.

(5) O'DONOHUE, J.P. and CAMERON, A. Friction and temperature in rolling sliding contacts. ASLE Trans, 1966, 9, 186.

(6) DOWSON, D. and HIGGINSON, G.R. The fundamentals of roller gear lubrication - elastohydrodynamic lubrication. Pergamon, 1966.

(7) CROOK, A.W. The lubrication of rollers. Phil.Trans., 1963, A255, 281.

(8) MAGI, M. On efficiencies of mechanical co-planar shaft power transmissions. Report from the Division of Machine Elements, Chalmers Univ. of Tech., 1974.

(9) EDGE, K.A. The characteristics of engine-hydrostatic transmission systems. PhD Thesis, Univ. of Bath, 1975.

(10) HUCKVALE, S.A. The simulation of heavy vehicle transmission systems incorporating epicyclic gear trains and hydrostatic elements. PhD Thesis, Univ. of Bath, 1978.

(11) TUPLIN, W.A. Gear Design. Machinery Pub. Co., 1962.

(12) CAMERON, A. Principles of lubrication. Longmans, 1966.

(13) TABOR, D. The mechanism of rolling friction. Phil. Trans., 1955, A229, 198.

(14) JOHNSON, K.L. Rolling resistance of a rigid cylinder on an elastic-plastic surface. Int. Journal Mech. Science, 1972, 14, 145.

(15) PALMGREN, A. Ball and roller bearing engineering. SKF Industries, 1959.

(16) DOREY, R.E. Hydrostatic split power transmissions and their application to the city bus. PhD Thesis, Univ. of Bath, 1983.

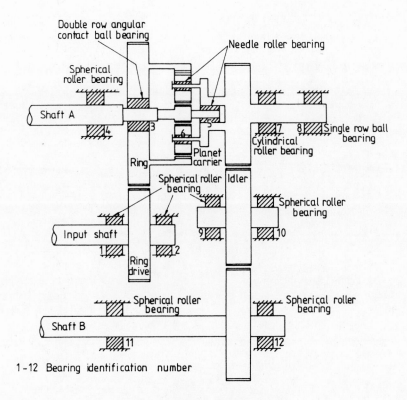

1-12 Bearing identification number

Fig 1   Heavy vehicle gearbox

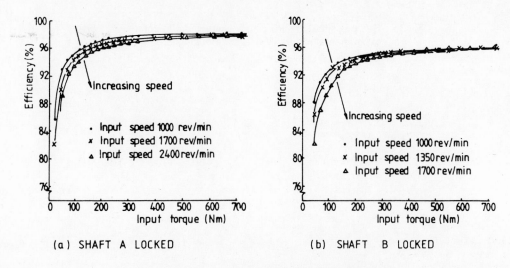

(a) SHAFT A LOCKED

(b) SHAFT B LOCKED

Fig 2   Gearbox experimental efficiency characteristics

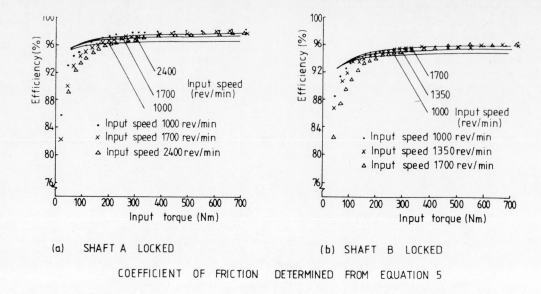

(a)   SHAFT A LOCKED

(b)   SHAFT B LOCKED

COEFFICIENT OF FRICTION DETERMINED FROM EQUATION 5

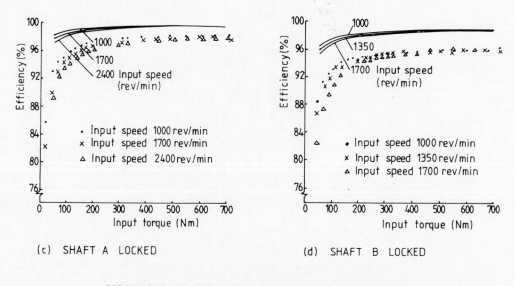

(c)   SHAFT A LOCKED

(d)   SHAFT B LOCKED

COEFFICIENT OF FRICTION DETERMINED FROM EQUATION 6

Fig 3   Gearbox simulated efficiency characteristics comparison with experimental results (Merrit and Buckingham's model for gear friction)

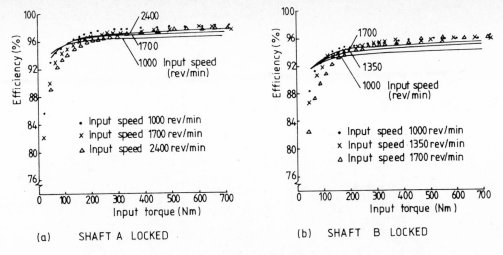

(a) SHAFT A LOCKED

(b) SHAFT B LOCKED

CHIUS MODEL FOR GEAR FRICTION

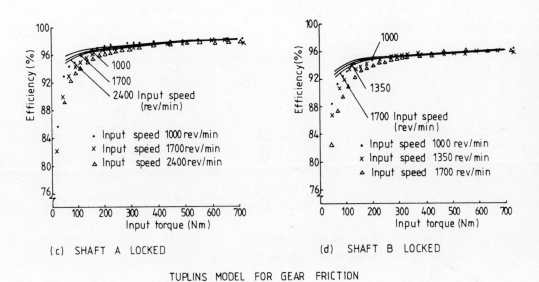

(c) SHAFT A LOCKED

(d) SHAFT B LOCKED

TUPLINS MODEL FOR GEAR FRICTION

Fig 4   Gearbox simulated efficiency characteristics comparison
with experimental results

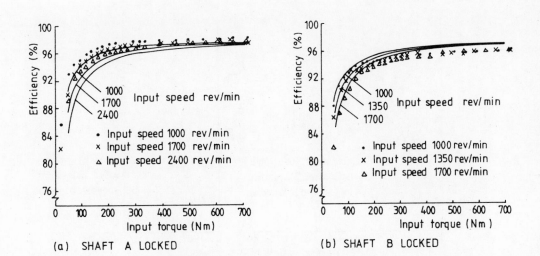

(a) SHAFT A LOCKED

(b) SHAFT B LOCKED

Fig 5   Gearbox simulated efficiency characteristics comparison
with experimental results (modified Tuplin model for gear
and bearing friction)

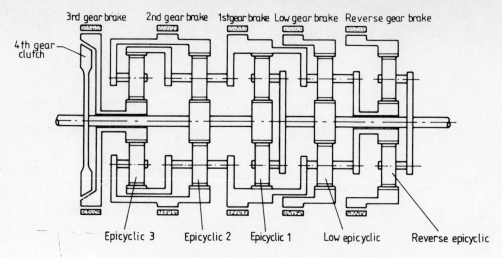

3rd gear brake   2nd gear brake   1st gear brake   Low gear brake   Reverse gear brake

4th gear clutch

Epicyclic 3   Epicyclic 2   Epicyclic 1   Low epicyclic   Reverse epicyclic

Fig 6   Simplified schematic view of compound epicyclic transmission

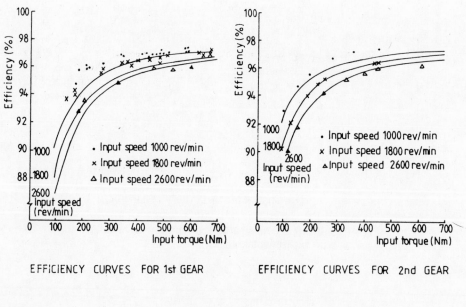

EFFICIENCY CURVES FOR 1st GEAR

EFFICIENCY CURVES FOR 2nd GEAR

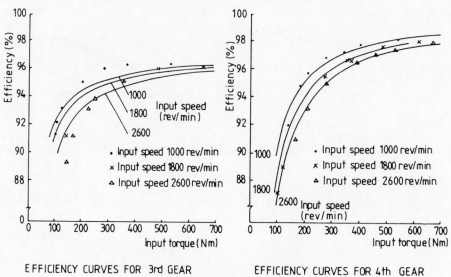

EFFICIENCY CURVES FOR 3rd GEAR

EFFICIENCY CURVES FOR 4th GEAR

Fig 7   Compound epicyclic transmission simulated efficiency characteristics comparison with experimental results

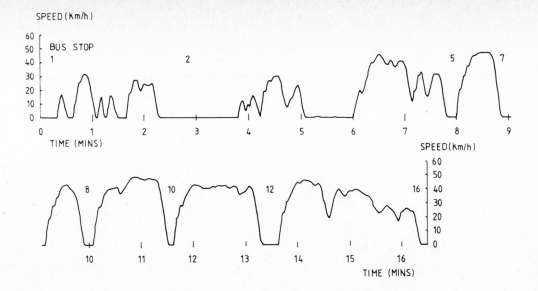

(a) RUN 4

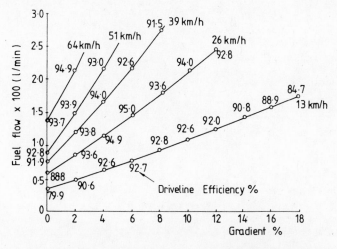

(b) RUN 6

Fig 8   City bus velocity time profiles

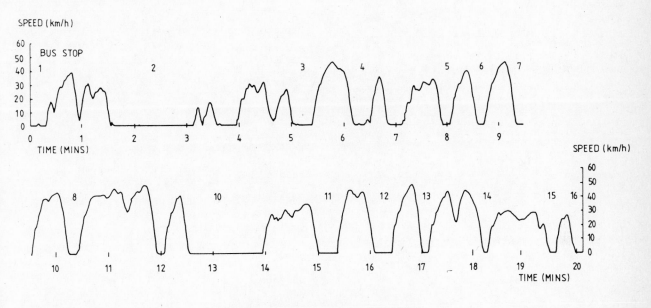

Fig 9   Variation of driveline efficiency with vehicle speed and route gradient and effect upon engine steady state fuel consumption

Table 1 Ball and roller bearing loss coefficients

Bearing Type	f_1
radial groove ball bearings	$\beta = 0°$ $\quad .0009(F_r/Co)^{.55}$
self-aligning ball bearings	$\beta = 10°$ $\quad .0003(F_r/Co)^{.4}$
angular contact ball bearings	$\beta = 30°$ $\quad .001(F_r/Co)^{.33}$
	$\beta = 40°$ $\quad .0013(F_r/Co)^{.33}$
cylindrical roller bearings	$0.00025 - 0.0003$
self-aligning roller bearings	$0.0004 - 0.0005$
needle roller bearings	$0.0005 - 0.001$

Note: Co is the static load rating
β is the contact angle of the bearing
LOAD DEPENDENT LOSS COEFFICENTS

Bearing Type	f_o
single row deep grove ball bearings	$1.5 - 2$
double row self-aligning ball bearings	$1.5 - 2$
single row angular contact ball bearings	2
double row angular contact ball bearings	4
single row cylindrical roller bearings	$2 - 3$
single row tapered roller bearings	$3 - 4$
double row spherical roller bearings	$4 - 6$
needle roller bearings	$2 - 8$

SPEED DEPENDENT LOSS COEFFICIENTS

Table 2 Details of gears and bearings

Gears in Mesh	Pitch circle Diameter (mm)	No. of teeth
ring drive	182	43
to ring(external)	428	101
ring (internal)	207	69
to planets	72	24
planets	72	24
to shaft A	63	21
planet carrier	381	90
to idler	309	73
idler	309	73
to shaft B	220	52

Pressure angle 20°
GEAR CHARACTERISTICS

Bearing Type	Identity number	Pitch Diameter of rolling elements
spherical roller	1,2	89 mm
double row angular contact ball	3	89 mm
spherical roller	4	89 mm
needle roller	5	32 mm
needle roller	6	40 mm
cylindrical roller	7	110 mm
single row ball	8	110 mm
spherical roller	9,10	89 mm
spherical roller	11,12	89 mm

BEARING CHRACTERISTICS

© IMechE 1986 C190/86

Table 3 Gear and bearing loss coefficients for the
modified Tuplin model

GEAR MESH	NO. OF TEETH t_1	t_2	LOSS FACTOR $.133(1/t_1+1/t_2)$
ring drive - ring gear	43 -	101	.0044
ring gear - planets	69(int) -	24	.0036
planets - shaft A	24	21	.0119
			.0199

SHAFT	BEARINGS	LOAD LOSS FACTOR f_1
input	spherical roller	.00045
ring gear	double row ball	.0005
planets	needle roller	.0010
planet carrier	needle roller	.0010
shaft A	spherical roller	.00045
		.0034

Gearbox loss = .0233 $\left[1 + \left(.5\left(\frac{\omega}{\omega_{max}}\right)^{.7}\left(\frac{T_{max}}{T}\right)\right)\right]$

(b) SHAFT B LOCKED

ω_{max} = 2400 rev/min
T_{max} = 700 Nm

GEAR MESH	NO. OF TEETH t_1	t_2	LOSS FACTOR $.133(1/t_1+1/t_2)$
ring drive - ring gear	43 -	101	.0044
ring gear - planets	69(int) -	24	.0036
planet carrier - idler	90 -	73	.0033
idler - shaft B	73 -	52	.0044
			.0157

SHAFT	BEARINGS	LOAD LOSS FACTOR f_1
input	spherical roller	.00045
ring gear	double row ball	.0005
planets	needle roller	.0010
planet carrier	needle roller + cyl. roller + ball	.00045
idler	spherical roller	.00045
shaft B	spherical roller	.00045
		.0033

Gearbox loss = .019 $\left[1 + \left(.5\left(\frac{\omega}{\omega_{max}}\right)^{.7}\left(\frac{T_{max}}{T}\right)\right)\right]$

(a) SHAFT A LOCKED

Table 4 Predicted Bus Fuel Consumption

Bus Stop	Total Distance (km)	Stage Distance (km)	Fuel Consumption (ℓ/100 km)					
			Run 1	Run 2	Run 3	Run 4	Run 5	Run 6
1								
2	.48	.48	39.1	27.3	50.3	47.2		46.2
3	.90	.42	80.5	69.6			90.2	75.1
4	1.35	.45	23.6	27.3	51.9		28.5	27.9
5	1.77	.42	24.8	26.9	38.7	34.9	32.1	32.7
6	2.01	.24	32.9					38.1
7	2.33	.32	40.9	48.1	45.8	46.8	48.8	48.2
8	2.74	.41	26.9	30.1	27.7	25.4	29.6	29.1
9	3.27	.53	61.5	60.7				
10	3.86	.59		36.6		42.7		40.8
11	4.43	.57	27.9	33.9	31.8			38.1
12	4.91	.48	18.3	17.1	13.6	21.5	30.5	18.6
13	5.20	.29			45.5			52.6
14	5.78	.58						31.2
15	6.29	.51	45.6	44.9	54.8		45.3	92.9
16	6.36	.07	88.8	76.8	99.1	39.1	99.5	89.1
Average fuel consumption (ℓ/100 km)			39.0	39.9	41.3	36.4	38.2	44.0

C196/86

Design and performance characteristics of the laboratory differential compound engine at Bath University

F J WALLACE, MSc, PhD, DSc, FEng, FIMechE, D PRINCE, BSc, D HOWARD, BSc and
M TARABAD, BSc, MSc, PhD
School of Engineering, University of Bath, Avon

SYNOPSIS The paper describes the main components of the latest version of the Differential Compound Engine (DCE), an integrated engine transmission system having a number of unique features, which is now ready for testing. The process of optimization of the operating characteristics appropriate to this particular form of continuously variable engine transmission system is described in outline, together with the control strategy adopted both for steady state and transient optimization. The resulting performance characteristics of the DCE, both steady state and transient, are discussed in the concluding sections of the paper.

1 INTRODUCTION

In the latest of many papers (1,2,3,4) on the differential compound engine (DCE), the main components and operating characteristics were described in some detail (1). The DCE concept combines, in integrated form, the benefits of thermodynamic compounding, (i.e. the possibility of excess turbine power feedback to the output shaft when both power turbine and supercharging compressor are connected with engine and output shaft through gearing), with the characteristics of a continuously variable transmission system. In the DCE this is achieved by employing a fully floating epicyclic gear train between engine, compressor and output shaft, and gearing the turbine to the output shaft either directly, or in the latest form of the DCE, through a subsidiary CVT. At the time of writing of (1) the funds for the complete rebuilding of the DCE unit at Bath University had not yet been secured. The major change which has occurred since that time is that the relatively small Perkins 6.354 6 cylinder D.I. engine of 5.8ℓ displacement has now been replaced by the larger and more highly rated Leyland 500 engine of 8.2ℓ displacement and equipped with low compression ratio (12.8:1) pistons.

With this major change of build, it has been possible to increase the predicted rating of the complete plant from 203 kW to 275 kW and, by taking advantage of the much higher max. cylinder pressure of the Leyland engine (approx. 150 bar cf. 100 bar), in conjunction with the L.C.R. pistons, to increase the degree of torque back up. So far as the other mechanical details of the complete plant are concerned, the changes are as follows :-

(a) The fully floating epicyclic gearbox has been modified, particularly with respect to the compressor drive, in that the sunwheel now drives an improved single rotary positive displacement compressor through a single step up gear from the sunwheel, having a step up ratio of 2.872.

(b) The original 2 small rotary positive displacement compressors have been replaced by a single unit having delivery of 8m³/sec at

12,000 rev/min. and 3:1 pressure ratio.

Mention was also made in ref. (1) of a turbine CVT to allow the variable nozzle power turbine to operate at max. efficiency under all operating conditions. The final form of this CVT has not yet been decided, but such a device will undoubtedly be incorporated in the final scheme. The build is as summarised in the following section, the plant layout being shown diagrammatically in Fig 1, with an external view in Fig 2.

2 BRIEF DESCRIPTION OF PLANT (Figs 1 and 2)

2.1 Mechanical components

The most important components of the plant are as follows :-

(i) Engine
Leyland 500 6 cylinder D.I. Diesel engine
swept volume   8.2ℓ
rated speed   2,600 rev/min.
rated power   266 kW at 3:1 boost
max. torque speed   1,673 rev/min.
max. torque power   229 kW at 3.8:1 boost

(ii) Compressor
1 Compair high efficiency rotary positive displacement compressor
max. output   0.870 kg/sec; rated output 0.477 kg/sec
max. speed   11,500 rev/min; rated speed 6,606 rev/min.
max. pressure ratio 3.95:1; rated pressure ratio 3.171:1
max. power absorption 173 kW; rated power absorption 73.97 kW

(iii) Power turbine
Napier CO 45 radial inflow turbine with variable nozzles
rated output   101.7 kW at 50,000 rev/min.
rated inlet temp. 660°C
rated pressure ratio 3.17:1
max. torque output 156.4 kW at 46,500 rev/min.
max. torque inlet temp. 414°C.   (min.
max. torque pressure ratio 3.95:1

(iv) Epicyclic gearbox
Fully floating epicyclic : Annulus to sun
ratio 3.074
Engine input direct to annulus gear
Sungear to compressor - step up ratio
2.872
Planet carrier to output shaft - step up
ratio 2.44

(v) Turbine step down gear
Initially by fixed gear ratio to output
shaft
Ultimately by CVT to output shaft

(vi) Absorption Dynamometers
2 Sundstrand axial piston pumps
type SPV 25, operating in parallel
(300 kW at 2,400 rev/min) driven by
splitter gearbox.

(vii) Output shaft operating conditions
Max. speed and power : 769 Nm at 3409 rev/
min $\equiv$ 274.4 kW
Max. torque   : 2718 Nm at 682 rev/
min $\equiv$ 194 kW

2.2 Control System (Fig 1)

The DCE system incorporates a fully floating
epicyclic gear train between the engine and the
output shaft so that engine speed N_E is independent of output shaft speed $N_{o/s}$. Furthermore,
the choice of N_E, for any given value of
$N_{o/s}$, determines the sun, and hence also the
compressor speed N_C. The choice of a rotary
positive displacement, rather than a centrifugal compressor, is dictated by the wide speed
range resulting from this particular method of
driving the compressor, and the freedom of positive displacement machines from surge and choke.
Furthermore, the thermodynamic linkage between
engine, compressor and turbine imposed by the
speed and torque balance conditions inherent in
the epicyclic gear train, enables the system as
a whole to be optimized for any demanded output
shaft speed and torque combination, $N_{o/s}$ and
$\tau_{o/s}$, at least for steady state conditions. [In
practice the output shaft torque signal is
replaced, for reasons of cost and reliability,
by a fuel rack position signal, as measured by
LDVT]. This optimization is achieved by control
of 3 variables which determine the speed and
torque relations of the plant, viz. (Fig 1) :

(a) power turbine nozzle setting - this primarily affects the boost level at which the
plant operates.
(b) turbine CVT setting - this allows the
turbine to operate at its best efficiency
under all conditions.
(c) injection timing - this allows the engine
to operate either at max. torque on the
plant limiting torque curve (LTC) without
exceeding permissible max. cylinder pressure
or, under part load conditions, at its best
efficiency.

All 3 controls are interactive and therefore
demand a common control strategy (Fig 3).
Although Fig 1 also shows a variable bypass
valve, its use is limited to transient operation,
previous experience having shown that under
steady state conditions it should always be wide
open. Each of the 3 devices listed above is
under electrohydraulic control, operated in turn
by analogue control loops, receiving their

voltage input either from manually operated
potentiometers (for purposes of initial manual
optimization) or via A/D converters from the
central microprocessor (LSI 11) which stores the
numerical arrays representing the optimum
control voltages for each of the 3 devices as a
function of input variables as shown in Fig 3,
i.e. output shaft speed $N_{o/s}$ and fuel rack
position XR, expressed as analogue voltages.

The instrumentation is still in process of
implementation, but will be very similar in
principle to the system which has been successfully implemented on a large (11.2ℓ) Diesel
engine equipped with a variable geometry turbocharger and injection timing control (5).

It is anticipated that the above system will
have to be supplemented, under fast transient
conditions, by the provision of special transient controls. This is shown diagrammatically in
Fig 4. The main feedback signals are still output shaft speed $N_{o/s}$ and fuel rack position XR.
Under steady state conditions these would result
in a uniquely determined engine speed N_E, which
can also be stored as a numerical array in the
central microprocessor. This 'desired' speed
N_E is compared with the instantaneous actual
speed, and the difference signal ($N_E - N_E'$) is
used to close a transient switch in the auxiliary boost control system, which demands a boost
level p_{Blow} lower than the steady state value
consistent with adequate air fuel ratio but designed to permit more rapid system acceleration.
This desired value p_{Blow} is compared with the
actual measured value p_{Bact} and applied as a
supplementary transient signal to the turbine
nozzle actuator.

3 STEADY STATE PERFORMANCE CHARACTERISTICS

The performance characteristics are summarized
in Figs 5a - e, each with output shaft torque
$\tau_{o/s}$ as ordinate and output shaft speed $N_{o/s}$ as
abscissa. They are based on computer predictions
using a comprehensive simulation package with
well tested engine, compressor, turbine and gear
subroutines, and represent fully optimized
steady state operation. [Some preliminary experimental performance characteristics will be
presented at the conference].

Fig 5a gives contours of overall, i.e. system
efficiencies allowing for epicyclic gear and
turbine CVT losses. It is evident that the
torque envelope gives a continuous and steep
rise of approx. 3.63:1 over the output shaft
speed range of 5:1. This does not quite achieve
the desired constant horsepower characteristic,
but since it is achieved steplessly, system
flexibility will nevertheless be superior to
that of a conventional turbocharged engine
coupled to a multi speed gearbox. It should be
noted that the 'gap' between output shaft stall
and $^1/5$ $(N_{o/s})_{max}$ is bridged in vehicle applications by the output torque
converter (Fig 1) which has a built-in torque
ratio of 3.6, giving an overall torque ratio
between stall and rated conditions of 13.07.
The system efficiency contours must be considered very satisfactory, with the 35% contour
covering well over one third of the total operating field. True compounding conditions, i.e.
excess of turbine over compressor power, are
achieved over approximately the same region,

but in spite of this, system efficiency is depressed somewhat by the relatively low engine brake thermal efficiencies associated with the low compression ratio (LCR) pistons (12.8:1) designed to allow high boost operation (up to 3.79:1) without exceeding a max. cylinder pressure of 150 bar.

Fig 5b gives boost pressure ratio contours showing that on the limiting torque curve (LTC) this varies from 2.91 under rated conditions to 3.73 at the max. torque condition. However, in spite of the very high boost under these latter conditions, max. cylinder pressure does not exceed 150 bar due to a combination of LCR pistons and retarded injection. Below the LTC, boost pressure ratio is approximately proportional to power level. It should be noted that on the system LTC, the calculated turbine nozzle angle varies between 8.4° under rated conditions, and 10.2° at max. system torque. Overall the extremes of the range of nozzle angle adjustment are 5.3° and 10.6°; the variable nozzle facility being particularly important under transient conditions (see Fig 7a).

Fig 5c gives engine BMEP contours. As the compounding principle yields its best results under high boost, high BMEP conditions, engine rating at max. output shaft speed and power has been fixed at 14.93 bar at 2600 rev/min. In order to avoid compressor overspeeding as output shaft speed $N_{o/s}$ is reduced, engine speed is also reduced, whilst boost and BMEP are increased, as the DCE moves towards the max. torque conditions on the system LTC., resulting in 20 bar BMEP at 1673 rev/min. at the max. torque point. Below the system LTC engine BMEP follows a very similar trend to boost, i.e. it is broadly proportional to system power demand, as might be expected.

Fig 5d shows contours of overall turbine gear ratio, designed to achieve best turbine efficiency over the full range of operating conditions, with the aid of the turbine CVT. On the system LTC the range of overall step down gear ratios required is from 20 under rated conditions to 93 at the max. torque point. This overall CVT range of 4.65:1 is entirely feasible with both belt type and 'Perbury' type CVT's. The final choice of turbine CVT still remains to be made. It will be noted that at max. output shaft speed, the overall step down ratio continues to decrease with reduction in demanded torque. The resultant increase in the overall CVT range may cause some difficulty, and a matching compromise may therefore be necessary.

Finally, Fig 5e shows contours of dynamic injection timing showing that on the system LTC, this is retarded progressively from 29° BTDC to 15° BTDC, the max. injection advance calculated under part load conditions being 30° BTDC. This overall range of 15° is by no means excessive and has already been achieved in the case of the microprocessor controlled variable geometry turbocharged engine described in ref. (5).

Although matching in the case of a rotary positive displacement compressor is far less critical than with centrifugal compressors with their surge and choke limitations, it is still important to operate in an efficient part of the compressor map.

Fig 6 gives operating lines covering the full range of system load/speed conditions, and shows that these lie mainly within the 70% island of the compressor map with the exception of low part load conditions.

4 TRANSIENT PERFORMANCE CHARACTERISTICS

In addition to its unique steady state characteristics the DCE also possesses outstanding transient response largely again as a result of the epicyclic gear coupling between engine and compressor which allows very rapid increase in the speed (and hence delivery pressure) of the low inertia compressor, while the high load inertia attached to the output shaft causes the latter to accelerate much more slowly. As already stated, the requirements of transient control differ somewhat from those for steady state optimization, a possible control system being that shown in Fig 4. The main objective is to achieve more rapid acceleration than would be possible with the unmodified steady state system by demanding a lower level of boost during the transient than the steady state value, consistent with a minimum acceptable air-fuel ratio. The resultant reduced compressor torque demand is transmitted through the epicyclic gear train as a reduced engine torque demand, and hence gives rise to more rapid engine acceleration. The resultant transient responses compared with those of the unmodified steady state system are shown in Figs 7a to 7e. In each case numbers 1 and 2 refer to a slightly modified steady state control strategy (Fig 3) whilst 3a and 4a refer to the results obtained by using the transient control system, Fig 4, with gains K of 5 and 10 respectively. All results apply to an increase in load from 25 to 100% at fixed minimum output shaft speed of 0.2 $(N_{o/s})_{max}$, i.e. with infinite load inertia.

Fig 7a shows turbine nozzle angle response. The steady state system translates the rack position and output shaft speed inputs (Fig 3) into a demand for an instantaneous increase in nozzle angle from 8.4° to 10.3°. The transient system (Fig 4), on the other hand, first results in a sharp decrease in nozzle angle, to 6° for K = 10, followed by a gradual opening to 12° over the first 1.5 sec., and when the transiently demanded boost pressure is matched by actual boost pressure, by a sudden drop to the finally demanded steady state value of 10.3°.

Fig 7b shows the much better boost response obtained with the transient system, as opposed to the steady state system, over the first 1.5 sec.

Fig 7c shows that, as a result of the improved boost response, engine torque rises immediately to its final value of 1300 Nm as opposed to less than 1100 Nm when under steady state control.

Fig 7d shows output shaft torque response, again significantly better under transient as opposed to steady state control. Finally Fig 7e shows the trapped air-fuel ratio response, with the steady state system resulting in an initial drop to 15.9 while the high gain (K = 10) transient system leads to the satisfactory minimum value of 21, rising rapidly to the final value of 28.

There is thus no doubt that the transient control system (Fig 4) confers results in significantly better transient response overall, and that, compared with turbocharged engine response, the DCE system proves greatly superior particularly with respect to rate of torque take-up and minimum air fuel ratios.

5 CONCLUSIONS

(1) The Differential Compound Engine (DCE) in its latest form has been set up on a comprehensively instrumented test bed and is ready for exhaustive steady state and transient testing with a view to validating the performance predictions given in the present paper.

(2) The steady state characteristics, in particular continuous torque back up over a 5:1 output shaft speed range as the associated values of system efficiency render the DCE concept uniquely attractive as an integrated continuously variable transmission system for heavy trucks and off highway vehicles.

(3) The DCE possesses outstanding transient response characteristics due to the method of coupling engine, supercharging compressor and load. These permit full load take up by the engine virtually instantaneously, and by the output shaft within approx. 1.5 sec.

ACKNOWLEDGEMENT

The invaluable support provided for this DCE project by the Science and Engineering Council is gratefully acknowledged.

REFERENCES

1. Wallace, F.J., Tarabad, M. and Howard, D. "The differential compound engine - a new integrated engine transmission system concept for heavy vehicles". 1983, Proc.I.Mech.E., Vol 197A.

2. Wallace, F.J., Tarabad, M and Howard, D. "Continuous microprocessor control of the differential compound engine and development possibilities". 1984, Symposium on Advanced and Hybrid Vehicles, University of Strathclyde.

3. Wallace, F.J. "The Differential Compound Engine". Proc.I.Mech.E., 1973, Vol 187, 48/73, p548

4. Wallace, F.J. and Kimber, R.M. "Optimization of the differential compound engine using microprocessor control". SAE, Detroit, Paper 810 336, Feb. 1981.

5. Wallace, F.J., Roberts, E.W. and Howard, D. "Variable geometry turbocharging optimization and control under steady state conditions". Turbocharger & Turbocharging Conference, I.Mech.E., April 1986.

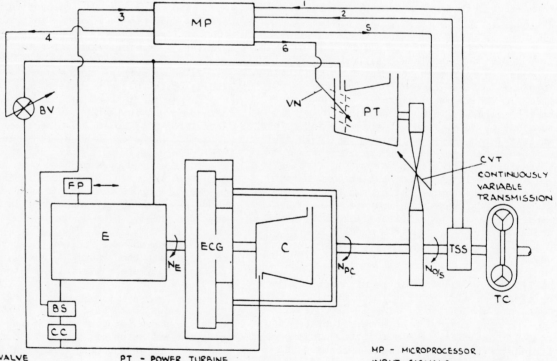

BV - BYPASS VALVE
BS - BOOST SENSOR
C - COMPRESSOR
CC - CHARGE COOLER
E - SEMI ADIABATIC ENGINE
ECG - EPICYCLIC GEAR TRAIN
FP - FUEL PUMP

PT - POWER TURBINE
TC - TORQUE CONVERTER
VN - VARIABLE TURBINE NOZZLES
TSS - OUTPUT TORQUE & SPEED SENSOR
N_E - ENGINE SPEED
N_{OS} - OUTPUT SHAFT SPEED
N_{PS} - PLANET CARRIER SPEED

MP - MICROPROCESSOR
INPUT SIGNALS
  1. TORQUE TRANSDUCER
  2 SPEED TRANSDUCER
  3 BOOST TRANSDUCER
OUTPUT SIGNALS
  4. BYPASS VALVE CONTROL
  5 CVT CONTROL
  6 NOZZLE CONTROL

Fig 1 Differential compound engine (DCE) layout, final version

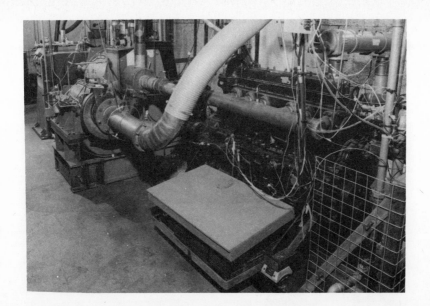

Fig 2   External view of experimental DCE

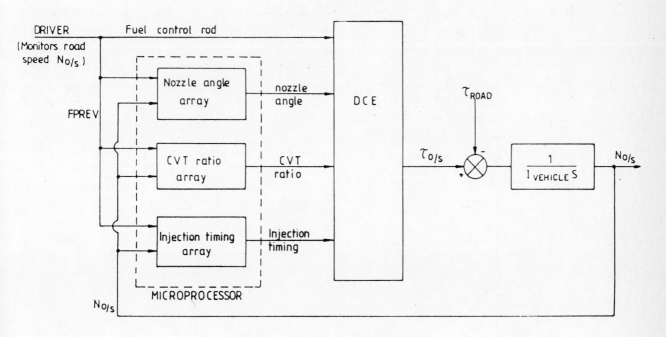

Fig 3   Steady state control scheme

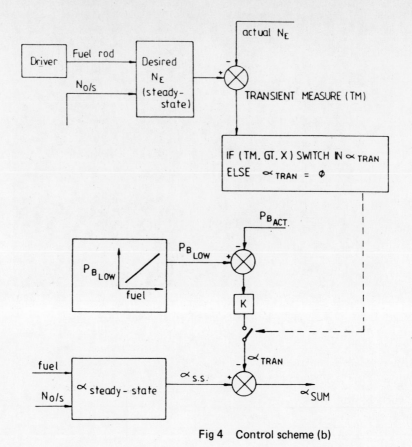

Fig 4 Control scheme (b)

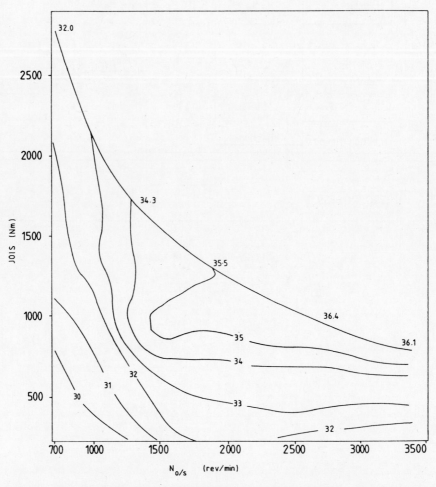

Fig 5a Output shaft thermal efficiency contours

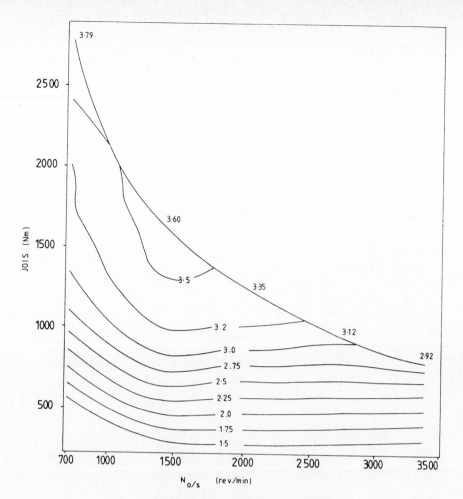

Fig 5b Boost pressure ratio contours

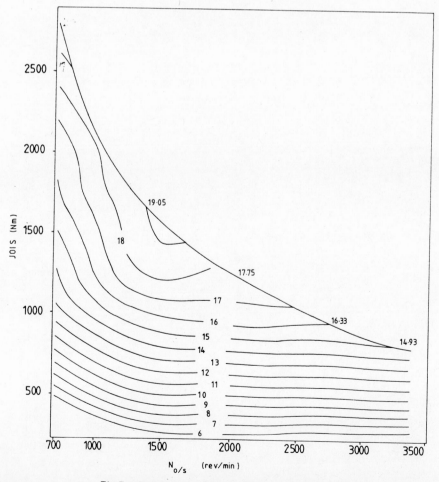

Fig 5c Brake mean effective pressure contours (bar)

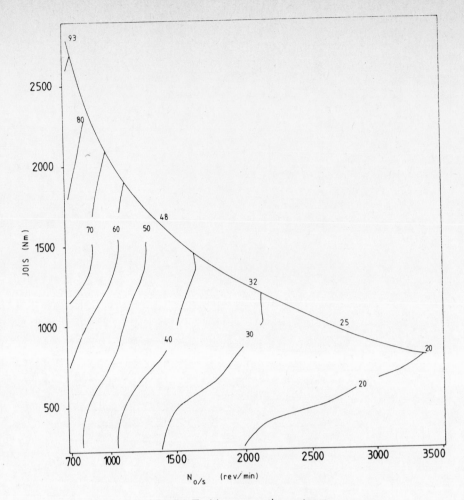

Fig 5d Turbine gear ratio contours

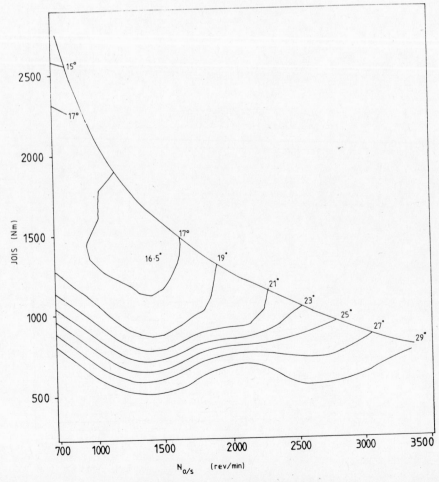

Fig 5e Dynamic injection timing

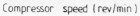

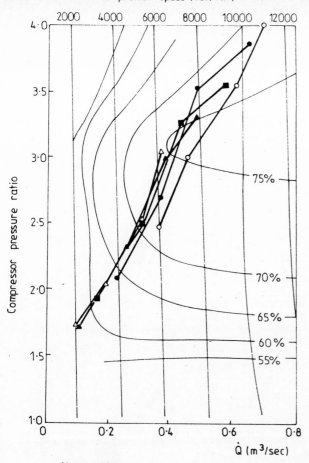

Fig 6   Compressor characteristics with operating points
(compressor speed)$_{max}$ = 11030 r/min
(compressor speed)$_{min}$ = 2014 r/min

○   No/s = 680
●   No/s = 1360
■   No/s = 2040
▲   No/s = 2720
△   No/s = 3400

SCHEME (b)

CASES 1, 2, 3a, 4a

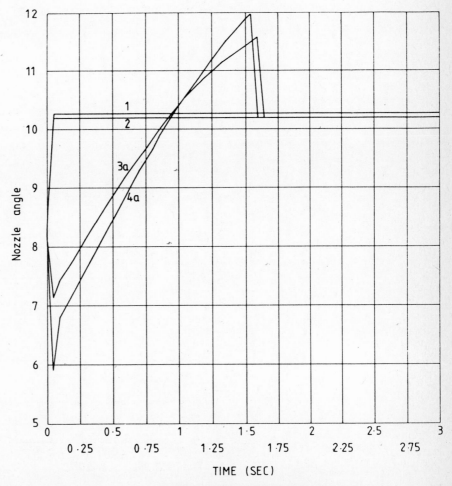

Fig 7a Nozzle angle response

CASES 1, 2, 3a, 4a

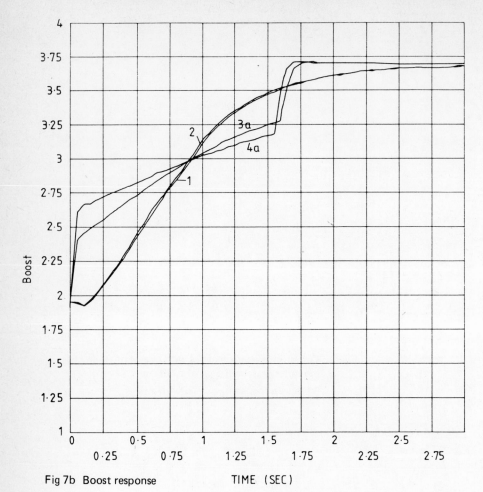

Fig 7b Boost response   TIME (SEC)

CASES 1, 2, 3a, 4a

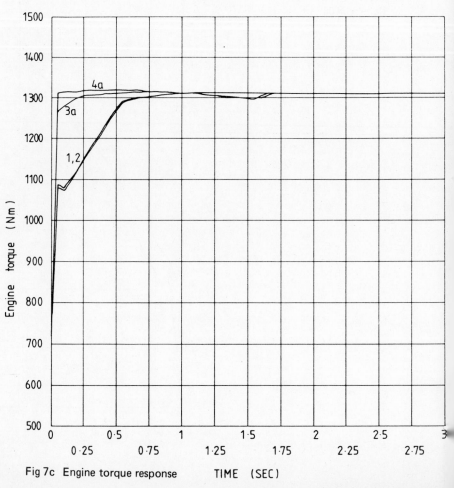

Fig 7c Engine torque response   TIME (SEC)

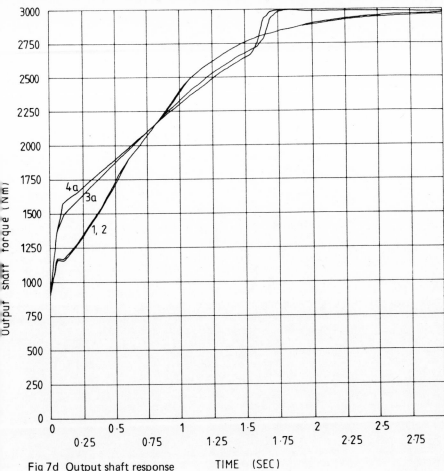

CASES 1, 2, 3a, 4a

Fig 7d Output shaft response   TIME (SEC)

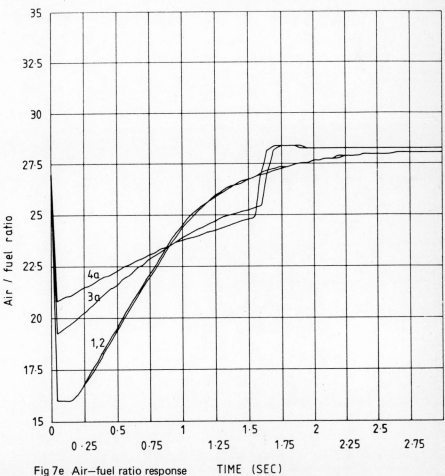

CASES 1, 2, 3a, 4a

Fig 7e Air—fuel ratio response   TIME (SEC)

C192/86

Development of Class 141 engine transmission system

P E J SPENCER, BSc
British Railways Board, Railway Technical Centre, Derby

SYNOPSIS

In the pursuit of a lightweight and fuel efficient vehicle, British Railways have equipped their new two axle railbuses with a mechanical transmission system. In this paper, the elements of the transmission system are described and their subsequent development in service discussed. The concept of gearshift quality is explored and the influence of system integration upon this is considered.

INTRODUCTION

Formerly, the British Rail policy towards Diesel Multiple Unit (DMU) mechanical transmission systems has been one of individual engines driving single axles through speed change gearboxes (Fig 1). A complete two or three car set may thus have had up to four separate transmission systems. Although certain foreign railway administrations have chosen to maintain this philosophy, for future DMU vehicles BR has chosen to have one transmission system per vehicle with the various elements gathered together (Fig 2). The control will be automatic, largely removing from the driver responsibility for transmission management [1].

The first of the new BR DMU vehicles is the class 141 twin-car railbus developed from a series of lightweight two-axle, single- and twin-car prototypes all having one powered axle per car. A fleet of 20 twin-car sets was introduced into service with the West Yorkshire PTE in May 1984 based at Neville Hill depot Leeds.

In this paper, the various elements of the engine-transmission system are considered and their development discussed. As will be seen, when creating an integrated system, there are important principles to be considered. During the course of class 141 development, certain lessons were learnt and the railbus series that has followed has drawn on this experience.

TRANSMISSION CONTROLLER

The Transmission Controller chosen for the class 141 railbus is the Leyland Bus G2 development, manufactured by Butec [2]. The design is based around two frequency to voltage convertor modules receiving the axle speed inputs, a series of voltage level switches to govern gearshift points and numerous relays and timer modules to control the gearshift logic (Fig 3).

A speedometer driving circuit is incorporated, providing a vehicle speed indication to the driver.

The Controller forms the interface between the driver and the various elements of the engine-transmission system, receiving direction, throttle and 'hold-gear' inputs from the cab controls. Speed inputs are provided from both driven and trailing axles. This gives a level of redundancy in fault conditions and also a means of axle speed comparison during wheelslip: when the driven axle speed exceeds that of the trailing axle by a set proportion, the throttle signal is removed for an interval. If sufficient axle speed is attained, a higher ratio is selected and retained for 10s before reselecting the appropriate gear. Since on certain gradients, it is possible to 'hunt' between adjacent gears when the balancing speed is near to a gearshift point, the driver is provided with a 'hold-gear' button. Originally, the function inhibited upshifts so that the train would climb the gradient without interruption through gear cycling. Subsequently, in order to improve the control of tractive effort during wheelspin, the 'hold-gear' button was given an additional function whereby, if operated when starting from rest, detection of spin would cause gear 2 to be selected and retained until the driver released the 'hold-gear' button.

The Controller has outputs to the throttle control system and also to the gearbox solenoid valves. Provision is made also for fault indication by means of 'train' and 'local' warning lights. According to the indication, the driver can interpret the nature of the fault concerned.

Although not required in the original vehicle specification, it became necessary to provide the driver with a visual indication of the gear selected. This was achieved by an LED display in parallel with the gearbox solenoid outputs.

Protection in the event of both axle probes failing or being left disconnected after maintenance is given by the Controller requiring to detect a minimum speed signal (7 mile/h) within 20s. Failure to achieve this, results in selection of gear 4. This is to remove the possibility of gearbox overspeeding through the vehicle being towed at too high a speed by the rest of the train. Originally, selection of gear 4 in this way was not accompanied by any throttle inhibition. In order to remove the possibility of torque oscillations at the gearbox input, it became necessary to configure the controller to select throttle-OFF in these conditions. Additionally, the detection interval was extended to 30s, and drivers were instructed to use the 'hold-gear' function in conditions of reduced adhesion as this inhibits the probe protection.

It became necessary to revise the electrical supply and return arrangements for the Controller since it was discovered that a loss of negative connection could result in a potential drop across the gearbox solenoid coils. Whilst this was of little consequence to the Controller, it was then possible in certain conditions for the gearbox to suffer two-gear engagement. The solution lay in improving the durability of the connections and employing +ve fused protection only.

It is important that any item of electronic equipment is fully able to withstand the vibration environment found in rail vehicle. During the course of development of the Controller the design was revised to increase relay and module security. Additionally, wiring arrangements and general robustness were improved.

DIESEL ENGINE

The engine chosen for the Class 141 Railbus is the Leyland TL11. This is a turbo-charged development of the 11 litre, 6 cylinder normally aspirated Leyand 680 design. In this application, a maximum power of 148 kW. at 1950 r/min and a maximum torque of 840 Nm at 1300 r/min. are achieved. This engine incorporates features required for rail traction duties and has proved well suited for the railbus application [3].

A CAV Majormec fuel pump with a mechanical governor is fitted which combines a two-speed (MIN-MAX) characteristic with a speed governed long range idle from 400 r/min to 850 r/min. (Fig 4a) This was chosen to give good low speed control for shunting purposes and scope for wheelspin control under adverse adhesion. The transition between modes of governing depends on spring rates and occurs at a throttle lever travel of approximately 35^0 out of a full displacement of 50^0.

A four stage electro-pneumatic throttle control system is used with independent regulation for each throttle step (Fig 4b). The pressure is fed to a proportional cylinder connected in turn to the governor lever. The system incorporates a quick release valve designed to exhaust the cylinder rapidly on descending steps.

This valve had to be modified from its original 0.6 bar (8.7 lbf/in^2) sensitivity to 0.2 bar (2.9 lbf/in^2) to ensure that throttle dip was consistent between intermediate steps and during gearshifts.

Additionally, the regulators were modified to incorporate a 0.0029 m^3/min bleed to increase sensitivity. These developments were essential to achieve consistent control in the two-speed governed range as this occupies only a small proportion of the lever travel.and so requires certain throttle steps to be closely grouped.

GEARBOX

The gearbox chosen for the Class 141 Railbus is the Self Changing Gears RRE5. This is a design drawing on SE4 experience from former DMU vehicles, having similar running gear but hydraulic as opposed to pneumatic actuation. The freewheel, reverser and four ratio speed-change section are incorporated into a self contained unit with a single, electrical connection [4]. Gears 1, 2 & 3 are of compound epicyclic form with brake-band engagement. The actuating linkage incorporates an automatic adjuster. Gear 4 is clutch engaged and causes the epicyclic pack to rotate as a whole. The reverser is of clutch engaged planetary form, rotating as a whole in forward and contra-rotating in reverse (Fig 5).

When using a mechanical transmission of this kind, attention must be paid to gearshift quality as this is crucial both to the standard of ride and also the longevity of the transmission itself.

Assessment of gearshift quality should consider:

TORQUE SPIKE — The impulse generated by the transmission due to change in state whilst engaging a gear or changing ratio.

GEARSHIFT DURATION — The total interval from initial interruption of power to resumption of steady state transmission.

The principal parameters influencing gearshift quality are defined as follows:

NEUTRAL GAP (NG) — The interval between de-energising a gear electrical signal and the energising of the subsequent one.

THROTTLE DIP (TD) — The interval between de-energising throttle electrical signals and the commencing of re-energising the steps in sequence.

Following bus transmission practice, an attenuation feature was incorporated, whereby a pneumatic signal would cause a reduction in hydraulic pressure from 8.28 bar (120 lbf/in^2) to 4.83 bar (70 lbf/in^2) during gear engagement. In this way, the work done in the gearbox is controlled, reducing torque spikes and so improving gearshift quality. The signal for attenuation was given by the Transmission Controller via an EP valve and was employed when starting from rest and for gearshift durations.

In bus applications, rapid gearshifts and hence short NG timings are unavoidable since only momentary interruptions in power transmission can be tolerated [2]. Since this constraint does not apply for railbus, NG timings can be longer. In turn, the necessity for attenuation is reduced and so in August 1984 this feature was deleted. This resulted in more impulsive gearshifts and somewhat reduced gearshift quality but this was not initially considered significant.

It is during the Neutral Gap that the crankshaft speed falls to prepare for engagement of the next gear. Fig 6a shows clearly the influence of NG timings that are too short when applied without attenuation. It can be seen that decelerations at the gearbox input of some 750 r/min within fractions of a second can be produced. This uncontrolled dissipation of energy can cause high torque spikes of up to three times the nominal maximum rating of the gearbox.

Clearly, this condition should be avoided. By increasing NG timings, very much lower levels of torque spikes are generated (Fig 6b). Whilst these become small for gear 2-3 and gear 3-4 shifts, the timer modules within the Controller had insufficient capacity to further improve the gear 1-2 shift, where a torque spike some 75% of maximum engine torque prevailed. This however was not discernable to the passenger and has not been a source of any transmission distress.

The influence of TD timings is also considerable. Too short an interval results in inadequate crankshaft deceleration. This in turn can be shown to cause high torque spikes. Too great an interval however will result in unnecessarily long gearshift durations. In either case, gearshift quality is impaired.

From the above it can be seen that NG and TD intervals require to be chosen carefully. In the case of class 141, both these parameters are preset in the Transmission Controller by timer modules. This constrains the choice of NG and TD values to those which best accommodate variations in engine characteristic from vehicle to vehicle (Table 1).

Subsequent classes of railbus however, are equipped with a microprocessor based Transmission Controller. This is capable of monitoring gearbox input speed and so anticipating crankshaft deceleration. Consequently, neutral gaps can be actively governed and throttle dip minimised. In this way, fully optimised gearshifts can be generated (Fig 6c).

TABLE 1   Class 141 Gearshift Quality

SHIFT	NG s	TD s	DURATION s	TORQUE-SPIKE kNm
ORIGINAL				
1-2	0.2	1.5	5.0	max.2.25
2-3	0.2	1.5	5.0	max.2.50
3-4	0.2	2.5	5.0	max.2.65
REVISED				
1-2	2.0	1.5	4.0	max.0.65
2-3	1.75	1.25	3.5	max.0.20
3-4	1.25	1.5	3.0	max.0.40

As the vehicle decelerates, the Controller will sequence down the gears. To avoid a 'snatch' occurring, when braking or coasting to a stand, the gear 2-1 shift has been replaced by gear 2-Neutral. Gear 1 is then only re-engaged when the driver moves the throttle handle away from 'IDLE' and so calls for power.

Hydraulic pressure is generated within the gearbox by a main pump, driven from the input shaft. Consequently, it is vital that input stall is kept to a minimum. Such a condition is inevitable when starting from rest but the inherent accumulation of the system sustains engagement during this phase. When the vehicle stalls due to lack of tractive effort however, as in the case of the gear 4 selection through the probe protection referred to earlier, it is important that the throttle signal is inhibited to 'IDLE'. Failure to do this results in cyclic application of high torque spikes at approximately 1Hz frequency (Fig 6d).

In a gearbox of this form, it is crucial that the integrity of the hydraulic circuit is maintained. Furthermore, since the hydraulic and lubrication circuits share the same oil, the quality of filtration must be sustained in all conditions. These requirements have led to improved filter and seal specifications.

FLUID COUPLING

Although mounted on the engine, the fluid coupling may be considered together with the gearbox. In the railbus, a standard automotive component is used although in this application it is filled with a special synthetic oil for non-flammability reasons. A consequence of this is a rather stiffer characteristic when hot.

It is most important for the fluid coupling not to be subjected to undue stall as this leads to rapid overheating. Leakage of oil can then occur which makes possible an avalanche effect leading to total coupling failure (Fig 6e). Correct configuring of the Controller has removed most of the conditions adverse to the fluid coupling and as an additional measure, the temperature specification of the sealing components has been raised.

FINAL DRIVE and AXLE SUSPENSION

The Final Drive fitted to the Class 141 Railbus is the Self Changing Gears RF42i. This is a new design and comprises main hypoid gears and an input- shaft isolation device.

In comparison with a bogie arrangement, a single axle suspension must be permitted a much higher degree of freedom to ensure good curving response [5]. This in turn means that the Final Drive is subject to significant movement and early experience showed that greater traction-rod restraint was needed to prevent excess travel.

Torque restraint is provided by a resiliently bushed link between the underframe and the top of the Final Drive. During the trials to monitor gearbox torque levels, it became apparent that at certain speeds in particular gears, very high amplitude oscillations were being seen in the propshafts. After much analysis, the most consistent forcing function was found to be the 2nd harmonic of the universal joint frequency.

Whilst under power, the Final Drive rotates due to torque reaction and this leads to a discrepancy in propshaft flange alignment, termed 'residual angle' (Fig 7). This angle is greatest at initial vehicle start but the oscillatory force is frequency dependent and has greater influence at higher shaft speeds where resonant responses were observed. In 4th gear particularly, resonance was detected consistently at a shaft frequency of 62Hz. Over the range 53Hz-62Hz it was possible to detect torque oscillations of amplitude up to twice the nominal mean torque.

This in turn means that the gearbox output becomes unloaded on a cyclic basis. Whilst no failures to date are thought associated with this, such high fatigue loadings could be detrimental to the long term durability of the gearbox. Consequently, fatigue life testing is being undertaken to establish what influence these loadings have. Various revisions to the torque restraint and vehicle suspension can be considered to limit Final Drive movement and consequent residual angle thereby reducing shaft oscillations. There exist also a variety of Constant Velocity Joint arrangements that could be applied. This latter option however would however require further development in order to be suitable for this application.

THE SYSTEM AS A WHOLE

During the course of development of the vehicle engine-transmission system, it has been the gearbox that has suffered greatest distress. Consequently, the reliability of the system as a whole has depended largely on the performance of this element.

Fig 8 reveals the gearbox performance since introduction to service in May 1984 and the influence of the various actions taken. A 'failure' has been defined as a fault necessitating complete gearbox replacement.

The major actions are detailed below:

a)   Deletion of Controller -ve fuses
b)   Deletion of Attenuation feature
c)   Revised Filter Seal profile
d)   Revised rivet and bonding specification for clutch and brake band linings
e)   Revised Gearshift Parameters

In particular, after action (e) which corrected the major deficiency in system integration, there has been a consistent improvement in reliability.

Assuming an annual mileage of 70,000 miles, a vehicle will take 3.57 years to achieve the specified minimum life between gearbox overhaul of 250,000 miles.

Hence for a fleet of 40 vehicles a target average of a maximum of 11.2 overhaul failures per year or 0.93 per month is set. This rate depends proportionally on the actual average annual mileage achieved and only constitutes a rough indicator of the standard required.

Since December 1985, a programme of gearbox refurbishment has been underway so that any damage suffered during a vehicle history but not yet revealed will be addressed. By mid 1986, all vehicles should be fitted with gearboxes to a common rebuild standard, incorporating hydraulic and mechanical revisions.

As part of a general vehicle refurbishment package due to start in mid 1986, the original Transmission Controller will be replaced by the microprocessor based unit developed for the Class 142 and 143 Railbus vehicles. It is intended that common software will be used throughout.

It is anticipated that these factors will result in an engine-transmission system well able to meet the specified reliability. The outcome of the fatigue life testing will dictate whether any suspension or torque restraint modifications are needed.

FUTURE DEVELOPMENTS

The majority of a further 75 twin-car Railbus sets have now been delivered to BR. These are designated Class 142 (50 sets of Leyland Bus/BRE.Ltd manufacture) and Class 143 (25 sets of Alexander/Barclay manufacture) and although similar to Class 141, full width bodies and revised suspension are fitted.

The same basic TL11 engine is used but the power has been increased to 157kW and a throttle control system with 7 preset steps is fitted. The gearbox is designated R500 and differs in detailed respects from the RRE5, incorporating hydraulic and mechanical revisions to improve performance and reliability. The final drive is very similar to the RF42i and is designated RF420i.

A microprocessor based Transmission Controller is used which is capable of receiving a gearbox input speed signal, allowing self-diagnosis of the transmission performance.

© IMechE 1986 C192/86

Detection systems for wheelslip will now be based on axle acceleration rates, giving improved sensitivity. The Controller will also be able to optimise tractive effort re-application so that wheelspin conditions are not recreated.

CONCLUSIONS

An automatically controlled mechanical transmission system of the form used on class 141 type vehicles must have all its elements carefully integrated. Any revision within the system, whether in the pursuit of improved performance or reliability must take due account of the interaction of the system as a whole

Attention must be paid to the following areas:

Elimination of Torque Spikes

Timing of Gearshift Events

Avoidance of Stall

Resonance in the Driveline

Good gearshift quality can be achieved with a Transmission Controller employing fixed value timer modules to govern gearshift events. To achieve optimum gearshifts requires the use of an Interactive Controller that can anticipate engine characteristics.

ACKNOWLEDGEMENTS

The author wishes to thank the Director of Mechanical and Electrical Engineering, British Railways Board for permission to present this paper.

REFERENCES:

[1]   CROXFORD M.C & SPENCER P.E.J.
       Diesel Multiple Units - Current Driveline
       Developments.
       I Mech E Traction Drives Seminar
       November 1985

[2]   DUNKLEY M.W.
       Railbus Transmission Control and Controls
       Development
       I Mech E Railbus Conference November 1982

[3]   TUCKER J.S.
       Developments in Commercial Vehicle
       Automotive Power Units.
       I Mech E Diesel Engines for Rail Traction
       Conference September 1982

[4]   VARLEY R.J.
       An Approach to Railbus Transmission
       Engineering
       I Mech E Railbus Conference November 1982

[5]   SMITH B.L.
       Development of Railbus Suspension
       I.Mech E Railbus Conference November 1982

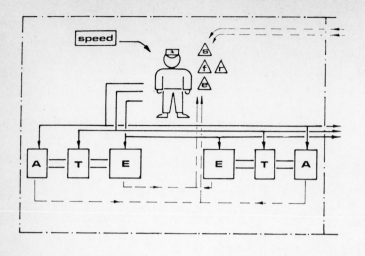

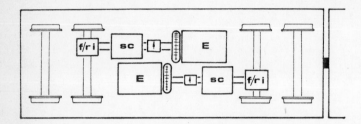

KEY:

E:	**Engine**	f/r :	**Forward/Reverse**
T:	**Transmission**	i :	**Drive Isolation**
A:	**Axle Drive**	s :	**Engine Stopped**
↕:	**Freewheel**	e :	**Engine Speed**
sc:	**Speed Change**	△ :	**Warning Lamp**

Fig 1   Former layout – diesel multiple unit (DMU)

←

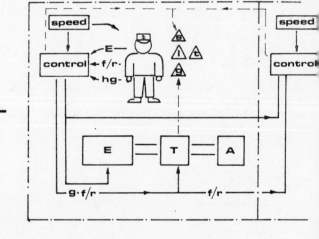

←

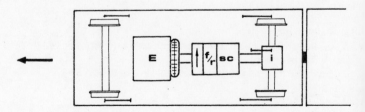

KEY:

hg : **Hold Gear**

g :   **Gear Indication**

l :   **Local Fault**

t :   **Train Fault**

Fig 2   New layout – railbus

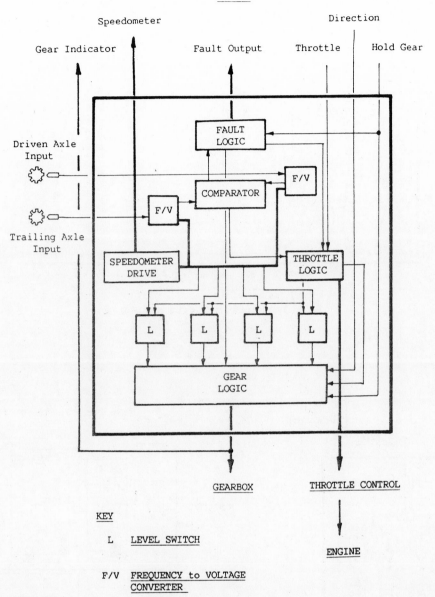

KEY

L   LEVEL SWITCH

F/V   FREQUENCY to VOLTAGE
      CONVERTER

Fig 3   Transmission controller

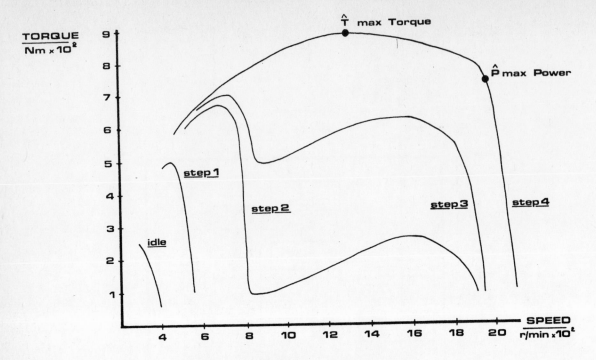

Fig 4a   Leyland TL11 engine characteristic

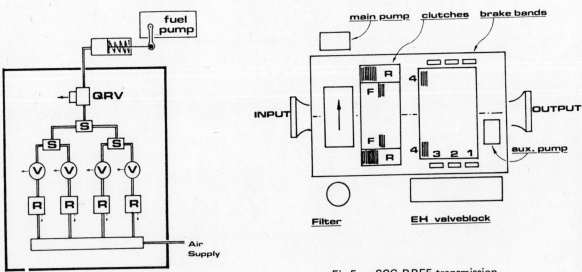

Fig 5   SCG RRE5 transmission
Ratios:
1st : 4.25:1
2nd : 2.41:1
3rd : -159:1
4th :   1:1
F/R   ±1:1

Key

R   Regulator   S Shuttle valve

V   EP Valve   QRV Quick Release Valve

Fig 4b   Throttle control

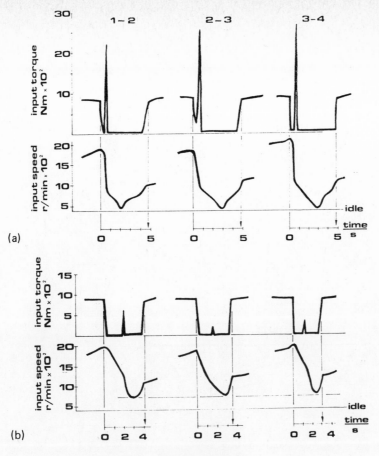

(a)

(b)

Fig 6   Torque responses
(a)   original
(b)   revised

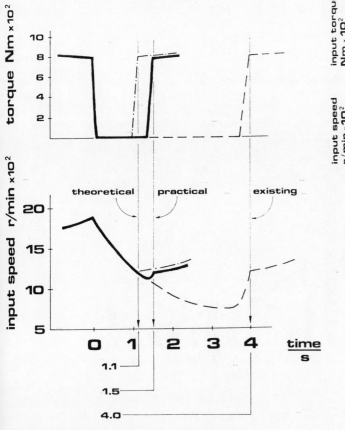

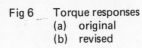

Fig 6c   Gearshift optimization

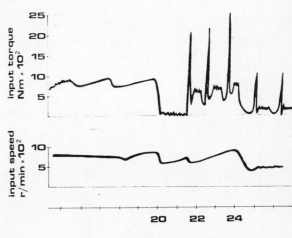

Fig 6d   Input stall

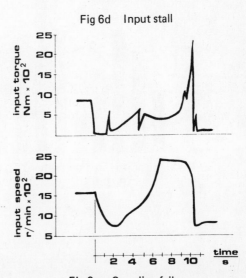

Fig 6e   Coupling failure

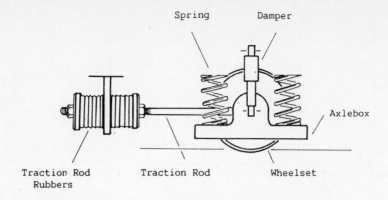

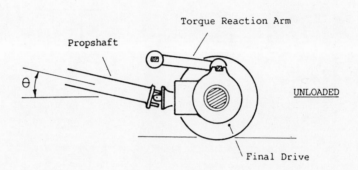

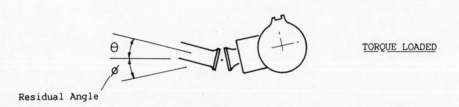

Fig 7   Final drive and axle suspension (not to scale)

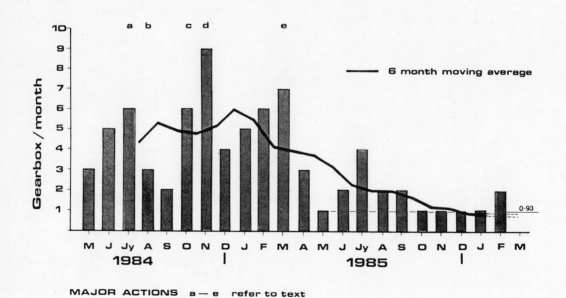

MAJOR ACTIONS a — e refer to text

Fig 8   RRE5 transmission failures

Hydraulic accumulator energy storage in a city bus

N D VAUGHAN, BSc(Eng), PhD, CEng, MIMechE and R E DOREY, BSc, PhD
School of Engineering, University of Bath, Avon

SYNOPSIS. This paper is concerned with the sizing and selection of an hydraulic accumulator system for regenerative braking in a city bus and with an evaluation by computer simulation of alternatives for its integration in the vehicle driveline. The paper builds upon earlier work published by the authors which has considered typical duty cycle and performance data for the bus. This is reviewed and used to justify the choice of accumulator system. Here the accumulator system is considered in conjunction with both conventional and hydrostatic split power transmissions, and the effect upon bus performance determined for operation over a typical route.

1 INTRODUCTION

The use of a regenerative braking scheme is most appropriate to vehicles which have a duty cycle involving frequent stop start operation. Road vehicles which might benefit most are those operating in a predominantly urban environment and these include the commuter car, taxi, delivery van and truck and the city bus. The operation of the city bus necessarily involves frequent stops and starts in addition to the external influences of traffic and pedestrians, thus making it a most suitable application for a regenerative scheme. In addition there has over the years been a trend towards heavier buses and higher traffic speeds bringing with it a consequent increase in fuel consumption (1). The potential to improve fuel consumption is both evident and highly desirable.

Schemes for regenerative braking have included electrical energy storage in batteries and mechanical energy storage in both flywheels and hydraulic accumulators. Systems for vehicles based on all three methods are under development but at present weight and energy transfer rate limitations are a disadvantage of the electrical solution. A direct comparison between flywheel and accumulator storage on an energy density basis shows a considerable advantage for the flywheel. However the accumulator shows advantages over the flywheel in other respects. To transfer energy from the vehicle and back requires only a hydraulic pump/motor unit, and a variable displacement unit of this type is simple to control. If accumulator sizing is carried out carefully and advantage taken of modern material developments then the accumulator solution certainly has considerable potential.

The use of hydraulic accumulators for urban vehicle applications is not new and has been reported a number of times (2,3). In the particular references given here the proposals considered the accumulator to be used as a temporary energy store in the main vehicle driveline allowing a reduction in engine size. This meant that the additional weight of the

regenerative system was partially offset by a reduction in engine weight. However this is not generally a suitable solution for the bus because of the inevitable loss in performance, particularly hill climbing ability, with reduced engine power.

For the city bus there have been several proposals in the UK for the application of a hydrostatic transmission (4) and for regenerative braking with hydraulic accumulators (5). Other work in Europe has included MAN and Volvo who have both pursued schemes to service trials. In both cases the original work (6,7) involved comparative studies between accumulator and flywheel schemes for energy storage. Whereas more recent publications from both companies (8,9) have shown a preference for accumulator based systems. In the Volvo scheme the regenerative system is used in conjunction with a conventional transmission whereas MAN use a hydrostatic based continuously variable transmission as the main drive with a regenerative facility.

In this paper variants on both these schemes are compared using computer simulation techniques. Particular importance is attached to correct selection of accumulator size, and after initial discussion the use of the simulation techniques is shown as a valuable aid in this context.

2 ACCUMULATOR SELECTION

It is of paramount importance that considerable care is exercised in the choice of both the energy storage capability and method of construction of the hydraulic accumulator to keep any weight penalty to a minimum. Sizing the energy capability is particularly important and although initial selection can be approached in a simple way it will be shown that this can be amended in the light of the actual working cycle. In addition it is shown below that a careful design of the accumulator system can also significantly reduce the weight for a given storage capability.

2.1 Accumulator energy storage

Consideration of the energy storage of an accumulator requires a representation of the typical process laws followed during a charge discharge cycle. The normal design process assumes that the gas volume follows an isothermal compression followed by an adiabatic expansion following the ideal gas law relationship:

$$pv^n = \text{constant}$$

For this application this representation is not entirely accurate with considerable uncertainty on the value of the index to be used. This will vary with both temperature and pressure as shown in Fig. 1 for the adiabatic index of nitrogen, the gas normally used. The behaviour of the accumulator will therefore vary during the cycle and be dependent on the immediate history of events to establish the working conditions. Although methods have been proposed to make allowance for this, an alternative heat transfer approach (10) has been used here for the detailed dynamic modelling of the accumulator and is described in detail below.

The index approach is however useful in demonstrating the dependence of various design parameters on the accumulator size and weight. It can be shown (11) that the energy stored per unit volume may be expressed as

$$E_v = p_{max} \left(\frac{r^{1/n} - r}{1-n} \right)$$

where p_{max} is the maximum accumulator pressure
   r is the ratio of minimum (discharged) to maximum (charged) pressures
   n is the polytropic index

A sensible maximum working pressure based on the availability of hydraulic components of 345 bar was chosen and for this value Fig. 2 shows the variation of the above expression for energy per unit volume. This clearly indicates that a pressure ratio of approximately 0.3 will maximise the energy stored per unit volume. An expression can also be derived for energy stored per unit mass (12), and indicates a similar pressure ratio and dependence on polytropic index. This then establishes a working pressure range for the accumulator with a minimum of 100 bar and a maximum of 345 bar, as well as the desirability of a gas with a low index if a suitable alternative to nitrogen could be found.

2.2 Stored energy requirements

The actual energy level used as a basis for accumulator selection is a key factor in the regenerative system design. Whilst bearing in mind the aim of keeping the accumulator as small as possible it must still be capable of storing a significant proportion of vehicle energy during braking and returning this to the vehicle during subsequent acceleration. The amount of vehicle energy available at the beginning of any braking event will be dependent on vehicle mass and speed at initiation. In the case of a two deck city bus the mass may vary from an unladed weight of the order of 10 tonne to a maximum laden weight of

nearer 16 tonne. Initial ideas might suggest that a vehicle speed of 48 km/h (30 mph) might be taken in conjunction with an average loading to specify the energy available. In practice of course, braking will be initiated from a variety of speeds, in general below the level chosen. Although there were a number of sources indicating an average loading on a city bus, information on braking sequences and duty cycles in general was very limited. It was therefore decided to collect typical duty cycle information with the cooperation of a local operator.

This information was obtained from a service bus operating on a route covering the city centre to suburbs and a total of six return journeys were monitored at various times throughout the day. Recordings from the bus speedometer were made on a magnetic tape giving a continuous record of vehicle speed with elapsed time for the complete round trip length of 12.8 km (8 mile). A sample of the hard copy produced from an outward leg of the journey is shown in Fig. 3. In addition passenger loading between stops was noted and a height and gradient profile constructed from a large scale ordnance survey map. The route had been chosen because it was fairly flat with few sections exceeding a gradient of 4%.

There was a marked consistency between the six sets of data and although variations in road and traffic conditions meant that no two journeys were identical they were all composed of similar sets of velocity profiles. It was of particular interest to note the almost complete absence of any extended periods of steady speed running.

These data formed an invaluable source of statistical information on vehicle braking and provided a realistic sequence of velocity profiles which could be used in the simulation work described below. In terms of a more general application, a comparison with some overall statistical data typical of London bus routes had shown (12) sufficient similarity to justify a wider application of the more detailed Bath route information.

From the hard copy traces 292 braking events were identified, giving an average of 3.8 brake applications per kilometre. For each of these the energy available for recovery was calculated as the kinetic energy of the vehicle at the start of the event less an estimate of the vehicle drag loss over the subsequent braking period. A further adjustment was made for any energy loss or gain associated with the local road gradient during each braking sequence. The net energy available from each event was categorised in intervals of 0.1 MJ and a histogram of the number of events in each category is shown in Fig. 4. It can be seen that the number of events requiring a high energy storage are a relatively small proportion, only 5% of the events having 1.1 MJ or greater.

It has never been the intention to replace completely the conventional vehicle service brakes by a regenerative system. In which case it is an important safety feature that the service brakes are in good working order at all times and to ensure this they must be used on a regular basis. Therefore it is most desirable that the accumulator system should not be capable of meeting all the vehicle braking requirements. Selection was then based on the energy available from 90% of the total braking events and ensured something of the order of 10% service brake use. Statistically this was shown (12) to lie between 0.9 MJ and 1.1 MJ.

This then represents the energy available at the rear wheels but may still represent an overestimate for accumulator sizing because of the losses occurring due to the mechanical transmission and hydraulic conversion in transferring the energy to the accumulator. Braking will occur over a very wide range of torques and speeds with an equivalent range in hydraulic pressures and flows. The losses occurring over these ranges are difficult to quantify with an overall approach and so the simulation methods were used here to predict the energy transfer. Simple braking sequences were simulated using the modelling techniques described below and assuming a storage capacity of 1 MJ. This showed (12) that on average only about 75% of the available energy was being stored in the accumulator with the remainder dissipated in mechanical and conversion losses. On this basis the energy requirements for the accumulator were lowered to 0.75 MJ. Using Fig. 2 and assuming an index of 1.6 gives an accumulator volume of 75 L.

2.3 Vehicle deceleration

One aspect of the braking sequence not yet discussed is the actual deceleration rate achieved. It has been stated (13) that a deceleration of around 1.1 m/s^2 defines a threshold above which passenger discomfort becomes increasingly obvious. The analysis of the Bath route data showed that events exceeding this were relatively few and occurred from higher initial speeds. The braking torque achieved with the regenerative transmission will depend on the capacity of the pump unit used to transfer fluid to the accumulator and the opposing pressure which will be determined by the state of accumulator change. It is interesting to note that the reduction in accumulator size from 1.0 MJ to 0.75 MJ actually increases the deceleration capability of the transmission. This was shown by an increase from 1.2 m/s^2 to 1.4 m/s^2 in the average deceleration achieved from 48 km/h in the simple braking sequence described above. This occurs because the accumulator pressure rises more rapidly for the smaller size and hence allows a higher decelerating torque to be achieved. There will then be circumstances when the smaller capacity accumulator will recover more energy because of its greater energy transfer rate. The significance of such a compromise can only be determined by comprehensive experimental work or more easily by the detailed simulation techniques described below.

2.4 Accumulator construction

The total volume of an accumulator comprises two components, a swept volume and a gas volume. In current commercial designs one of two methods is used to separate these systems and prevent the gas dissipating in the

hydraulic fluid. The more common method is the use of a flexible diaphragm or bladder and the second is the use of a moveable piston. Although bladder accumulators are frequently contained within a single pressure vessel the size required for this application indicates the use of a separate back-up bottle for the gas volume. In the case of the piston type these are generally two interconnected vessels representing physically the swept and gas volumes. Both these accumulator types are cylindrical in shape and although this represents a weight penalty in relation to the ideal spherical vessel, their shape is most appropriate for incorporation within the existing bus structure.

It is generally accepted that bladder accumulators have the higher energy density although economical piston accumulator designs do not show a large penalty. In the application to a regenerative transmission there are operational advantages for the transmission favouring the choice of a piston type which are described below. If an arrangement incorporating both high and low pressure accumulators is adopted as shown in Figs. 6 and 7 then this will minimise the volume of working fluid required and completely eliminate the necessity for a low pressure gas bottle with consequent weight savings. In addition there are advantages for control purposes if the piston position can be used to indicate the state of accumulator charge.

A further weight saving could be made if composite materials were used in place of steel for the pressure vessels. Manufacturing methods and costs of composites have now developed to the stage where this will be a competitive alternative to steels. Still another technique which would lead to a lower volume and weight is the use of a wax impregnated fill for the gas space which has been shown (10) to give near isothermal process conditions. This could reduce accumulator volume and weight by a further 10 - 20%.

3 TRANSMISSION SYSTEMS

Previously the choice of transmission and methods for integrating the hydraulic accumulator system into the vehicle drive have been examined (11, 12). Here it is appropriate simply to review the principal features of the scheme and to draw attention to major design issues.

The basic transmission system considered for the bus duty is shown in Fig. 5. This is a single planetary hydrostatic split power transmission. It was chosen to provide a continuously variable drive with a good overall level of efficiency suitable for inclusion of the regenerative system.

The speed range required of the transmission in the bus duty is 5.2:1. This has been achieved with a basic transmission range of 2.28:1 in combination with a two speed series gear change. The maximum power transferred through the variable drive is approximately 0.64 of the input. That is 83 kW, based upon a full engine power of 130 kW. The duty was fulfilled by hydrostatic units of 52 cc/rev capacity operating at a maximum speed of 3500 rev/min and pressure of 350 bar. The gear ratios chosen for the transmission system are shown in the Table accompanying Fig. 5.

The modification of the single planetary transmission for regenerative duty is shown in Fig. 6 The accumulator system is connected to the main transmission pump/motor set (units X and Y) and to an additional hydrostatic unit (Z) used to provide supplementary retardation and assistance in braking and acceleration. The hydraulic circuit for the third unit operates independently of the main transmission and this is important for three reasons. First, in braking, it allows the displacement of the units to be scheduled to provide a progressively increasing level of braking torque, which until unit X comes into operation occurs without engine motoring and the inherent energy loss that this represents. Second, in acceleration, it allows the high pressure accumulator to be discharged fully independently of the operating pressure necessitated in the main transmission loop to enable power delivery from the engine. Third, it improves transmission efficiency to be able to off load unit Z when the high pressure accumulator is exhausted and the transmission is operated in its non-regenerative mode.

Further important features of the regenerative scheme are the cross coupled high pressure and low pressure accumulator pistons and the non-return valves situated in the high pressure accumulator line. The former allows the low pressure oil storage capacity to be matched closely to the high pressure oil volume, whilst the latter prevents the possibility of accumulator discharge during braking or accumulator charge during acceleration.

To enable the benefit obtained from the split power transmission to be properly assessed the conventional bus transmission was also considered in modified form with regenerative braking provided by hydraulic accumulator. Details of this scheme are shown in Fig. 7. The hydrostatic unit used to charge and discharge the high pressure accumulator is geared directly to the transmission output. This enables the smooth and continuous delivery of power from the accumulator system throughout the vehicle acceleration sequence. The accumulator system was sized to be the same as that employed in the split power transmission. The capacity of the hydrostatic unit was selected to be equivalent to the combined capacities of units Y and Z. For completeness the gear ratios used in the transmission are also shown in the table accompanying Fig. 7.

4   COMPONENT MODELLING

In the vehicle performance investigation undertaken for the route simulation work discussed later in the paper the engine, transmission and vehicle load characteristics were described by individual component models. The computer program of the system was comprised of a discrete subroutine structure of the individual models. These were linked according to the kinematic and torsional requirements of the system. This method of modelling has previously been described by the

authors (14); here it is important to explain the level of component behaviour that was represented.

4.1 Engine model

The engine model used in the work was based upon the operating characteristics of a commercial six cylinder turbocharged diesel engine. The engine developed torque was expressed as a function of the difference between the actual engine speed, the governor set speed and the governor droop characteristic, as shown in Fig. 8a, where:

$$M_{e1} = (\omega_s - \omega_e)g_e$$

ω_e is the engine speed
ω_s is the governor set speed and
g_e is the slope of the governor droop characteristic

The maximum and minimum (motoring) torques and the torque absorbed in driving ancillaries were described by quadratic relationships of the form:

$$M = a + b\omega_e + c\omega_e^2$$

Within the limiting bounds of torque the engine torque delivery was calculated as:

$$M_{e2} = M_{e1} - M_{anc}$$

4.2 Epicyclic and transfer gear models

The equations of motion of epicyclic gearsets and simple transfer gears are well known. However, to demonstrate the inclusion of frictional loss mechanisms into the torque transfer relationships it is useful to consider the particular gearing configurations shown in Fig. 8b. For the epicyclic, the kinematic relations of the members may be written as:

$$\omega_s = \omega_c(1+R) - \omega_r R$$

$$\omega_p = \frac{\omega_r R - \omega_s}{R-1}$$

where ω_c is the speed of the carrier
   ω_p is the speed of the planets
   ω_r is the speed of the ring
   ω_s is the speed of the sun
and R is the epicyclic ratio

Which may be differentiated to find the interrelationship of the component accelerations. Assuming that there are load dependent losses associated with the gear meshes and speed and load dependent losses with the bearings, then the torque transfer relations may be written as:

$$M_{r1} = M_r - f_{or}\omega_r - f_{ir}M_r$$

$$M_{r2} = M_{r1} - j_r \dot{\omega}_r$$

$$M_{r3} = M_{r2}(1 - C_r \text{sign}(M_{r2}\omega_r))$$

$$M_{s3} = \frac{M_{r2}}{R} - \frac{2}{R-1}(j_p\dot{\omega}_p + f_{op}\omega_p + f_{1p}M_r \frac{(R+1)}{Rr_c})$$

$$M_{c2} = 2j_p\dot{\omega}_c\left(\frac{R+1}{R-1}\right)^2 - \frac{R+1}{2R}(M_{r3} + RM_{s3})$$

$$M_{s2} = \frac{M_{s3}}{(1 - C_s\,\text{sign}(M_{s3}\omega_s))}$$

$$M_{c1} = M_{c2} + j_c\dot{\omega}_c$$

$$M_{s1} = M_{s2} + j_s\dot{\omega}_s$$

$$M_c = M_{c1} + f_{oc}\omega_c + f_{1c}M_{c1}$$

$$M_s = M_{s1} + f_{os}\omega_s + f_{1s}M_{s1}$$

where C is the gear mesh loss coefficient
$\quad f_o$ is the speed dependent bearing loss
$\qquad$ coefficient
$\quad f_1$ is the load dependent bearing loss
$\qquad$ coefficient
$\quad j$ is the member inertia
$\quad r_c$ is the radius of the carrier
and $\quad$ M is the torque applied to the member

The subscripts c, p, r and s refer respectively to the carrier, planet, ring and sun members. Where double subscripts are shown for torques, the torque acts on the member indicated by the first subscript from the member indicated by the second. The above relationships may be re-written to allow determination of any of the component torques based upon the knowledge of one such value and two component accelerations.

Similar relationships may be developed for the simple transfer gear and these are:

$$\omega_2 = -\frac{r_1}{r_2}\omega_1$$

$$M_{11} = M_1 - j_1\dot{\omega}_1 - f_{o1}\omega_1 - f_{11}M_1$$

$$M_{21} = \frac{r_2}{r_1}M_{11}(1 - C_1\,\text{sign}(M_{11}\omega_1))$$

$$M_2 = M_{21} - j_2\dot{\omega}_2 - f_{o2}\omega_2 - f_{12}M_2$$

Where r_1 is the radius of gear 1
and $\quad r_2$ is the radius of gear 2

4.3 Band brake and clutch models

The band brake and clutch models used in the work simply described the drag losses associated with these components. The losses were assumed to take the form:

$$M = M_c + f\omega$$

where M_c is a constant torque value
and $\quad f$ is a coefficient dependent upon speed

4.4 Fluid coupling model

The fluid coupling model was developed from performance data obtained for a commercial coupling. These data were reduced to the characteristic shown in Fig. 8c and the torque transferred by the coupling modelled according to the relationships:

$$\frac{M}{\omega^2} = (a - b\nu) \qquad \text{for } 0 < \nu \leqslant 0.525$$

$$\frac{M}{\omega^2} = c(1 - e^{-d(1-\nu)}) \qquad \text{for } 0.525 < \nu \leqslant 1$$

where ω is the speed of the input member
$\quad \nu$ is the speed ratio
and a, b, c and d are constants

4.5 Hydrostatic drive model

The major components to be modelled in the hydrostatic drive are the pump and motor. The effective operation of the transmission is affected significantly both in terms of power delivery and energy storage by the efficiencies of the units. Their performance was modelled using an extended form of the classical Wilson model, previously described (15), fitted to experimentally determined flow and torque characteristics. The relationships used in the model (quoted here for the case of a pump) were:

$$Q = \omega xD - C^*_s\frac{PD}{\mu} - \frac{\omega PD}{B}\left(v_r + \frac{1+x}{2}\right)$$

$$M = PxD + C^*_v\,\mu\omega D + C^*_f PD$$

where B is the fluid bulk modulus
$\quad C^*_f$ is the coulomb friction coefficient
$\quad C^*_s$ is the slip coefficient
$\quad C^*_v$ is the viscous friction coefficient
$\quad D$ is the volumetric diplacement per
$\qquad$ radian
$\quad M$ is torque
$\quad P$ is pressure
$\quad Q$ is flowrate
$\quad v$ is the volume ratio: ratio of
$\qquad$ clearance volume to swept volume
$\quad x$ is the fraction of maximum unit
$\qquad$ capacity
$\quad \dot{\omega}$ is speed
and $\quad \mu$ is the absolute viscosity of the fluid

The star notation used with the coefficients indicates that these parameters were in turn described in terms of the units' operating conditions. This technique enabled non-linearities in flow and torque to be taken into account, and also the dependency of the flow loss upon speed and the torque loss upon displacement setting.

4.6 Hydraulic accumulator model

In the bus application where the accumulator is charged in a braking sequence preceding a bus stop, the delay to let passengers on and off before subsequently discharging the accumulator results in a fall of gas temperature and pressure and a degradation of energy storage. To represent this effect accurately and to take into account the operational efficiency of the accumulator system, a heat transfer model based upon the work of Otis (10) was used. Changes in state of the accumulator gas were described by the relationships:

$$\dot{T} = \left(\frac{T_o - T}{\tau} - \frac{P\dot{V}}{ms} + \frac{T\dot{v}}{bvs}\frac{\partial s}{\partial p}\right)\left(\frac{s}{s + \frac{T\partial s}{\partial T} + \frac{aT}{b}\frac{\partial s}{\partial p}}\right)$$

$$\dot{p} = \frac{a}{b}\dot{T} - \frac{\dot{v}}{bv}$$

where

$$a = \frac{1}{T} + \frac{1}{Z}\frac{\partial z}{\partial T} \qquad b = \frac{1}{p} - \frac{1}{z}\frac{\partial z}{\partial p}$$

    m is the mass of the gas
    P is the gas pressure
    s is the specific heat at constant volume
    T is the gas temperature
    T_o is the temperature of the surroundings
    V is the gas volume
    z is the compressibility factor
and τ is the thermal time constant

The variation of S and Z with pressure and temperature was determined from tables of properties, and described according to the relationships shown in Fig. 8d.

4.7 Load model

The vehicle load characteristics were based upon data published by TRRL (16) and accounted for rolling resistance, windage and route gradient. These were modelled using the relationship:

$$M = M_c + C_1\omega + C_2\omega^2$$

where C_1 is a coefficient dependent upon speed
    C_2 is a coefficient dependent upon speed squared
and M_c is a constant torque value

5 ROUTE SIMULATION AND PERFORMANCE ASSESSMENTS

The computer simulation program was used to establish the performance of the bus over the route using the split power and conventional transmission systems in their regenerative and non-regenerative forms. The models were run over the range of loading conditions encountered on the route and the vehicle speed in each case made to follow the velocity profiles of the type illustrated in Fig. 3. This procedure ensured that the transmissions were subjected to similar performance conditions.

5.1 Control strategies

In the case of the conventional transmission the input to the non-regenerative model was simply the engine governor set speed. This was varied to control the engine power delivery and in turn the vehicle acceleration and speed. The gear changes were scheduled to occur automatically as a function of the gearbox drive speed. For the conventional transmission modified for regenerative duty the system was controlled to make preferential use of the accumulator. This was supplemented in acceleration by the engine delivery and assisted in deceleration by the vehicle braking system.

For both regenerative and non-regenerative split power transmissions the engine was controlled to operate along its line of minimum specific fuel consumption. This was achieved by varying the transmission ratio to operate the engine independently of the vehicle loading conditions. For the regenerative system the same strategy, involving the preferential use

of the accumulator in acceleration and braking was employed.

5.2 Fuel consumption and energy level comparisons

The fuel consumption obtained over the route using each of the transmission systems is shown in Table 1. Overall the best performance is provided by the split power transmission, which shows a nett improvement of 4.9% over the conventional transmission without the regenerative system and 21.7% with the regenerative system. Modification of the conventional transmission to include the regenerative system enabled a fuel saving of 12.1% to be made.

The better reduction in fuel consumption achieved by the regenerative system when used with the split power arrangement relates in part to the higher level of energy storage that was achieved and in part to improved engine running conditions. The first of these effects is shown in Table 2 which provides a breakdown of accumulator energy recovery and energy utilisation for each of the stage journeys comprising the bus route. The total energy recovery with the split power transmission was approximately 14.3 MJ, whilst with the conventional transmission it was about 12.6 MJ. This improvement, of some 13.5%, is a measure of the additional braking torque that is available through the use of hydrostatic unit X in the split power transmission. The second factor, that of improved engine operation, arises as a result of running the engine under favourable fuelling levels in the split power transmission and comparatively unfavourable conditions in the conventional transmission.

The great benefit offered by the split power transmission is that when the accumulator is delivering power the transmission ratio can be varied and the engine run at low speed commensurate with the ideal operating condition for whatever additional power is required. In the conventional transmission this is not the case. Reduced engine power must be achieved by operating the engine at reduced torque at the speed determined by the current vehicle speed and the engaged gear. Under such conditions the engine fuelling levels can be poor.

Comparing individual stage journeys the regenerative system shows most benefit over those parts of the route where there are appreciable downward grades. Particular sections which may be identified are between stops 3-4, 16-17 and 19-21. There are only two stage journeys where the regenerative system imposes a penalty in fuel consumption and both of these, between stops 10-11 and 15-16, are associated with significant upward grades.

Considering accumulator energy storage then in most braking sequences the accumulator was either empty or very close to this condition at the start of the sequence. For both the split power and conventional transmissions there were few instances of the accumulator becoming fully charged before the end of a braking sequence. Of the small proportion of braking events so affected most were associated with the low energy levels present at low vehicle speeds. As a percentage of the total number of braking events, the split power transmission achieved 70% of the cases through transmission braking alone or combined braking involving some small usage of the main vehicle brakes; 63% of events were similarly achieved with the conventional transmission. In terms of the useful utilisation of accumulator energy both transmission systems showed a good level of return. Measured from the start of the route, where the accumulator was discharged, to an equivalent point within the last stage journey the utilisation of stored energy for both systems lay between 93 and 94%.

6 CONCLUSIONS

The use of an accumulator regenerative system in conjunction with a split power main transmission shows considerable additional fuel savings over a similar regenerative facility when added to a conventional transmission.

Careful attention to the sizing of the accumulator allows the energy capacity to be reduced by a factor of a half over that obtained with a simplistic estimate of energy requirements. Simulation for a particular vehicle route profile has shown that the smaller accumulator is an acceptable choice with a satisfactory energy exchange and utilisation.

The duty cycle used here has been established as representative of other routes, however further work is required to investigate the proposed solution over a wider range of operating conditions.

REFERENCES

(1) SMITH, C.E. Exhaust emissions and noise. Land Transport Conf. Instn. Mech. Engrs., 1977.

(2) ELDER, F.T., OTIS, D.R. & DEWEY, C. Accumulator-charged hydrostatic drive for cars saves energy. Hydraulics & Pneumatics, 1974, 180-183.

(3) SVOBODA, J.V. Analogue and digital modelling in the design of a hydraulic vehicular drive. Proc. Instn. Mech. Engrs. **193,** 1979, 277-286.

(4) CUNNINGHAM, S.U., JACKSON,D. & McGILLIVRAY, D.C. Hydrostatic transmissions and city vehicles. Automatic and semi-automatic gearboxes for heavy commercial vehicles, Instn. Mech. Engrs, 1978.

(5) SCOTT, D. Regenerative braking system could cut fuel consumption. Automotive Engg., 1976, 12-13.

(6) EVANS, P.A. & KARLSSON, A. The Volvo city bus. Hydrostatic transmissions for vehicle application, 1981.

(7) SCOTT, D. Regenerative braking cuts bus fuel needs. Automative Engg., 1979, 102-107.

(8) HAMMARSTROM, L. VTS-Hydrostatic transmission: experiences from the first field test. Int. Symp. on Advanced and Hybrid Vehicles, Strathclyde, Univ. of Strathclyde 1984.

(9) MARTINI, S. The MAN hydrobus: a drive concept with hydrostatic brake energy recovery. Int. Symp. on Advanced and Hybrid Vehicles, Strathclyde, Univ. of Strathclyde, 1984.

(10) OTIS, D.R. & ELDER, F.T. Accumulators: the role of heat transfer in fluid power systems. 4th Int. Fluid Power Symp., 1975.

(11) BOWNS, D.E., VAUGHAN, N.D. & DOREY, R.E. Design study of a regenerative hydrostatic split power transmission for a city bus. Hydrostatic transmissions for vehicle application, Warwick. Mech. Engg. Pubs., 1981.

(12) DOREY, R.E. & VAUGHAN, N.D. The computer aided investigation and performance evaluation of a regenerative hydrostatic split power transmission for a city bus. Int. Symp. on Advanced and Hybrid Vehicles, Strathclyde, Univ. of Strathclyde, 1984.

(13) BROOKS, B.M. et al. Passenger problems on moving buses, TRRL, SR 520, 1980.

(14) DOREY, R.E. & VAUGHAN, N.D. Computer aided design of split power hydrostatic transmissions. Proc. Instn. Mech. Engrs., **198B,** 1984, 61-69.

(15) McCANDLISH, D. & DOREY, R.E. The mathematical modelling of hydrostatic pumps and motors. Proc. Instn. Mech. Engrs., **198B,** 1984, 165-174.

(16) WILLIAMS, T. Energy losses in heavy commercial vehicles. TRRL, SR 329, 1977.

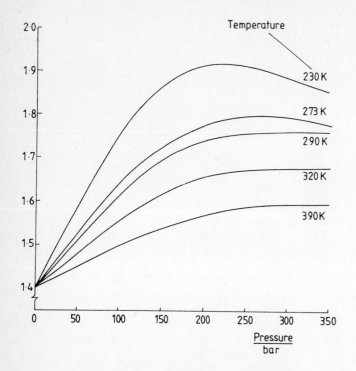

Fig 1   Variation of adiabatic index with pressure and temperature for nitrogen

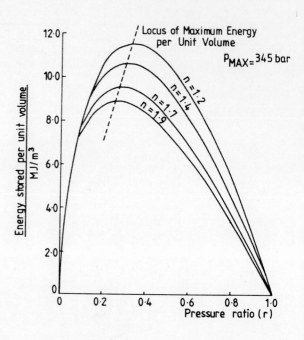

Fig 2   Hydraulic accumulator energy storage as a function of pressure ratio and polytropic index

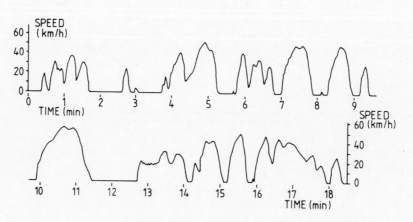

Fig 3   Bath bus route

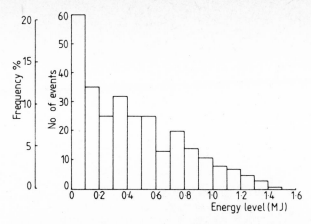

Fig 4   Distribution of energy available from braking events

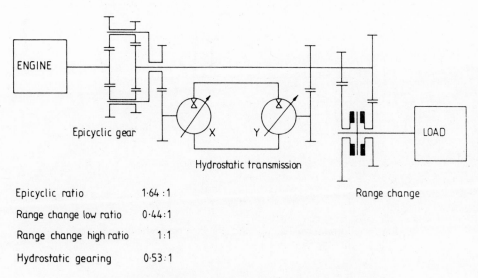

Epicyclic ratio	1·64 : 1
Range change low ratio	0·44 : 1
Range change high ratio	1 : 1
Hydrostatic gearing	0·53 : 1

Fig 5   Single planetary multi-range hydrostatic split power
transmission

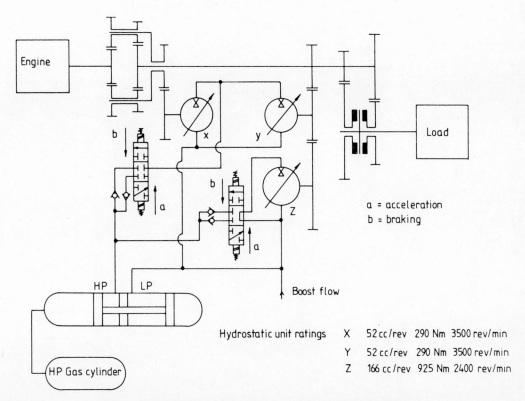

Hydrostatic unit ratings	X	52 cc/rev	290 Nm	3500 rev/min
	Y	52 cc/rev	290 Nm	3500 rev/min
	Z	166 cc/rev	925 Nm	2400 rev/min

Fig 6   Regenerative single planetary multi-range transmission

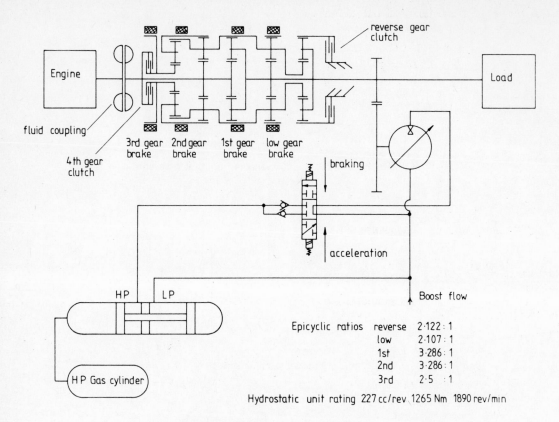

Epicyclic ratios reverse 2·122 : 1
                    low   2·107 : 1
                    1st   3·286 : 1
                    2nd   3·286 : 1
                    3rd   2·5   : 1

Hydrostatic unit rating 227 cc/rev 1265 Nm 1890 rev/min

Fig 7   Conventional compound epicyclic transmission modified
         for regenerative duty

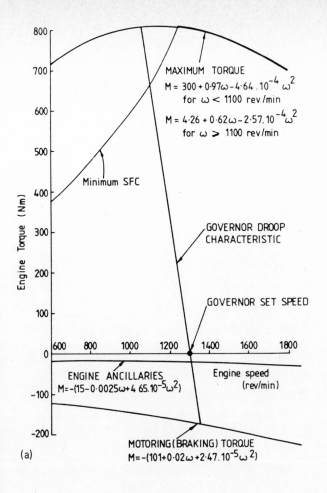

MAXIMUM TORQUE
$M = 300 + 0.97\omega - 4.64 \cdot 10^{-4}\omega^2$
for $\omega < 1100$ rev/min

$M = 4.26 + 0.62\omega - 2.57 \cdot 10^{-4}\omega^2$
for $\omega > 1100$ rev/min

Minimum SFC

GOVERNOR DROOP
CHARACTERISTIC

GOVERNOR SET SPEED

ENGINE ANCILLARIES
$M = -(15 - 0.0025\omega + 4.65 \cdot 10^{-5}\omega^2)$

Engine speed
(rev/min)

MOTORING (BRAKING) TORQUE
$M = -(101 + 0.02\omega + 2.47 \cdot 10^{-5}\omega^2)$

(a)

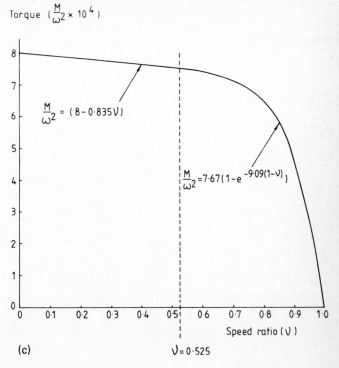

Torque $\left(\dfrac{M}{\omega^2} \times 10^4\right)$

$\dfrac{M}{\omega^2} = (8 - 0.835\text{V})$

$\dfrac{M}{\omega^2} = 7.67(1 - e^{-9.09(1-\text{V})})$

Speed ratio (V)

(c)   V = 0.525

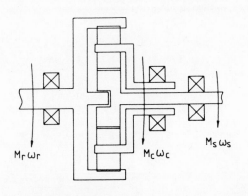

Epicyclic gearset

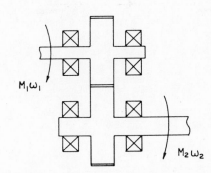

(b)   Simple transfer gear

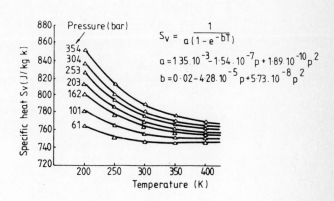

$S_v = \dfrac{1}{a(1 - e^{-bT})}$

$a = 1.35 \cdot 10^{-3} - 1.54 \cdot 10^{-7}p + 1.89 \cdot 10^{-10}p^2$

$b = 0.02 - 4.28 \cdot 10^{-5}p + 5.73 \cdot 10^{-8}p^2$

Pressure (bar)
354
304
253
203
162
101
61

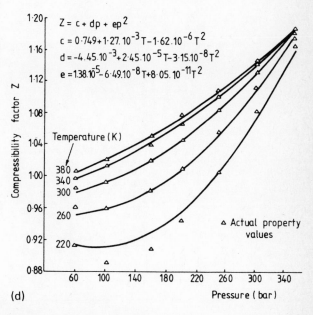

$Z = c + dp + ep^2$

$c = 0.749 + 1.27 \cdot 10^{-3}T - 1.62 \cdot 10^{-6}T^2$

$d = -4.45 \cdot 10^{-3} + 2.45 \cdot 10^{-5}T - 3.15 \cdot 10^{-8}T^2$

$e = 1.38 \cdot 10^{-5} - 6.49 \cdot 10^{-8}T + 8.05 \cdot 10^{-11}T^2$

Temperature (K)
380
340
300
260
220

△ Actual property
   values

(d)   Pressure (bar)

Fig 8   Details of driveline components for computer modelling
(a) diesel engine torque—speed characteristic
(b) possible bearing arrangements for epicyclic and
    transfer gears
(c) fluid coupling characteristic
(d) specific heat and compressibility factor for nitrogen

Table 1 A comparison of fuel consumption for all transmission systems

| | | Fuel Consumption L /100 km | | | |
| | | Non-regenerative | | Regenerative | |
Bus Stop	Stage distance km	Conventional transmission	Split power transmission	Conventional transmission	Split power transmission
1					
2	0.48	50.3	44.5	47.2	41.0
3	0.87	51.9	51.7	53.3	48.2
4	0.42	38.7	33.0	22.3	14.3
5	0.56	45.8	48.0	42.1	44.5
6	0.40	27.7	25.2	20.6	20.4
7	1.69	31.8	29.9	30.6	24.5
8	0.48	13.6	12.5	11.7	7.8
9	0.23	45.5	47.0	36.3	34.2
10	1.09	54.8	49.7	48.8	43.3
11	0.06	99.1	100.5	99.7	101.6
12	0.10	33.2	28.7	33.7	29.1
13	1.51	30.1	27.2	25.1	15.3
14	0.48	61.5	54.3	56.3	44.4
15	1.63	41.4	42.2	37.6	38.9
16	0.37	58.8	66.9	56.6	61.1
17	0.45	24.3	24.2	18.3	16.4
18	0.51	68.1	60.0	57.0	54.7
19	0.53	31.3	34.2	26.0	24.5
20	0.31	36.8	35.3	26.3	22.7
21	0.63	27.1	22.5	17.3	12.8
Overall fuel consumption L /100 km		40.5	38.5	35.6	31.7
Improvement over conventional transmission %		—	4.9	12.1	21.7

Total route distance 12.8 km

Table 2 A comparison of energy recovery and utilization over the route

| | | Conventional transmission | | Split power transmission | |
Bus stop	Stage distance km	Energy recovered MJ	Energy used MJ	Energy recovered MJ	Energy used MJ
1+					
2	0.48	.4416	.3243	.4825	.3414
3	0.87	1.0336	.4557	1.0415	.4888
4	0.42	.9214	.8883	1.2267	1.2925
5	0.56	.4011	.3713	.3400	.3503
6	0.40	.4969	.3783	.6516	.3230
7	1.69	.5601	.8148	.6925	.9370
8	0.48	.7380	.2818	.6927	.3581
9	0.23	.3818	.5960	.6313	.6115
10	1.09	.4620	.8360	.6309	1.2077
11	0.06	–	–	–	–
12	0.10	.1790	–	.2345	–
13	1.51	1.4810	1.2051	1.8034	1.5941
14	0.43	.0656	.2853	–	.2508
15	1.63	1.7330	1.5229	1.7602	1.3398
16	0.37	.5182	.2588	.6211	.3110
17	0.45	.5739	.4608	.3950	.5392
18	0.51	.2623	.6353	.2420	.5837
19	0.53	1.1300	.9733	1.3421	.8332
20 §	0.31	.4277	.5757	.4469	.5928
21	0.63	.7504	.6544	1.0749	.9850
Total of energy recovery and utilisation		12.5576	11.5181	14.3098	12.9399

+ Accumulator initially discharged
§ Accumulator discharged within this stage journey

© IMechE 1986 C186/86

C197/86

Energy storage systems for public service vehicles

C H CURTIS, BSc
London Buses Limited, Chiswick, London

SYNOPSIS This paper outlines the consideration of alternative energy storage application for a modern Public Service Vehicle leading to the fitment of the Volvo Cumulo system to a Volvo under-floor engined "Citybus". Test results are included indicating the degree of savings experienced on different types of routes showing that this system cannot be justified on a universal basis. Only service operation will determine the maintenance level required for the system which is now to be obtained.

INTRODUCTION

Fuel economy has always been to the forefront in Bus Operation within London Buses and its predecessors but the underlying philosophy has changed somewhat. Naturally with a fleet at one time of over 8000 buses even a small improvement per bus made a large scale difference. However over the post war years wage rates have increased considerably more than anything else such that today they represent over seventy per cent of the operating costs. Adoption of one person operation has helped to some extent but the savings are not in direct proportion to the men saved. Fuel prices including taxation have of course risen but with the elimination of tax on stage carriage operation only, this has helped as far as the Bus operator is concerned in London. On the other hand traffic congestion is getting worse every year with the increase of car ownership, both privately and company owned, such that the average speed of the bus is reduced. It has been calculated that an increase of average speed of one mile per hour in the speed of the London Bus would generate a saving of over £½ million per annum.

Apart from identifying factors over which London Buses have little or no control, a further fact has come into the picture concerning the availability on hydro-carbon fuels. Various estimates have been given but thirty years seems to be a reasonable estimate of the continued availability of such fuels. Depending upon the various controls that might be employed, this period can vary either way.

London Buses saw fit in the execution of its operation to look at various ways to extend this period by its own efforts in fuel economy and the other option of alternative fuels. This paper is concerned with the efforts in economy by utilising a form of energy storage.

PRELIMINARY REVIEW

The bus does not have the advantage of retaining energy in the system as does a trolleybus and an alternative is to carry batteries which can be charged up during braking. This has the disadvantage of excessive weight and generally needs a prime mover as well an electricmotor/dynamo on the vehicle. Bearing in mind that there are weight limits on a two axle vehicle of sixteen tons, the passenger capacity is seriously reduced. At one time the flywheel system appeared to be the way to go. Discussions were undertaken with Volvo of Sweden who had produced such a vehicle which showed up to fifteen per cent fuel savings and tests were conducted in Sweden with this vehicle, by the writer, which showed promise.

On the test vehicle it was arranged that the flywheel could be speeded up before starting off. This ran the flywheel up to 10 000 r.p.m. when the bus could be driven without additional energy input. The other alternative was to have the engine such that when the flywheel speed dropped to a minimum figure the engine would speed up again to re-charge the flywheel, irrespective of road speed.

Additionally hard braking would re-charge the flywheel.

This was achieved by utilising a clutch mechanism such that the flywheel was coupled to the transmission which was engaged when the brakes were applied. For ideal operation the flywheel should be in a vacuum to reduce frictional losses but this is hardly practical in this type of installation. With a flywheel there are always fears of over-speeding and the flywheel design was such that it was made of several discs pressed on to a shaft such that if over-speeding did ever occur, then the discs would slip on the shaft. A typical installation is shown in Figure 1.

There was always the question that a smaller engine could be utilised but since the bus always had to have the same acceleration whether or not the flywheel was in circuit, the smaller engine was ruled out.

At the time London buses was purchasing some Volvo B55 double deck buses for evaluation purposes along with a similar number of Leyland Olympians, Dennis Dominators and Metrobuses. Work was started on utilising one of the B55 vehicles for such a flywheel installation to be made. Figure 2.

A computer analysis was then undertaken by Volvo on typical London Bus operation and it was shown that with so much idling in gear brought about by traffic conditions a good deal of energy stored in the flywheel would be lost and there would not be the improvement in fuel consumption originally expected.

It was therefore decided not to proceed with this scheme in one of the B55 vehicles which was instead delivered in standard form.

FURTHER PROPOSALS

It so happened that Volvo have an extensive Hydraulic division and it was natural to expect that the question of hydraulic storage would be considered.

A system was proposed that a combined pump/motor be installed in the transmission line between the gearbox and rear axle. (Fig. 3b) The pump (shown as 12) would charge up an accumulator (shown as 13). Therefore as the bus braked fluid would be stored in the accumulator under pressure exerted by the nitrogen accumulator (shown as 14). When the system was fully charged the pump would cut out. On acceleration the pump (12) would become a motor and put its energy into the drive line. As the stored energy was used up the engine (7) would speed up and make up the deficiency utilising the gearbox (8). This was to be the system proposed and five vehicles were equipped for operation in Copenhagen and are returning savings up to twenty-five per cent in fuel consumption.

PROTO-TYPE INSTALLATION

It so happened the Volvo (Great Britian) were introducing a new underfloor engined deck vehicle as opposed to the current rear engined vehicle that had become commonplace with the introduction of one person operation. London Buses were interested in this concept having had to abandon their own development and therefore felt that it might be worthwhile to examine the Volvo Citybus, as it was known, and incorporate the hydraulic energy storage at the same time. Arrangements were therefore made to lease one such vehicle to achieve their assessment.

THE VOLVO CITYBUS

The full specification is detailed in the Appendix. 1

EXPERIMENTAL SET-UP OPERATION

A full description and operation of the system is described in Appendix. 2

TESTS RESULT - TRACK

A.   First a calibration of the speeds was undertaken and the results indicated speeds to actual were as follows:-

Indicated m. p . h.	Actual m. p. h.
20 m. p. h.	18.47
30 m. p. h.	29.30
40 m. p. h.	39.82

Which was regarded as acceptable for the accuracy required for this test.

B.   Next an acceleration test was performed showing the cooperation performance of the Diesel and Hydraulic Drives.

The latter had now been named Cumulo.

	Speed	Time (Secs.) Diesel	Time (Secs.) Cumulo
Unladen	10 m.p.h.	2.74	2.99
	20 m.p.h.	6.12	7.01
	30 m.p.h.	13.67	13.62
	40 m.p.h.	26.93	25.63
Laden	10 m.p.h.	3.80	3.90
	20 m.p.h.	9.18	9.34
	30 m.p.h.	19.80	19.35
	40 m.p.h.	36.91	35.71

C.   Fuel Tests

  i) Saw Tooth

The test involves full acceleration and then brake at 30%g.

Unladen	Mode	M.P.G.	Laden	M.P.G.
	Diesel	3.457		3.042
	Cumulo	4.697		3.794
Fuel	Saving	35.87%		24.72%

  ii) 6 Stop/mile & 20%g braking for 20 m.p.h.

Unladen	Mode	M.P.G.	Laden	M.P.G.
	Diesel	6.064		5.549
	Cumulo	7.731		7.008
Fuel	Saving	27.49%		20.82%

iii) 4 Stops/mile & 20.g braking for 30 m.p.h.

Unladen	Mode	M.P.G.	Laden	M.P.G.
	Diesel	5.963		5.000
	Cumulo	7.788		6.472
Fuel	Saving	30.61%		29.44%

D.   TEST RESULTS - SERVICE ROUTES (UNLADEN)

i) Route 11

			M.P.G.
Brook Green - Aldwych	Diesel Mode		4.83
Brook Green - Aldwych	Cumulo Mode		5.78
	Saving		23.8%

ii) Route 170

Aldwych - Roehampton	Diesel Mode		5.13
Aldwych - Roehampton	Cumulo Mode		6.97
	Saving		35.9%

iii) Route 406 (L.C.B.S.)

Kingston - Reigate	Diesel Mode		7.23
Kingston - Reigate	Cumulo Mode		7.45
	Saving		3.04%

TEST RESULTS - SERVICE ROUTES (LADEN)

iv) Route 11

Brook Green - Aldwych	Diesel Mode		3.87
Brook Green - Aldwych	Cumulo Mode		5.34
	Saving		37.98%

DISCUSSION OF RESULTS

As would be expected the Cumulo system saves fuel but the extent is governed entirely by the route profile and of course passenger load. The more intensive service, such as Route 11, does not get the opportunity of high speeds because it runs in the highly congested part of the Capital. With the West End - suburban service the saving is greater. In the case of L.C.B.S. Route 406 it has a high speed but fewer stops, clearly showing the small saving achieved.

What has yet to be assessed is the maintenance cost of operating what is a more complex vehicle. At the present costing it would seem that on the basis of the extra cost of the equipment a period of about five years is required to off-set this by anticipated fuel savings. This will of course be affected by the maintenance costs which are not known sufficiently accurately.

All that now remains is to put the bus into passenger service.

ACKNOWLEDGEMENTS

The author wishes to express his thanks to London Buses for permission to publish this work and to his staff, particularly Mr G V R·obertson who has carried out a good deal of the test work. Also to Volvo (Sweden) for their co-operation in the application of this Cumulo system to London Bus operation.

APPENDIX 1

BASIC CITYBUS SPECIFICATION

Length mm

WB	Wheelbase	4953
OAL	Overall Underframe Length	9514
J	Front Overhang	2263
AF	Rear Overhang	2298

ENGINE

The Volvo THD100EC, six cylinder, horizontally mounted Turbo charged, 4 stroke diesel engine with overhead valves and direct injection, specifically developed for economy and bus application.
Maximum Power   174KW at 2000 rpm.
Maximum torque 845Nm at 2000 rpm

ENGINE DETAILS

Bore	120.65 mm
Stroke	140 mm
Swept volume	9.6 Litres
Compression ratio	15.1:1
Oil capacity	30 Litres
Cooling system capacity (without saloon heaters)	48 Litres

Engine performance set in accordance with BSAU 141(A), ISO 2534 and SAEU 270.

Smoke requirements conform with EEC regulation 24, BSAU 141A and Federal Register of Swedish regulations.

COOLING SYSTEM

Front mounted radiator includes temperature sensing fan.

TRANSMISSION SYSTEM

ZF HP500
4-Speed fully automatic transmission with torque converter and in-built retarder.

Torque converter ratio	2.36:1
1st Gear ratio	2.81:1
2ns	1.84:1
3rd	1.36:1
4th	1.00:1
Reverse	3.97:1

FINAL DRIVE

Heavy duty single reduction hypoid crown wheel and pioion differential unit mounted in straight rear axle.

Standard ratio 4.86:1 providing top speed of 45 miles per hour with 2000 rpm governed engine.

BRAKING SYSTEM

Compressor

Westinghouse twin cylinder water cooled engine gear driven compressor.
Air Tank Capacity

Front Brakes	25 Litres
Rear Brakes	30 Litres
Parking Brakes	30 Litres
Auxillary Tank	30 Litres

BRAKING SYSTEM

Braking system incorpoates separate circuits for front and rear axles.

Extensive use is made of reinforced plastic piping.

SAB automatic slack adjusters are fitted.

Brake Dimensions

Brake Liner Width

Front	203 mm (8in.)
Rear	254 mm (10in.)
Brake Drm Diameter Front and Rear	393.7 mm (15.5in.)
Liner Thickness	19 mm ($\frac{3}{4}$in.)
Friction Area Front Brakes	3055 mm^2 (474sq. in.)
Rear Brakes	3810 mm^2 (590sq. in.)
Total Friction Area	6865 mm^2 (1064sq. in.)

Parking brake operated by type 30 spring brake chambers on rear axle.

STEERING GEAR

Power assisted steering is incorporated with engine gear driven pump and remote mounted steering box fitted away from immediate front of chassis for protection.

Approximately five turns lock to lock with front wheel angle of fifty degrees.

FRAME

Jig welded dual central spine design incorporating full peripheral framing.

SUSPENSION

Full air suspension of rolling bellows type.

Number	Front	Rear
Air Bellows	2	4
Levelling Valves	2	2

Heavy duty anti-roll bars are incorporated to front and rear axle.

Double acting hydraulic shock absorbers are fitted, two to front axle, four to rear axle.

FUEL SYSTEM

Rear mounted fuel tanks (2x) with capacity 300 litres (2 x 150 litres) - 66 gallons.

WHEELS AND TYRES

10-stud spigot fixing single piece stell rims.
Size 8.25 x 22.5 inches.

ELECTRICAL EQUIPMENT

24 volt earth return system.

CAV AG203 alternator rated at 60 amp output.

INSTRUMENTATION

Electronic speedometer

Dual air pressure guage

Temperature guage

Following warning lights are provided dependent upon level of equipment fitted to chassis and body.

Turn indicators

Headlamp main beam

Low air pressure

High coolant temperature

Battery charging light

Lubrication oil pressure

Coolant level

Parking brake engaged

Gearbox temperature (when automatic transmission fitted).

All safety circuits wired to buzzer.

MISCELLANEOUS EQUIPMENT

APPENDIX 2

VOLVO CITYBUS ENERGY STORAGE SYSTEM

PRINCIPLE OF THE SYSTEM

The major working units of the system are the low pressure accumulator, the pump/motor unit and the high pressure accumulator. The pump/motor unit is connected to the drive shaft to the rear axle by an oil-immersed chain drive box. As the bus is braked, oil is drawn from the low pressure accumulator and pumped to the high pressure accumulator where it is retained by a shut-off valve. When drive is required, the shut-off valve is opened to allow the pressure to drive the motor to accelerate the bus.

The degree of acceleration or deceleration of the bus is determined by the "yoke angle" of the pump/motor unit. This is controlled detecting the position of either the brake or accelerator pedal and adjusting the pressure in a separate servo circuit to maintain the yoke at the desired angle. The servo pump is belt-driven from the front of the engine and draws its oil supply from the low pressure accumulator.

An electronic control unit (ECU) monitors the output of sensors throughout the system and controls the overall operation of the system. This unit is situated below the stairs and has a digital display which identifies any system faults by showing a failure code number.

SYSTEM UNITS

Low Pressure Accumulator

This is the supply reservoir for the system and is situated centrally, below the floor on the off-side of the chassis. It is a large cylindrical tube containing a piston which divides the volume into an air chamber and an oil chamber. The air side is initially charged from the bus air system to force feed the main pump/motor unit so that it operates more efficiently. Three switches are attached to the outer surface of the vessel to detect the position of the piston as oil is drawn off and returned during operation. The vessel also incorporates a temperature switch to cut out the system if overheating occurs.

Main Pump/Motor Unit

This unit is situated centrally below the floor towards the near side of the bus and is connected to the cardan shaft between the gearbox and rear axle. Drive is transmitted via an oil-immersed chain box and a clutch which disengages when the system is not in use or at high road speed.

The unit has a number of pumping elements which can be inclined on a drive plate to vary the output from a maximum drive at +40 degrees yoke angle through neutral at zero and to a maximum deceleration at -40 degrees yoke angle.

High Pressure Accumulator

This is another cylindrical tube containing a piston to divide the volume into gas and oil chambers. As presurised oil is received from the pump the piston is forced back to compress a nitrogen precharge. To increase the storage capacity, the piston can travel the full length of the tube and the nitrogen is forced into remote pressure bottles. The entry to the oil side of the accumulator has a shut-off valve to retain the pressure and can be opened to allow reverse flow during drive.

Servo Pump

This is belt-driven from the front of the engine and draws oil from the low pressure accumulator.

Servo Valve block

This is situated centrally on the near side of the bus adjacent to the engine oil tank. The unit comprises an oil filter, small accumulator (to be deleted) relief valves and a by-pass valve to control the servo circuit operation.

Pump/Motor Valve Block

The valves within the pump govern the yoke angle of the unit as determined by the pedal position, by regulating the pressure in the servo circuit. The unit also contains an overflow valve to return oil to the low pressure accumulator when the high pressure accumulator becomes fully charged during prolonged periods of braking.

Pedals

Both brake and accelerator pedals have connecting links which operate potentiometers to signal the position of either pedal. When the accelerator is fully depressed, maximum drive yoke angle is selected for acceleration. As the brake pedal is depressed, the retardation yoke angle is increased until the air brakes come into operation (detected by an increase in pedal load) and maximum yoke angle is attained in addition to some air braking.

"Soft" Throttle Cylinder

On the chassis there is a mechanical throttle linkage, but to prevent operation of the fuel pump rack when driving hydraulically, an air cylinder incorporated in the linkage is exhausted. The cylinder is situated below the cab floor.

High Idle Solenoid

This solenoid is in the throttle linkage just forward of the engine and is used to set the engine at 1300 r.p.m. This is required during changeover from hydraulic to diesel drive and is also used to provide a faster air system build up when the reservoirs are exhausted.

Electronic Control Unit (ECU)

This unit is situated below the stairs and monitors signals from all parts of the system i.e. pedal positions, yoke angle, road speed, oil temperature, soft throttle, high idle, stored oil volume, servo pressure etc. This unit masterminds the operation of the system, such as when to select hydraulic or diesel drive and also carefully controls a precise sequence of events to ensure a smooth transition from hydraulic to diesel drive when oil storage is depleted.

Operation of the System

Starting

The ECU detects when the engine is started and that servo pressure is available and carries out a calibration sequence. Sensors are checked and the yoke is moved from one extreme to the other to establish the neutral position. During this calibration stage, the red "system fail" light on the drivers console remains on. The gear selector should be in neutral and the pedals should not be touched otherwise calibration is interrupted. If any faults are evident, a failure code is displayed by the ECU so that the fault can be determined. A failure code may be shown if calibration is interrupted and in this situation the engine

should be stopped and restarted to allow calibration to be completed.

Initial Acceleration

When a forward gear is selected, the pump/motor clutch is engaged. If no hydraulic storage is available, the bus can be driven away normally using the conventional diesel and automatic gearbox. At speeds above 43 miles per hour the pump/motor clutch disengages to prevent overspeeding the unit.

Hydraulic Retardation

At speeds above 30 miles per hour the hydraulic system is not working so the normal air brakes are used to slow down the bus. At 39 miles per hour the clutch is re-engaged and as 30 miles per hour is reached, the hydraulic retardation is slowly introduced by increasing the yoke angle to the desired degree over a period of about four seconds. This enables the driver to react to the increase in braking effort so that the air brake effort can be reduced and the degree of hydraulic retardation regulated by the pedal position.

At speeds below 30 miles per hour, hydraulic braking is immediately available and regulated by the position of the brake pedal. If heavy braking is required, the pedal can be depressed further to supplement the hydraulic brake with some air braking.

If a rear wheel skid occurs, the hydraulic braking is discontinued so that the more balanced front-to-rear distribution of the air brakes can be used to control the bus.

Initial Braking (Figure 4)

The piston in the low pressure accumulator normally rests near the "San 0" switch. As the bus slows down, the pump is turning and transferring oil from the low pressure accumulator to the high pressure accumulator. It is high pressure that provides a resistance to the pump to produce braking effort. As oil is transferred, both pistons move along their tubes and the ECU detects the passage of the low pressure piston past another two switches. Until the piston reaches the "San 2" switch, there is insufficient oil storage to warrant the selection of hydraulic drive should acceleration be required. For this reason, the gearbox remains in the correct gear to correspond to the road speed and the throttle linkage is intact.

Intermediate Braking (Figure 5)

Once the piston has passed the "San 2" switch the gearbox is set to neutral and the soft throttle cylinder is exhausted to interrupt the connection to the engine fuel pump. Now hudraulic drive is available if selected by depressing the throttle pedal.

© IMechE 1986 C197/86

Extended Braking (Figure 6)

In periods of extended braking, the high pressure accumulator will become fully charged and the overflow valve will open to allow oil to be pumped directly back to the low pressure accumulator while the oil is retained in the high pressure accumulator by the shut-off valve. The overflow valve provides sufficient pressure to maintain pump resistance and therefore retardation but does cause the oil to become heated. A temperature switch in the low pressure accumulator cuts out the system if the temperature gets too high and conventional braking takes over.

Terminal Braking

When the bus reaches about 5 miles per hour, the yoke angle is slowly reduced to decrease the hydraulic braking effort. This allows the driver time to react and apply some air brake effort to bring the bus finally to a standstill. The handbrake must then be applied to hold the bus.

Acceleration (Figure 7)

When there is sufficient storage in the high pressure accumulator, hydraulic drive is selected by engaging a forward gear and depressing the throttle pedal. The position of the pedal determines the yoke angle which governs the rate of acceleration.

At this stage, the soft throttle cylinder is exhausted so that the engine is idling and the gearbox is in neutral.

As the bus speed increases, the oil returning to the low pressure accumulator pushes the piston back, towards its starting position.

Changeover (Figure 8)

As the piston passes the "San 1" switch, the ECU detects that stored energy is nearly exhausted and starts a carefully timed sequence to reinstate the diesel drive.

The "high idle" solenoid sets the engine speed to 1300 r.p.m. and the correct gear speed begins to engage. The yoke angle is slowly decreased and at the same time, air pressure is gradually allowed into the soft throttle cylinder to allow operation of the fuel pump. Finally the gearbox is locked up and normal diesel drive continues the motion of the bus.

Wheel Spin

If the ECU detects that the wheels are slipping during hydraulic drive, then the yoke angle is alternately reduced and increased again until traction is regained.

Override

In certain circumstances, insufficient acceleration is available from the hydraulic drive and in these instances the ECU automatically reinstates diesel drive.

Figure 3 (a) illustrates the chassis with the storage system installed before the body was built.

SYSTEM DATA

High Pressure accumulator precharge	–	200 Bar (2900 psi)
High Pressure relief pressure	–	360 Bar (5220 psi)
Pump/motor torque (Type V21)	–	1000 Bar (738 lb ft) @ 360 Bar
Pump/motor displacement (max)	–	160 cc/rev
Low pressure accumulator precharge	–	2 Bar (30 psi)
Low pressure accumulator relief pressure	–	10 Bar (145 psi)
Servo operating pressure	–	45 Bar (650 psi)
Pump chain drive – ratio	–	26:1
– lubrication	–	Dexron ATF
System oil	–	Shell ellus 46T

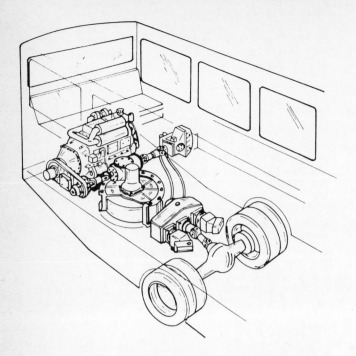

Fig 1 General arrangement of flywheel energy storage system in single deck bus

Fig 3a The chassis of the Volvo Citybus with the storage system installed before the body was built

Fig 2

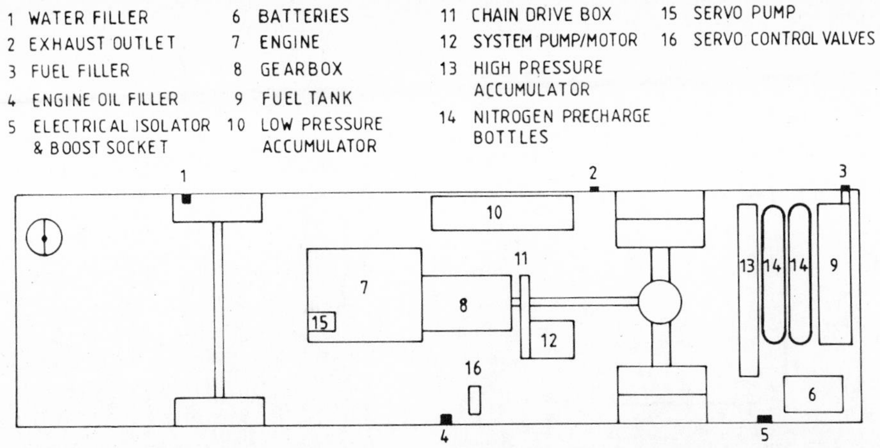

1 WATER FILLER
2 EXHAUST OUTLET
3 FUEL FILLER
4 ENGINE OIL FILLER
5 ELECTRICAL ISOLATOR & BOOST SOCKET
6 BATTERIES
7 ENGINE
8 GEARBOX
9 FUEL TANK
10 LOW PRESSURE ACCUMULATOR
11 CHAIN DRIVE BOX
12 SYSTEM PUMP/MOTOR
13 HIGH PRESSURE ACCUMULATOR
14 NITROGEN PRECHARGE BOTTLES
15 SERVO PUMP
16 SERVO CONTROL VALVES

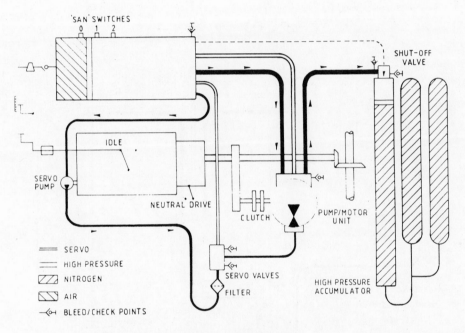

Fig 3b Volvo Citybus with hydraulic energy storage system

'SAN' SWITCHES
0 1 2
SHUT-OFF VALVE
IDLE
SERVO PUMP
NEUTRAL DRIVE
CLUTCH
PUMP/MOTOR UNIT
SERVO VALVES
FILTER
HIGH PRESSURE ACCUMULATOR
SERVO
HIGH PRESSURE
NITROGEN
AIR
BLEED/CHECK POINTS

Fig 4 Initial braking

'SAN' SWITCHES
0 1 2
SHUT-OFF VALVE
IDLE
SERVO PUMP
NEUTRAL DRIVE
CLUTCH
PUMP/MOTOR UNIT
SERVO VALVES
FILTER
HIGH PRESSURE ACCUMULATOR
SERVO
HIGH PRESSURE
NITROGEN
AIR
BLEED/CHECK POINTS

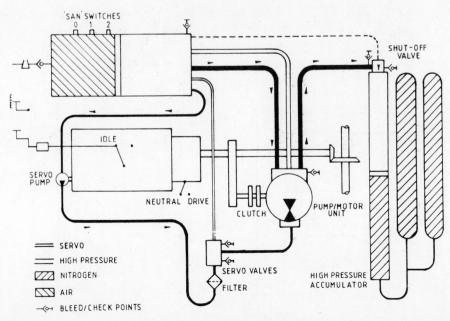

Fig 5 Intermediate braking

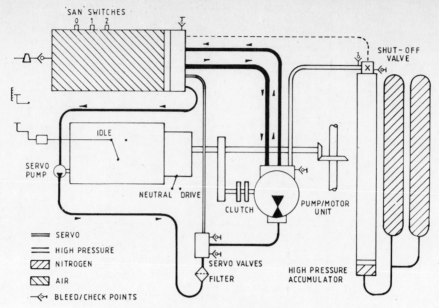

Fig 6   Extended braking

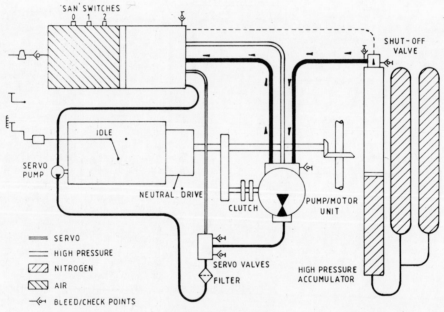

Fig 7   Accelerating

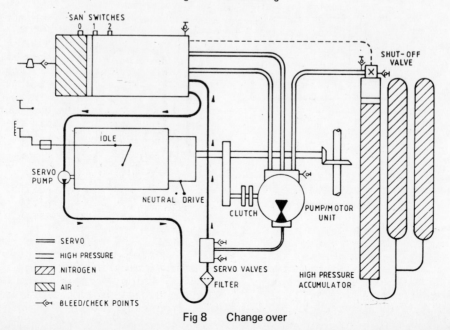

Fig 8   Change over

Integration of a commercial vehicle regenerative braking driveline

C J GREENWOOD, BSc
Leyland Vehicles, Leyland, Preston, Lancashire

SYNOPSIS   The paper discusses the design options available for the production of a commercial vehicle regenerative braking driveline.   It is based on the experience gained during the joint development programme for the Leyland/BP regenerative bus, and, as such, concentrates on mechanical systems using a high-speed flywheel as the energy storage medium.   It covers the operational specifications for each of the driveline components and outlines the strategy adopted for their integration into the final system.   The operational characteristics of the bus are described, including the mechanically automated 'link' transmission that engages the engine and flywheel.

1   INTRODUCTION

Much has been written concerning the theoretical benefits available from a vehicle driveline capable of regenerative braking. The cyclic storage and re-use of kinetic energy, as a principal, is well understood.   This paper seeks to explore the practical implications of such a system and to propose a series of design concepts evolved during the Leyland 'REGEN-BUS' development programme.

All regenerative braking systems require a transmission capable of controlling the power flow between the driving wheels and energy store.   The function is derived from the appropriate control of ratio <u>and</u> rate of change of ratio and the transmission is invariably termed 'continuously variable' or CVT.

The   form   and   characteristics associated with the CVT will largely determine the driveline configuration and in particular the nature of the energy store.   As a basic principal, the number of energy form conversions should be minimised.   Thus, CVT's relying on pressurised fluid to transmit power will be most effective if energy is stored hydrostatically.   Equally, a mechanical CVT is best suited to a high speed flywheel system.

2   TRANSMISSION

Leyland has undertaken two overlapping projects to develop car and commercial vehicle sized CVTs.   Activity was started at   Rover   in   1973   on   the   smaller transmission, the results being reported in (1).   In 1979, a second programme (2) was started at Leyland, Lancashire, that culminated in a successful prototype demonstration in a National Bus.   Although the programmes were run independently and produced markedly different systems, they were   founded   upon   identical   variator technology.

The variable ratio mechanism adopted is   a   rolling   traction   drive   shown schematically in fig. l.   It exploits an elasto hydrodynamic oil film, generated at the disc/roller interface, to transmit torque without metal to metal contact. Ratio variation is produced by steering the   traction   rollers   to   alter   their precession angles.   Control is achieved by the usual microprocessor based electronics through the agency of an hydraulic control system   containing   a   purpose   designed control valve and ram (3).

It is a fundamental property of the roller steering system that the variator, and   therefore   complete   transmission, operates under torque rather than ratio control.   In essence, the application of a control demand will cause the transmission to produce an equivalent torque at either its input or output shafts. The effect is not influenced by the current ratio or rate of change of ratio and does not seek to control either.   Of course, all CVTs will control the power they transmit by the ultimate variation of input or output torque.   However,   those   transmissions adopting a ratio control strategy achieve the effect by externally defining the required ratio and rate of change of ratio.

The traction variator has a ratio spread dictated by the physical shape of its input and output discs.   However configured,   zero   ratio   (infinite reduction) is not possible and so additional   means   must   be   provided   to accelerate the vehicle from rest.   This was   achieved with the prototype bus transmission by incorporating a mechanical 'shunt' using an epicyclic gear train. The usefulness of such a system is limited by   its   recirculating   power   and   the resultant high variator loadings developed within the transmission whilst operating close to infinite reduction - termed geared neutral.

The effect was moderated by limiting the shunt operation between full reverse and 'second gear' ratios. The remaining ratio spread was provided by a direct mode with the shunt disengaged. The complete transmission, shown in fig. 2, was configured for synchronous shift between modes giving one 'cold' regime change for continuous variation of ratio between full reverse and deep overdrive.

The prototype transmission was fitted into a 16 tonne single deck city bus (National I) and was driven by the standard '500' engine rated at 160hp. Engine operation was via the conventional air throttle and mechanical fuel pump. In a series of back to back tests, with a standard vehicle, on the Leyland Technical Centre track, the CVT bus demonstrated a 10 per cent fuel saving at six stops per mile. It is believed that this is the only commercial vehicle CVT to have achieved a fuel saving without the addition of a regenerative braking system.

The success of the transmission development programme encouraged its extension towards a full regenerative braking system. Given the all-mechanical CVT, the only choice for energy storage was a high speed flywheel. Consequently, a joint project was inaugurated with the British Petroleum Company plc to develop a commercial, city bus regenerative braking driveline. Responsibility was divided between Leyland for the transmission, engine, vehicle and controls and the partner for the development of a high-speed flywheel, energy storage system.

3 FLYWHEEL

As a general principal, it was decided that the system should only store the kinetic energy of the vehicle. Whilst the potential energy due to route gradients is theoretically available, its storage would introduce two major problems. The capacity of the unit would increase drastically (the kinetic energy of a vehicle at 48 Kph is only equivalent to the potential energy at a height of 9.2 m), and the time of storage would greatly reduce its availability by parasitic loss. Consequently, the flywheel capacity was set at the kinetic energy available from a 16 tonne vehicle travelling at 48 Kph or about 0.5 kWhr.

The power rating of the unit was determined by consideration of both the drive and braking parts of the cycle. When driving, the energy store would replace the engine and, as such, should be capable of matching its power output. Since a CVT can transmit full engine power at virtually any vehicle speed, the flywheel must sustain maximum power at any energy storage level - i.e. rotational speed.

Retardation performance is more difficult to define. Foundation brake deceleration is obtained from all of the vehicle's wheels and is specified to provide emergency action. Replicating this performance with the transmission would not only increase the size of all driveline components (braking a 16 tonne bus from 48 Kph at 0.5g dissipates 1044 kW), but would be illegal since it would be done with the two driving wheels alone. A more realistic approach is to consider the deceleration levels encountered during normal passenger operation. Leyland bus studies have shown that 90 per cent of all retardation for city buses is produced at less than 10%g. This was taken as the maximum retardation required from the regenerative system alone. Even at this level, the driveline would have to handle a maximum 224 kW. However, this rating would be instantaneous, since the power is dependent on vehicle speed for constant rate retardation. The energy store is most likely to absorb maximum power at its minimum energy level - i.e. rotational speed.

It follows that the power rating of the energy store is dictated by its torque capacity at its minimum speed. The unit specification was set to a maximum 'continuous' power rating of 120 kW and a maximum 'intermittent' rating of 160kW.

It was decided that the energy store should mount directly onto the driveline casings, thereby avoiding the space requirements of drive shafts and separate suspension system. Accordingly, the store was required to withstand the vibration environment of the engine and transmission. Theoretical studies showed that :

(a) the vibration loads originating from the engine and transmission would be less than the expected flywheel out of balance forces

(b) vertical body motion would not impose any greater forces under normal operation

(c) the greatest flywheel loads would derive from the yaw motion when steering.

Consequently, three levels of operational stress were defined covering the full range of expected operation.

Normal passenger operation of the bus was taken to define the durability and reliability of the unit. The maximum precession loads occur with the bus at its tightest steering radius at the maximum stable speed. This condition was specified as 0.7 rad/sec and was to be achievable without detriment to storage life.

Category two operation was the worst vehicle evolution to be sustained by the flywheel without failure and represented an emergency condition. Again, it was defined as a maximum precession and was taken as the worst possible skid condition that would not necessarily result in vehicle damage. It was specified at 3 rad/sec.

Category three was taken as any incident causing flywheel failure and required that failure to be benign under any 'possible' circumstance. It could originate externally - vehicle accident or internally - component failure and really defined the effectiveness required of the storage containment systems.

4 ENGINE

The regenerative driveline engine is required to supply only that energy lost or additionally demanded by the vehicle. On a level road it will maintain motion after the energy stored from the last stop has been re-converted to kinetic energy. However, the gradient performance of the system is totally dependent upon the engine power available. If acceptable levels of vehicle speed are to be maintained, the engine rating cannot be reduced.

The capacity of current bus engines is largely determined by the arduous duty cycle provided by their inevitable stop start operation. Durability is inextricably linked with size. The pressure for larger engines is compounded by the rather narrow ratio spread of the transmissions used and the compensating emphasis on engine torque and torque curve shape.

However, the duty cycle experienced by a regen. engine will be radically altered by both the use of stored energy and the presence of a CVT. Most high power operation will be provided by the energy store as the vehicle accelerates from rest. The CVT will operate the engine on its 'ideal' economy line, fig. 3 - i.e. maintain minimum engine speed for the demanded power.

Since the CVT is totally insensitive to the shape of the engine torque curve and is itself responsible for the vehicle's gradeability (at zero ratio), a large engine is neither required for durability nor performance. In fact, a small engine running near its potential rating will be more economical, since the optimum fuel efficiency will occur at lower powers. A city bus requires less than 30 per cent of its rated power to maintain its normal maximum legal speed.

Thus, the additional weight, size and cost of the regen. driveline is largely compensated by a smaller, cheaper engine. The Leyland 'regen. driveline' could be specified with a 6½ litre '400' engine as a replacement for the current 11.1 litre 'TL11'.

5 SYSTEM INTEGRATION

With the availability of a practical CVT and energy store, the success of a regen. driveline is largely dependent upon the method of system integration adopted. Restricting engine operation to its ideal line imposes a response penalty in 'compensation' for improved economy. Variations in power demand can only be met by a commensurate change in engine speed. The time penalty will largely depend upon the engine rotational inertia and the resulting crankshaft acceleration. Inappropriately linking the energy storage flywheel to the engine would destroy the driveline response and performance. Equally, there is no point in diverting stored energy to the engine by leaving it connected into the system when not driving.

Engagement and disengagement of the engine and storage flywheel must be accomplished with minimal driveline shock and control disruption or delay. Reliance on the usual, oil filled, multiplate clutch for connection can create serious problems. The inevitable delay between initiation and application can make a smooth connection very difficult. The effect can become critical when the inertias are large, as would be the case with the storage flywheel and vehicle.

The system must maintain the current levels of driveability, retaining, wherever possible, conventional control function and 'feel'. Provision for 'cold start' - preferably turn key - and fail safe operation must also be incorporated.

6 SYSTEM CONCEPTS

A CVT is essential for the operation of the energy store and desirable for the optimised control of the engine. Thus, the simplest and most obvious driveline concept would be to fit separate engine and energy store CVT's, connected to a common axle drive shaft, fig. 4a. Provided adequate ratio spread to be available from each transmission, system control would merely require the correct activation of the appropriate transmission. Indeed, power could be directed between the engine, energy store and vehicle in virtually any combination.

Although impractical, it does suggest the 'perfect' transmission. Sometimes described as a 'three port' CVT, fig. 4(b), it would confer independent, variable ratio operation between the input ports and the output. However, such a system requires two variable ratio drives and is therefore little more practical than the first system.

It is possible to approximate a three port system by arranging dependent, but appropriate, operation of the engine and energy store. Unfortunately, it has not proven possible to define a form of dependency that is flexible enough to meet all of the needs of a real vehicle drive train.

As an example of the problems encountered, an epicyclic link can be arranged between the engine and energy storage flywheel. Termed a GYREACTOR transmission, the principal is shown in fig. 4c. The three epicyclic shafts are connected to the engine, flywheel and output, the resulting power flows being governed by the epicyclic relationship. Since this provides that any two shaft torques are defined by the third, the engine can be used to control the power flow from the flywheel. Appropriate choice of gearing will ensure that power from the engine will cause a decelerating torque to appear at the flywheel. Thus, the power at the output shaft will be the sum of engine and flywheel powers. The effect could be reversed by a change of gearing causing energy to be stored in the accelerating flywheel. The system is 'three port' in the sense that the engine, flywheel and vehicle are all operated simultaneously. However, vehicle acceleration <u>and</u> deceleration requires fuel to be <u>burnt</u> by the engine. The system enhances vehicle performance at the cost of increased fuel consumption!

A less ambitious approach retains the separate functions of engine and energy store by the addition of the regenerative system to an otherwise conventional drivetrain. The system shown in fig. 4d uses a 'standard engine and transmission' provided with a connection for the regenerative CVT. Any form of CVT and store is feasible, although historically a hydrostatic pump/motor and accumulators have been used.

The concept has the advantage of applying least emphasis on the CVT, since it is only used during the regenerative part of the cycle. However, since the regenerative power exceeds the normal engine rating and the CVT must provide hill climb torques, its capacity must exceed that of the standard transmission. Furthermore, the engine derives no benefit from the system. Retaining the conventional transmission rejects the opportunity for ideal line operation and improved engine utilisation. In economic terms the concept viability suffers, since no savings are made over the conventional drivetrain, to compensate for the additional cost of the regenerative system.

The most practical design approach to the problem extracts the greatest benefit from each driveline component. An efficient CVT must form the foundation of the system, incorporated so as to operate with both the engine and energy store. The only realistic approach is to switch between the two as circumstances demand. Clutches interposed between the transmission input and the engine and energy store, provide the means of selection, fig. 4e.

The feasibility of the arrangement is largely dependent on the smooth, rapid operation of the clutches. Accurate synchronisation at engagement is crucial. Although it is possible for simple multiplate clutches, controlled by a microprocessor, to be effective, the Leyland system was designed with a lower technical risk approach based on mechanical automation.

7 LEYLAND DRIVELINE CONCEPT

The complete regenerative driveline is shown schematically in Fig. 5. The engine is connected to the transmission via a sprag clutch that will only permit power flow from the engine. The flywheel connection is made at the transmission input via a second sprag clutch arranged to prevent power flow to the flywheel.

Energy storage is accomplished via a parallel multiplate clutch operated by the driveline control system. A flywheel disconnect clutch is incorporated to reduce the system parasitic losses whilst the flywheel is fully charged and the vehicle is stationary.

8 SYSTEM OPERATION

This sprag arrangement ensures that the transmission is automatically connected to that input (engine or flywheel) rotating at the greatest speed (assuming that the flywheel disconnect clutch is closed).

8.1 Engine driving, flywheel exhausted

With the flywheel running at its minimum energy level, its speed referred to transmission input will be less than or equal to 1000 rpm. Operation of the engine above this speed will automatically engage the engine sprag clutch, thereby disengaging the flywheel. Conventional operation of the driveline is then possible, since the flywheel is 'transparent'. It is also possible to switch from flywheel to engine operation, at any time, by accelerating the engine to a speed beyond that of the flywheel, should this be required.

8.2 Flywheel engagement and regenerative braking

A braking demand on the system must be preceded by a 'zero' throttle setting.

The resulting engine deceleration will eventually cause the engine speed to drop below that of the flywheel. At this point, the engine sprag will overrun and the flywheel sprag will engage. The flywheel cannot be connected until this speed reversal has occurred, but the engagement will be automatic and shock-free. The electronic control system will, at all times, monitor the speeds of transmission input and flywheel shafts. When the speeds coincide, it will engage the parallel multiplate clutch, rapidly locking the flywheel into the system. No clutch modulation will be required, since, by definition, the relative speeds across the plates must be zero. Regenerative braking may then commence by downshifting the CVT.

8.3 Flywheel driving

Energy can be withdrawn from the flywheel by reversing the transmission torques. Since the sprag locks under drive loads, the multiplate clutch, in parallel with it, may be released when appropriate, without interrupting the power flow. Once the clutch is open, drive may be reconnected to the engine simply by accelerating its crankshaft.

8.4 Cruising

Prolonged periods of engine operation will allow the flywheel parasitic losses to decelerate the energy store. This may be prevented by transmitting power across the parallel multiplate clutch. A partial 'engagement' at reduced hydraulic pressure will transmit the low power required. Such an operation would not interfere with the driveline performance other than by diverting a small proportion of engine power to the energy store.

8.5 Start up

With the flywheel stationary, the engine may be started, since only its sprag will connect, the engine providing the fastest input. The flywheel can then be initially charged to its minimum energy speed by the use of the cruise control.

8.6 Flywheel de-coupling

At any appropriate time, the flywheel can be disengaged from the system by opening its disconnect clutch. The transmission input shaft will then decelerate to engine speed, when the engine sprag will engage. The flywheel can only be re-engaged by the modulated application of the disconnect clutch, or by accelerating the engine to the referred flywheel speed.

8.7 Low power strategy

When cruising at city traffic speeds, the power required to sustain the motion of a bus will be considerably less than its engine rating. The fuel efficiency of the engine at very low output is inevitably poor and not amenable to improvement by the CVT. However, fuel efficiency can be improved by using the flywheel as a 'short term' energy store allowing the engine to operate in short high power bursts. The fuel consumption of the engine is thus improved, whilst the transmission draws energy from the flywheel as required. Thus, the flywheel acts as the 'prime mover' for the vehicle whilst the driveline control system monitors its speed and therefore energy level. When exhausted, the engine will be reconnected simply by opening its 'throttle', via its driving sprag clutch. Since, by definition, the engine power must exceed the loading imposed by the transmission, the surplus power will be used to accelerate the energy store. The speed at which the engine is disconnected will be determined as a function of vehicle speed, since sufficient energy capacity must remain to stop the bus.

8.8 Kick down

Switching drive from the flywheel requires the engine

(a) to accelerate from idle to the synchronous engagement speed under no load;

(b) when connected to the link transmission, to further accelerate to that speed at which it can supply the power demanded by the driver.

At maximum power demands, the engine must therefore accelerate from the flywheel exhausted speed (1000 rpm) to the engine rated speed (2000 rpm) before the demanded driving torque can re-appear at the bus wheels. Since the first acceleration from idle can be completed before the flywheel is released, it does not influence the 'power off time' and so the delay is dependent upon the required engine speed change between engagement and the final operating point.

The effect can be reduced by the early release of the flywheel at speeds closer to the engine operating point. Vehicle performance will be enhanced, but at the cost of lower fuel efficiency. Integration of kick down into the control strategy will be dependent on the inevitable degradation in economy which must be quantified in the bus environment.

9 PROGRAMME

An experimental version of the complete regenerative driveline has been built and successfully tested. It has recently been fitted into a National bus and has achieved limited track operation.

Development of the system control began with the 'cold start' activity and has progressed through each evolution required for full vehicle operation. The system is completely automatic, requiring no additional driver input. From the 'turn key' start to regenerative operation, the system is driven through conventional controls, whilst the driveline electronics monitor system 'health' and safety. Fuel consumption measurement and full scale traffic operation will follow later this year.

10 CONCLUSIONS

The inherent controllability and efficiency of the Leyland traction variator provides a practical approach to flywheel-based regenerative braking systems. The driveline concept adopted for the system avoids any engagement synchronisation problems returning smooth, shock-free operation under all conditions.

Providing CVT operation for both the energy store and engine allows complete system integration and produces a concept both effective and economically viable.

REFERENCES

(1) STUBBS, P.W.R. The Development of a Perbury Traction Transmission for Motor-car Applications. International Power Transmission and Gear Conference, San Francisco, USA, ASME, August 1980.

(2) GREENWOOD, C. J. The Design, Construction and Operation of a Commercial Vehicle Continuously Variable Transmission. Driveline-84, London, England, I.Mech.E., March 1984.

(3) DUNNE, J.E. and GREENWOOD, C.J. Integrated Control System. I.S.A.T.A., Milan, Italy, September 1984.

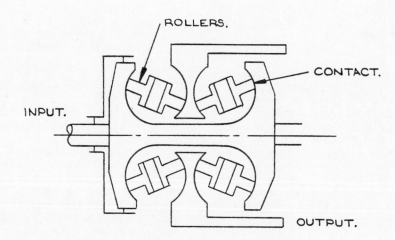

Fig 1   Schematic of traction vehicle

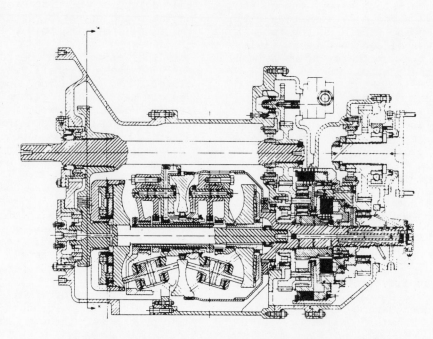

Fig 2   General assembly of continuously variable transmission (CVT)

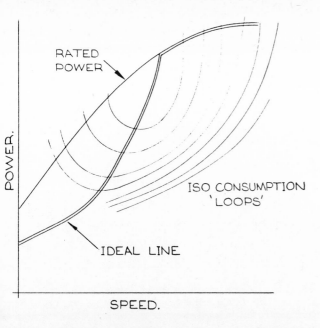

Fig 3   Typical diesel engine performance map with 'ideal' operating line superimposed

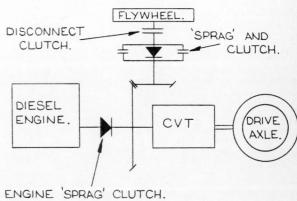

Fig 5   Schematic of regenerative driveline

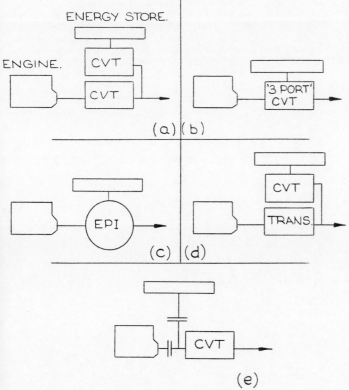

Fig 4   Possible regenerative driveline concepts

C195/86

The armoured fighting vehicle power pack

J C ALLINSON, BSc, CEng, MIMechE and **D A BALDWIN**
Royal Armament Research and Development Establishment, Chertsey, Surrey

SYNOPSIS   This paper discusses design policy for the power packs of armoured fighting vehicles and the various options available for engines and transmissions. It describes the automation of a layshaft transmission in a Comet tank and a design concept based on this work. It presents a novel design of mechanical steering system for a high speed track layer and finally it describes a two layshaft automatic transmission that is being produced in prototype form for armoured fighting vehicles.

1.   INTRODUCTION

Current United Kingdom policy on the design of Armoured Fighting Vehicles (AFV) propulsion systems is to adopt an integrated approach to the engine and transmission, and to extend this approach to both the cooling system and a controller for the entire package.

The AFV powerpack designer has to cope with all the constraints familiar to designers of powerpacks for civilian vehicles, and an additional set of priorities stemming from the military environment in which the vehicle will operate.

The AFV designer must consider the severe battlefield conditions under which the equipment must function reliably, and also must tailor his design solution to the very special duty cycles deriving from the proposed tactical use intended by the vehicle user. Battlefield ambients and duty cycles can vary widely when more than one national customer is involved. Early consideration of potential defence sales involves a further set of design constraints and increases the challenge to the designer seeking an optimum solution.

UK policy has for some years included a preparedness to trade-off ultimate automotive performance against improved firepower and protection. The Main Battle Tanks (MBTs) which result may traditionally draw a certain amount of criticism in peacetime, when high speeds on tarmac roads assume disproportionate importance, but provide a mix of fighting characteristics which is tailored to the requirements of the British Army in time of war, and which has proved also to fulfil the requirements of many other nations with a requirement for armour to fulfil a similar tactical role.

It may be difficult to believe, given the size of the vehicles, but there is a serious shortage of space for the powerpack in a modern AFV. The space constraints evolve from the limitation on width imposed by transportation requirements, the subsequent limitation on length for an agile vehicle, steered by its tracks, the tactical need for a low silhouette and the requirements of a large ground clearance.

In addition the hull size thus defined must carry heavy armour, particularly at the front of the vehicle, a large turret, which sweeps a significant volume inside the hull, and the maximum stowage of consumables such as fuel and ammunition. Room must also be found for the driver and an ever increasing volume of electronic equipment.

The requirement is therefore, clearly, to produce equivalent, or hopefully greater power at the track drive sprockets from a smaller, more compact powerpack. Developments and new technologies applied to engine and transmission may affect the powerpack volume directly or indirectly. Directly by using engines and transmissions of smaller overall dimensions to produce and transmit large powers; indirectly by improved efficiency, making the cooling equipment (a major contributor to the overall powerpack size) smaller. Reduced fuel consumption also reduces the size of the hull mounted automotives by allowing less fuel tank volume.

2.   THE ENGINE

There are two practical options for consideration as Main Battle Tank prime movers. The reciprocating diesel engine and the automotive gas turbine. The diesel engine has advantages in fuel consumption (particulary at part load), in development cost and time, and in production cost. The automotive gas turbine has advantages in size and weight although size benefit can be lost in large heat exchangers, required to give acceptable fuel consumption, and in larger air filters for the greater volume of engine air.

Battle tank power at the engine flywheel is now in the 750 to 1500 kW region. For these power outputs the gas turbine technology has the advantage of being generally downrated from more powerful aircraft ratings whereas the diesel technology requires uprating from civilian automotive applications.

Gas turbine engines tend to be built to give an output within a small range of powers, dictated by the need for internal matching and optimisation. Thus a range of power outputs would usually require a range of engine types. The diesel engine can be more readily adapted, by altering the number of cylinders and their rated power, to give a range of output powers. To enable demonstration of reduced power pack volume would therefore require a special gas turbine to be produced (given that no existing engine is available in compact form) whereas a diesel with fewer cylinders can be selected from the range available and uprated to the power required.

The factors deciding the power output of a diesel engine are the engine speed and the torque generated. To increase the performance of a given base engine either or both of these parameters may be uprated.

The scope of speed increase is limited for a compression ignition engine of the size being considered. The diesel engine is highly stressed, being based on high cylinder pressures to achieve good combustion. The components are large, with high inertias, and the increased frictional and inertia losses diminish the power increase achieved by running above an optimum speed. Higher speeds also impair the combustion process on direct injection diesels.

Increased power must be sought from a small speed increase with a large increase in torque produced. Increase in torque can be achieved by increasing the engine capacity and by improving its thermal and volumetric efficiency. Large capacities lead to greater frictional and inertia losses which inhibit speed increases. Thermal efficiency is largely a function of compression ratio. The extent to which the compression ratio can be increased is limited by the maximum cylinder pressure the engine can withstand. Variable compression pistons can improve thermal efficiency, but at a high cost in complexity and inertia. Volumetric efficiency can be improved by pressure charging, charge cooling, control of valve timing and manifold design to improve cylinder scavenging. These changes create the need to improve fuel supply, injection pressure, quantity and timing, and combustion chamber changes to improve swirl and aid combustion. To achieve ultimate ratings, engines and turbochargers will need heat insulated and precision cooled internal components to retain durability, and improvements to component strength and lubrication. Cold starting aids, such as manifold heaters, become essential to overcome the problem of the low compression ratios required to accept the high levels of boost envisaged.

The design of future tank engines is entirely the preserve of the engine supplier. Our task at the Royal Armament Research and Development Establishment is to encourage and assist in research in areas which we believe will lead to the incorporation of improvements on the engines available for fighting vehicle appli-

cation. We are investigating variable geometry turbocharging, low heat loss engines, involving use of ceramic insulation and precision cooling, variable valve timing, and further extension of digital control for both engine and transmission.

The short term research aim is to achieve ratings of some 22 bar brake mean effective pressure at 2500 r/min whilst retaining good engine response, torque back-up, startability, reliability and durability. We see future ratings being of the order of 25 bar brake mean effective pressure 2500 r/min. These engines will require to deliver between 750 and 1500 kW and will be multi-cylinder medium size units.

We have devised a possible future compact power pack to illustrate our thinking (Fig 1). This uses a transverse 17.6 litre vee eight diesel engine, coupled to a high efficiency layshaft transmission with mechanical steering, engine and transmission cooling by high thermal ratio coolers with a modulated fan, all under the control of a microprocessor based management system.

3. THE TRANSMISSION

The transmission for a modern battle tank such as Challenger is fully automatic using conventional technology of epicyclic gearing and multiple friction clutches with a torque converter. Transmissions of this type, although giving excellent driveability, are less efficient than the manually operated layshaft type which use dog clutches for gear engagement and a friction clutch as the coupling to the engine.

In order to achieve a smaller power pack obviously the transmission itself needs to be smaller, but transmission efficiency has an influence on the volume of other components in the power pack. If the losses in the transmission are reduced it is possible to deliver the same power at the sprockets with a smaller prime mover. The cooling system can, as we have indicated, be reduced in size as less heat is being rejected by the engine and transmission, and there is also a reduction of the amount of fuel that has to be carried under armour.

Dog engaged layshaft gearboxes with no synchronizing devices are used in older British tanks such as Centurion. They are reliable and highly efficient, but manual operation of the clutch and gear lever requires coniderable physical effort and a great deal of driver skill to synchronize the dog clutches.

In 1976 RARDE embarked on a research programme with the aim of converting a Centurion layshaft transmission to full automatic control to give a more acceptable level of driveability.

All the necessary modifications were external to the existing transmission. Hydraulic actuators were attached to the gear selector rods which also operated microswitches to signal gear engaged and neutral positions. Speed sensors were attached to the input and output shafts of the transmission.

A disc brake was added to the input shaft to synchronize the dog clutches during up shifts. Synchronism for down shifts was achieved by blipping the engine.

A microprocessor controlled the gearchange process in a semi-automatic mode, the driver making the decision of when to change the gear which he implemented by pressing a button either for upchange or downchange. There is a problem with providing full automatic control of the Centurion transmission due to the kinematics of the steering system, which reacts the steering forces at the input clutch, so steering of Centurion is not possible with the clutch disengaged. The driver's control was arranged such that gearchanging was inhibited while steering the vehicle.

The transmission was installed in a Comet tank with a mass of 33 tonnes.
A microprocessor control system was fitted.
The trials with the Comet have shown that good quality gearchanges are achieved in an average time of 0.5 seconds.
The success of these experiments gave us the incentive to perform further research into a layshaft transmission that could be optimised for full automatic control and suitable for a compact power pack in a modern main battle tank. For a tracked military vehicle which has a high rolling resistance on cross country terrain it is essential that power is interrupted at the drive sprockets during gearchanging for the shortest possible time.
In order to reduce gearchange times to our eventual aim of an average of 0.25 seconds consideration has been given to the following.

(a) The engine must be optimised to give good response to acceleration demands in order to synchronise the dog clutches for down-changing. This can be a problem with turbocharged diesel engines, particularly those of high specific power.
(b) The inertia of the transmission input components and the prime mover must be as low as possible.
(c) The dog clutches must be capable of being moved into and out of engagement rapidly.
(d) Each gearchange should require only one dog clutch to be disengaged and another engaged. This eliminates the use of range change and splitter arrangements.
(e) Computing time must be very short, and may require parallel processing in consequence.

A diagram of the ratio change gearbox integrated with a steering system is shown in fig 2. With this arrangement two dog clutches are in engagement for each ratio, but to change ratio only one dog clutch is put to neutral and another engaged. Ratio skipping can be achieved when desirable without violating this rule. There are a total of fifteen dog clutch combinations but only twelve of these give

sensible ratios, eight forward and four reverse.

A disadvantage of this ratio change gearbox is high power recirculation in the lower ratios, which increases the dimensions of the shafts and gears, but the reduction in the number of components gives a nett saving in volume.

In an integrated tracked vehicle transmission advantage can be taken of the effect the steering system has on the overall transmission ratios. as the steering system uses four differentials the calculation of speeds and torques is rather tedious, so a computer program, which includes a model of the dynamic behaviour of the dog clutches when they engage, has been written.

This model shows the transient torques in the transmission and would allow us to optimise the speed difference at the dog clutches before engagement, initial results show this to be about 300 r/min.

4. STEERING

The transmission for a tank is often of similar size to the engine. This is because it has to include a steering system which can account for about half the volume of the transmission.

There are many mechanisms available for skid steering a tracklayer but it was not until 1939 that a fundamental study of the problem was made by Dr Merritt, at the Department of Tank Design. (ref 1)

As a result of his investigations Merritt devised a system of three differentials which is used successfully on British tanks such as Centurion, Chieftain and Scorpion.

The three differential system is shown in fig 3. It has left and right hand summing differentials, each of which has a common input from the ratio change section of the transmission. One arm of each differential is the output to the track sprocket, the third arm is driven by the 'half shafts' of a central steering brake. The steering differential is driven from the prime mover. When one of the steering brakes is applied the output shaft on one side decreases its speed by the same amount, this difference in speed between the two tracks determines the radius of turn. This system has several advantages over simple clutch/brake mechanisms used on some previous tanks. Firstly it is regenerative, which means that power can be transferred from the slower moving inner track to the outer track, which enables the vehicle to sustain a high speed turn. It was shown by Merritt that the power required at the outer track in this condition could be as much as three times the maximum power of the prime mover. Secondly, and a significant improvement on previous designs, with the steering brake locked there is a different radius of turn for each ratio of the gear box, a small radius in low gear which increases as each higher ratio is selected. The Merritt system also allows the vehicle to pivot turn when the ratio change gearbox is in neutral, the sprockets rotating in opposite directions, though a true pivot turn is only obtained if the resistance to slewing of each track is equal.

For our illustrative compact power pack transmission, we have devised a steer system which is a development of Merritt's using four differentials, (see fig 4).

The additional differential sums the speed of the prime mover and the output speed of the ratio change gearbox. The resultant of these two speeds then drives the steering differential of a Merritt system.

The elements of the fourth differential are arranged such that as each higher gear ratio is selected, so the speed of the steer differential reduces. The effect of the fourth differential is to give a smaller radius of turn in low gear and a larger radius in top gear than can be achieved with a three differential system.

This effect can be illustrated by considering the rate of turn (fig 5) which, with the steering brake locked, is proportional to vehicle speed in each gear. for a three differential system the rate of turn at maximum speed in any gear is a constant.

For good agility at low vehicle speeds a high rate of turn is required but with a three differential system it is fixed at some compromise figure to avoid lateral skidding of the vehicle at high speeds.

Using four differentials gives a sloping characterstic to the maximum rate of turn (see fig 6) which allows the vehicle to have a high rate, hence small radius of turn at low vehicle speeds. The opposite effect occurs in reverse gears with the arrangement shown in fig 4, this is acceptable because the maximum speed of the vehicle is only thirty per cent of its maximum forward speed. The effect occurs because the reversing gears are situated within the ratio change gearbox. If, however, the reversing mechanism were placed before the drive to the fourth differential, the same steering characteristic would be achieved in both directions.

The radius of turn in any gear can be adjusted by allowing the steering brake to slip, but in doing so power is wasted in the brake and the steering is in force control. Force control means that the forces required at the tracks are being balanced by the torque on the brake. Since in general the same forces are required to slew the vehicle at any radius of turn the control is unstable. With microprocessor control it is possible to solve this problem. With the steer brake locked there is a speed difference imposed between the two tracks which defines the radius of turn, hence the steering is in speed control.

5. THE BRAKING SYSTEM

The main vehicle brakes are of the oil cooled multi disc type and are integral with the transmission. This does mean that when the power pack is removed for servicing the vehicle is without parking brakes, but it is more convenient to mount them on the transmission as they use a common oil for cooling and actuation. Oil cooling gives good heat dissipation from the surface of the plates, the heat being easily transferred to the power pack cooling system. A disadvantage of this type of brake is the power loss when it is released, due to viscous drag between the plates and oil churning. This is kept to a minimum by having a 'dry' sump lubrication system.

6. A PRE-ENGAGED TWO LAYSHAFT TRANSMISSION

This is a particular design of layshaft transmission that will have a high efficiency with automatic power shift gearchanging. Although the transmission is designed for an input power of 340 kW, the gearing and bearings are capable of transmitting 740 kW by running at twice the speed, so it has potential for use in a main battle tank.

For vehicle trials the transmission will be fitted in an FV432 armoured personnel carrier with a mass of 15 tonnes. This vehicle has a seperate 'cletrac' steering gearbox, which is convenient for testing a ratio change transmission without the complication and cost of a new steering system. A cross drive steering system can be integrated with the ratio change transmission at a later date. The prime mover will be a highly rated diesel engine, with two stage turbocharging.

The principle of operation can be described by reference to the block diagram fig 7.

The system is depicted as two seperate four speed dog engaged layshaft gearboxes in parallel with alternate ratios in each. There is a multiplate input clutch to each gearbox, so to change ratio the drive is switched from one gearbox to the other. This gives a power shift similar to conventional epicyclic automatic gearboxes.

The next ratio that is required, either higher or lower, is preselected in the idling gearbox at some predetermined point in the speed range of the engine. The synchronization of dog clutches is carried out in an idling gearbox and the actual shift time is not constrained by any limitations of the synchronizing process. There is a limit to the time that can be allowed for the dog clutch engagement if the idling gearbox is to avoid being caught in the wrong gear when the vehicle makes rapid changes in speed. There are two synchronizing clutches connecting the two gearboxes through a gear ratio such that engagement of one of the clutches will synchronize for upshifts in one gearbox and downshifts in the other.

Forward and reverse selection is achieved by dog clutches and spur gears at the engine side of the input clutches, thus giving eight ratios in each direction.

The schematic diagram fig 8 shows how the two gearboxes can be arranged on two layshafts with a common output shaft.

A microprocessor control system will be used to manage the gearchanging process, including synchronization of the dog clutches by speed measurement, and take off from rest using one of the input clutches.

7.   CONCLUSION

The power packs presented in this paper are research concepts for possible use in future vehicles. There are of course many options available for both the prime mover and transmission. The prime mover may be a highly rated diesel engine for which there are a number of pressure charging systems available, or it could be a gas turbine.

Both the single layshaft and the two layshaft transmissions offer an improvement in efficiency over conventional epicyclic ones. The two layshaft device is perceived as a low risk project, there being a certainty that the gear change will always be made, and with the minimum interruption of power flow.

The single layshaft project can be considered to have a higher risk, as synchronism of the dog clutch for down shift depends on the engine's ability to respond to acceleration demands. However the volume of a single layshaft transmission is less because there is only one layshaft and one input clutch.

The transmission and steering system of the future battle tank could be mechanical, hydraulic, electric, or a combination of these, all of which will depend increasingly on microprocessor control.

It is the task of the power pack engineer to optimise performance, volume, ease of control and reliability, in support of the battle tank designer who has the difficult job of finding the right compromise between firepower, protection and mobility.

ACKNOWLEDGEMENTS

The authors wish to thank the Ministry of Defence for granting permission to publish this paper.

REFERENCES

(1)   MERRITT H E   The Evolution of a Tank
                      Transmission.
                      Proc I Mech E 1946 Vol 154.

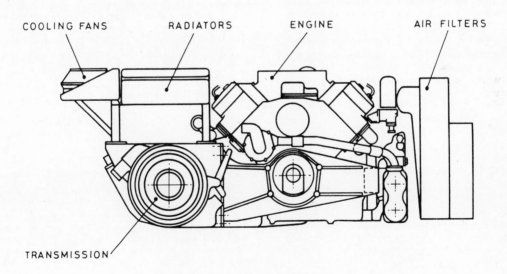

Fig 1   A compact power pack

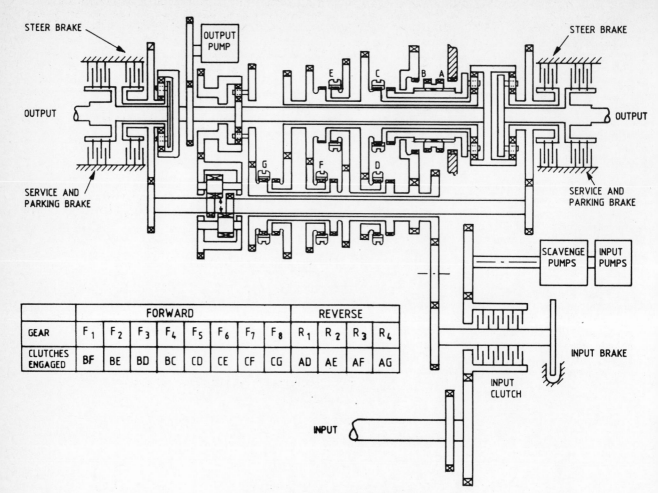

GEAR	FORWARD								REVERSE			
	F_1	F_2	F_3	F_4	F_5	F_6	F_7	F_8	R_1	R_2	R_3	R_4
CLUTCHES ENGAGED	BF	BE	BD	BC	CD	CE	CF	CG	AD	AE	AF	AG

Fig 2   Single layshaft transmission

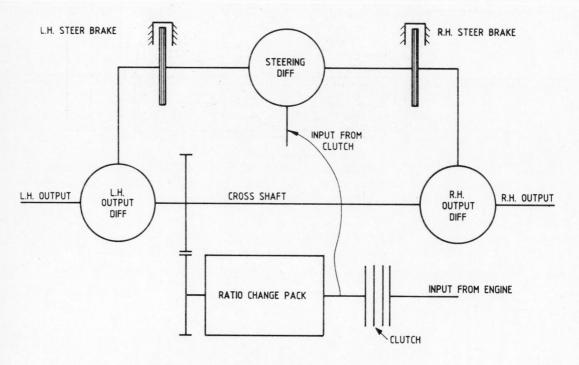

Fig 3   Merritt three differential steering system

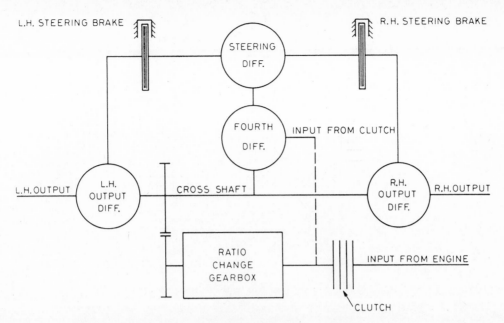

Fig 4   Four differential steering system

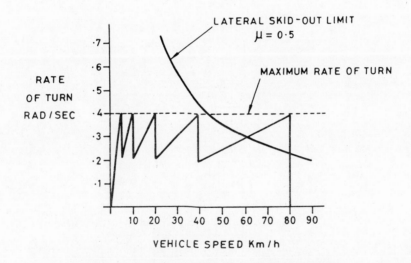

Fig 5   Rate of turn with three differential system

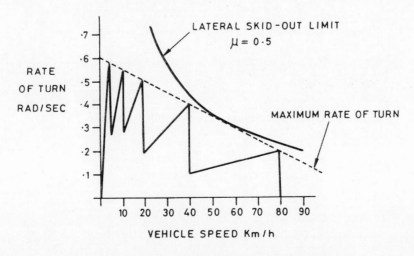

Fig 6   Rate of turn with four differential system

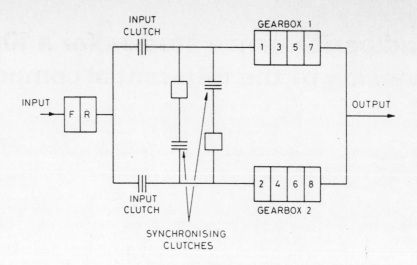

Fig 7   Pre-engaged two layshaft transmission

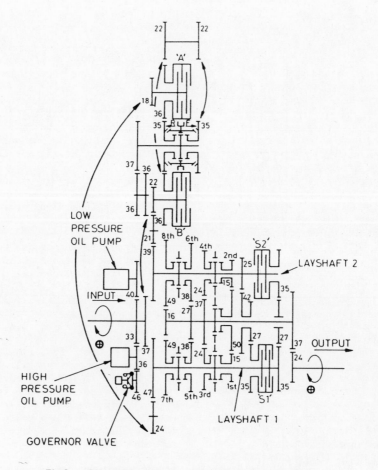

Fig 8   Schematic diagram of two layshaft transmission

C194/86

Design and performance studies for a 1000 h.p. military version of the differential compound engine

F J WALLACE, MSc, PhD, DSc, FEng, FIMechE, M TARABAD, BSc, MSc, PhD and D HOWARD, BSc
School of Engineering, University of Bath, Avon

SYNOPSIS The paper describes the main components of a military version of the Differential Compound Engine, the engine operating at very high boost pressure and bmep, and with a high pressure ratio, centrifugal compressor substituted for the rotary positive displacement compressor previously used on more moderately rated version of the DCE.   The second part of the paper deals with detailed steady state performance predictions and comparisons with an alternative very high output, two stage turbocharged engine followed by a 9 speed stepped transmission, showing the clear advantage of the DCE in terms of continuous torque back-up and superior fuel economy at higher speeds and loads.   In the final section, the paper presents transient response, both of the DCE alone and of the complete 40 tonne tracked vehicle.

1 INTRODUCTION

The main components of a 275 kW (387 hp) laboratory version of the differential compound engine (DCE) at Bath University, and their functional relationship, have been described in the companion paper (1).   The essential feature of the scheme is the differential coupling between engine, supercharging compressor and output shaft, achieved in the case of the laboratory engine by an epicyclic gear and in the case of the proposed 1000 hp military engine, by a differential gear, the exhaust turbine being connected in both versions to the output shaft through a continuously variable transmission (Fig 1).

The overriding objective of this arrangement is to achieve stepless output shaft torque-speed characteristics, i.e. to eliminate the need for a multi speed gearbox by the inherently steep torque rise characteristics of the system. A subsidiary objective is to take advantage of the mechanical connection between engine, compressor and turbine which permits thermodynamic compounding, i.e. the utilization of any excess of turbine power over demanded compressor power, making due allowance for unavoidable gear losses. A further advantage of the differential compounding arrangement is its outstandingly good transient response made possible by the fact that following a step input of fuel, the initial rate of acceleration of the low inertia compressor is extremely high compared with that of the high inertia load, resulting in a rapid increase in boost and a correspondingly rapid load acceptance. All these characteristics render the DCE potentially very attractive for military applications where a combination of high specific power, stepless transmission characteristics and excellent transient response are all highly desirable.

The present paper is based on a study commissioned by RARDE (Chertsey) to explore the possi-bility of a very high output DCE based on a 13.05ℓ 6 cylinder in line Diesel engine and developing 1000 s.h.p. as an alternative to a 'conventional' system using an equally highly rated two stage turbocharged engine having the same displacement volume used in conjunction with a 9 speed stepped transmission. The overrriding constraint was to accommodate the DCE in an engine compartment having a total volume of 4 m³.

Fig 2 shows the layout of the complete plant in diagrammatic form, while Figs 3a and 3b respectively show side and plan views of the engine compartment.

Fig 2 shows the transverse engine layout with a transfer gearbox transmitting engine power to a parallel shaft driving the differential gear train, one member of which drives the centrifugal compressor through bevel and step up gearing while the other drives the output shaft through a large bevel gear, which also transmits turbine power to the output shaft through the turbine CVT (of the 'PERBURY' type) and a combination of reduction and bevel gears. The DCE output shaft is connected to the final drive shaft through a torque converter with lock up facilities such that the torque converter is in use only at the very bottom end of the vehicle speed range. The sprocket drive and steering arrangements are 'conventional'.

Fig 3a shows the very compact layout in side view. The engine (3.1) is tilted forward and the transfer gear (3.4) at the flywheel end is clearly shown. The torque converter (3.5.2) and lock up clutch (3.5.3) are also visible although the final drive shaft and sprocket half shaft are omitted for clarity. The power turbine appears in end view with its twin exhaust supply pipes connected to the engine exhaust manifold in the conventional manner; the turbine reduction gear casing also appears in end view but the turbine CVT is hidden.

The centrifugal compressor (3.2) is mounted high

up in the engine compartment and tilted forward; it supplies air directly to the large charge air cooler (3.6), and draws atmospheric air through two admission pipes from two large filters (3.7.3) on either side of the engine compartment (not shown in Fig 3a). The oblique compressor drive from the differential gear is just visible. Finally Fig 3a shows the steer transmission (3.5.4) and one of the 3 fans each driven by hydraulic motors and drawing air through the radiator, charge air cooler and steering gear oil cooler which are mounted immediately below the intake louvres covering part of the engine compartment.

The plan view, Fig 3b taken from immediately below the cooler group, clearly shows the over-all disposition of the various components. Engine, turbine and compressor together with their connecting piping are clearly visible, as also are the main transmission (3.4), the turbine CVT (3.4.1), the torque converter (3.5.2) and the lock up clutch (3.5.3). Other components shown are the final drive transmission (3.5), the output epicyclic gearbox (3.5.1), the hydraulic steer transmission (3.5.4), the main brake (3.5.5), the air cleaners (3.7.3) on either side of the engine compartment, and the hydraulic pump for the fan drives (3.7.7). Thus the complete aggregate has been successfully accommodated in a space of no more than 4m³.

2 STEADY STATE PERFORMANCE PREDICTIONS AND COMPARISONS WITH A 'CONVENTIONAL' 2 STAGE TURBOCHARGED ENGINE WITH 9 SPEED TRANSMISSION

2.1 Specification of main components

(1) Engine
6 cylinder in line D.I. Diesel engine with low compression ratio (10:1) piston
swept volume 13.05ℓ
rated speed   2400 rev/min.)
rated power   732 kW   ) BMEP = 28.06 bar
max. torque speed 1710 rev/min) BMEP =
max. torque power 665 kW   )   35.78 bar

(2) Compressor
high pressure ratio centrifugal compressor
max. output   1.833 kg/sec
rated output   1.45 kg/sec
max. speed   49,500 rev/min
rated speed   39,500 rev/min.
max. pressure ratio 7:1
rated pressure ratio 4:1
max. power absorption 524 kW
rated power absorption 328 kW

(3) Turbine
high pressure ratio radial inflow turbine
   with variable nozzles
max. torque output 608 kW at 60,000 rev/min.
rated output 429 kW at 58000 rev/min.
max. torque inlet temp. 940 K
rated inlet temp. 977 K
max. torque pressure ratio 6.935
rated pressure ratio 4.947

(4) Output shaft operating conditions
max. speed and power 3700 Nm at 2000 rev/min
                                          ≡ 775 kW
max. torque speed and power 13148 Nm at
   500 rev/min   ≡ 689 kW

(5) Torque converter
(with lock up clutch above 500 rev/min.
 input speed)
Max. torque ratio at sprocket shaft stall:
   3.5184:1

Giving overall tractive effort ratio :

$$\frac{\text{Tractive effort at vehicle stall}}{"\quad"\quad"\ \text{max.vehicle speed}} = 12.74 : 1$$

2.2 Control system (Fig 1)

The control system for the military version of the DCE is basically similar to that of the laboratory version as already described in the companion paper (1). With reference to Fig 1, the controlled variables are :
a) power turbine nozzle setting - controlling boost
b) turbine CVT setting - ensuring max. turbine efficiency
c) injection timing - limiting max. cylinder pressure (on LTC) or ensuring best engine efficiency

and these are adjusted to achieve best overall, i.e. system efficiency. One major difference between the laboratory and the military versions of the DCE is the use of a centrifugal instead of a rotary positive displacement compressor in the latter case. This is made possible by the fact that at the very high ratings proposed for the military version, the ratio of rated engine to rated compressor power which may be shown to govern the degree of compressor overspeeding on the limiting torque curve with decreasing output shaft speed, decreases from

$$\frac{266}{74} = 3.59 \text{ to } \frac{732}{328} = 2.23 \text{ (see Section 2.1)}$$

This results in compressor speed varying between 39,500 rev/min. and 49,500 rev/min. at the extremes of the output shaft speed range, compared with 6,606 rev/min. and 11,500 rev/min. respectively for the laboratory DCE. Furthermore the high boost levels required for this very high BMEP application of the DCE can be achieved with a single stage centrifugal compressor whereas a two stage intercooled arrangement would be required if rotary positive displacement compressors were to be employed. It was found in the course of the layout study that the bulk of the latter system would have been prohibitive. The major control implication is that turbine nozzle angle has to be regulated so as to ensure operation well within the surge and choke limits of the rather narrow compressor flow map.

The range of the 3 controlled variables (nozzle angle, turbine CVT and injection timing) is shown in Figs. 4c, d and e, all with output shaft torque $\tau_{o/s}$ as ordinate and output shaft speed as abscissa, while Fig 4a gives the overall system efficiency in the same co-ordinate field.

2.3 Steady State operating characteristics (Figs 4a to 4e)

Fig 4a gives overall, i.e. system efficiencies allowing for gear and turbine CVT losses. The torque envelope gives a steep and continuous torque rise of 3.554:1 over the output shaft speed range of 4:1, i.e. very nearly constant horsepower. The gap between final drive shaft stall and the minimum DCE output shaft speed of 500 rev/min. is bridged by the output torque converter which has a built in torque ratio of

3.584:1 giving an overall torque ratio between stalled and max. speed conditions of 3.554 x 3.584 = 12.74:1. The system efficiency contours are good, with the 34% contour covering approx. one third of the full operating field. It is also noteworthy that compounding conditions obtain virtually over the whole operating field with output shaft power and efficiency exceeding the corresponding engine values except at very light loads. In this respect the centrifugal compressor scheme is superior to that with a rotary positive displacement compressor due to the inherently higher efficiencies of the former. Even higher efficiencies would have been reached if max. cylinder pressure had not been limited to 150 bar, this being achieved by the combination of low compression ratio pistons (10:1) with, at high boost levels, highly retarded timing.

Fig 4b gives boost and engine BMEP contours which are virtually coincident. Since the limiting torque curve is essentially a constant power curve, boost levels are seen to follow constant power contours as might be expected. The maximum boost ratio of 6.628 coinciding with max. torque is undoubtedly very high, as is the corresponding engine BMEP of 35.78 bar. However, it must be borne in mind that 1000 h.p from a 13.05ℓ engine represents an extremely high rating, whether the power plant is a DCE or a 'conventional' two stage turbocharged engine. The highest boost ratio of the latter similarly approaches 6:1.

Fig 4c gives the turbine nozzle angle contours which again follow a very similar trend to those for boost and BMEP, nozzle angles increasing with increasing power demand.

Fig 4d gives the overall reduction ratio between the turbine and the DCE output shaft achieved by a combination of reduction gearing and the turbine CVT. The extremes of the range are 120:1 at the high torque, low speed end of the range and 20:1 at the low torque, high speed end. An overall variation of 6:1 is probably rather extreme. However, the required range of

$$\frac{120}{29} = 4.14:1$$

along the limiting torque curve is well within the range of the proposed single stage 'PERBURY' type transmission.

Fig 4e gives contours of dynamic injection timing.

Figs 5a and 5b are sprocket power vs vehicle speed curves for a 40,000 kg vehicle equipped respectively with the 1000 hp DCE and a corresponding 1000 hp 2 stage turbocharged version of the same 13.05ℓ engine driving the sprockets through a 9 speed gearbox.

Fig 5a shows that the DCE delivers very nearly constant power between vehicle speeds of 65 and 16 km/hr. Below the latter speed the previously locked up torque converter is engaged. It will be seen that in the torque converter mode the vehicle is capable of negotiating gradients of 50% and more. At the same time at max. vehicle speed on the level road there is still a substantial power margin. Best vehicle s.f.c. of 0.241 kg/kW hr. occurs at max. speed and power

(see also Fig 4a) and must be considered very satisfactory.

Fig 5b shows the corresponding performance map for the 'conventional' power pack, with power envelopes for all 9 gears, but s.f.c. contours only for top, i.e. 9th gear. Best vehicle s.f.c in top gear of 0.247 kg/kWhr now occurs in the mid speed range rather than at max. speed, where consumption has increased from 0.241 to 0.262 kg/kWhr. It is evident that the stepless DCE system outperforms the 'conventional' system at higher speeds, and achieves substantially similar 'gradability'.

3 TRANSIENT RESPONSE

One of the outstanding characteristics of the DCE system is its excellent transient response. This is well illustrated by Figs 6a, 6b and 6c showing output shaft torque, boost and air fuel ratio response over a 3 sec. period for the following 3 cases :-

Case 1 :- 10% to 100% fuel step with stalled torque converter.
Output shaft torque $920 < \tau_{o/s} < 11580$ Nm

Case 2 :- 15% to 100% fuel step at rated output shaft speed.
Output shaft torque $540 < \tau_{o/s} < 3970$ Nm

Case 3 :- 25% to 60% fuel step with stalled torque converter.
Output shaft torque $2760 < \tau_{o/s} < 6960$ Nm

Torque response (Fig 6a) is excellent, the final torque value being reached in 1.5 sec. in Cases 2 and 3 and 2.5 sec. in the particularly severe Case 1. In each case the nozzle angle schedule is adjusted to remain well within surge of the centrifugal compressor and fuelling is initially limited to ensure that the trapped air fuel ratio does not fall below 20:1.

One of the chief operational differences between centrifugal and rotary positive displacement compressors is that the latter is free of surge limited speed and pressure ratio limitations. Hence transient scheduling of fuel and nozzle angle can be more drastic. However, the lower inertia of the centrifugal compressor more than compensates for these disadvantages.

Boost response (Fig 6b) follows a similar trend, boost again reaching its final value within the very short time scales of the torque response. Air fuel ratio (Fig 6c), boost limited at 20:1 for 0.9, 0.8 and 0.3 sec. in Cases 1,2 and 3 respectively then rises rapidly to final values of 30.5, 28 and 27 respectively.

Calculations for vehicle response show that the 40,000 kg vehicle can be accelerated from standstill to 40 km/hr. in 8 sec. This is clearly far ahead of corresponding figures for the 'conventional' system with its repeated gear changes.

4 CONCLUSIONS

(1) A detailed layout study shows that it is possible to accommodate a 1000 hp DCE engine transmission unit complete with all auxiliary devices in a 4 m³ compartment.

2) In this very high output application the
   bulky rotary positive displacement compressor
   can be replaced advantageously by a high
   pressure ratio centrifugal compressor.

3) The steady state performance curves show that
   a substantially constant horsepower envelope
   is possible with this stepless system.

4) Steady state economy is superior to a
   'conventional' system at higher speeds and
   loads, but inferior at low speeds.

5) Transient response is outstandingly good due
   to the differential method of coupling.

ACKNOWLEDGEMENTS

The paper is based on a study funded by RARDE,
Chertsey, whose assistance is gratefully acknowledged.   The layout and design work was
undertaken by Horstman Defence Systems Ltd.

REFERENCES

1) Companion Paper : Design and Performance
   Characteristics of Laboratory Differential
   Compound Engine (DCE) at Bath University.
   1986.

APPENDIX 1

The match over the full operating field in a
hypothetical high pressure ratio centrifugal
compressor map is given below . It will be
seen that a single line characteristic has been
achieved, making it possible to run the DCE in
the narrow flow field offered by the high
pressure ratio map.

APPENDIX 2

Tables 1 & 2 give the results of performance
calculations for the DCE covering the full load
and speed range, including the allowance for
pipe losses in the duct system as follows :

        pipe a) = compressor to inter-cooler
            b) = engine exhaust up to by-pass
                     junction
            c) = by-pass
            d) = exhaust junction with by-pass to
                     turbine

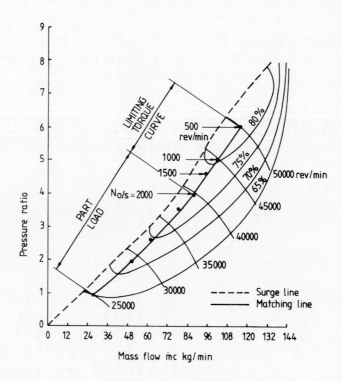

Centrifugal compressor map

Table 1

RR C6 DCE 1000hp with centrifugal compressor (inc. pipe losses(10cm i.d.))

ambient temperature (deg k) 300.0	inlet valve closing (degs) 223.0	compressor scale factor 1.00	
compression ratio 10.00	ambient pressure (bar) 1.00	cooler effectiveness 0.8000	
	engine diagram factor 0.9500	turbine flow loss factor 0.8000	

engine speed(r.p.m)	1668.02	1780.07	1990.60	2012.58	2102.65	2143.29	2270.71	2396.77
boost pressure ratio	1.897	2.842	1.897	4.260	2.842	5.207	3.787	4.733
delivered air to fuel ratio	39.392	27.792	39.677	24.961	27.600	24.256	25.935	24.504
delivery ratio	0.966	0.966	0.965	0.965	0.965	0.966	0.965	0.966
manifold temp (deg k)	320.251	330.677	320.251	341.508	330.677	347.162	338.189	344.567
engine power (kw.)	113.91	292.71	135.35	551.10	351.58	704.81	540.15	731.75
engine torque (n.m.)	658.15	1590.11	658.15	2622.71	1590.58	3144.08	2282.82	2928.48
b.m.e.p (bar)	6.2769	15.1144	6.2499	25.1688	15.3688	30.2256	21.8644	28.0621
s.f.c. (kg/kw hr)	0.290	0.248	0.289	0.240	0.245	0.248	0.239	0.242
b.thermal eff.	0.2874	0.3366	0.2884	0.3469	0.3401	0.3365	0.3490	0.3447
fuel / rev (kg.)	3.303	6.792	3.278	13.586	6.835	13.586	9.475	12.314
max cyl pressure (bar)	83.20	151.26	84.67	150.76	149.70	148.04	147.18	151.90
exhaust temperature(deg k)	670.31	865.83	683.46	1005.88	885.42	1078.96	971.66	1055.76
mass flow (kg/min)	21.704	33.600	25.888	55.122	39.668	70.631	55.801	72.318
percentage heat to coolant	30.84	23.94	27.75	17.98	21.67	15.59	17.80	15.33
compressor speed (r.p.m.)	25000.0	29000.0	25000.0	37300.8	29000.0	41967.1	35000.0	39500.0
compressor pressure ratio	2.000	3.000	2.000	4.500	3.000	5.500	4.000	5.000
mass flow (kg/min)	25.996	49.991	25.996	78.942	49.991	93.766	69.988	86.985
compressor power (kw.)	44.20	129.15	44.20	276.93	129.15	374.52	225.63	328.00
compressor torque (n.m)	16.88	42.51	16.88	70.87	42.51	85.18	61.53	79.26
delivery temperature (deg k)	401.25	453.39	401.25	507.54	453.39	535.81	490.94	522.84
compressor efficiency	0.650	0.720	0.650	0.771	0.720	0.791	0.760	0.780
turbine speed (r.p.m)	33000.0	43500.0	34000.0	54000.0	46000.0	58500.0	52000.0	58000.0
turbine pressure ratio	1.991	2.976	1.991	4.454	2.975	5.444	3.960	4.947
mass flow (kg/min)	26.589	51.245	26.692	81.244	51.494	96.813	72.207	90.060
turbine power (kw)	38.09	134.22	41.62	327.70	146.69	473.67	276.98	428.50
turbine torque (n.m)	11.02	29.45	11.68	57.93	30.44	77.29	50.84	77.52
inlet temperature(deg k)	629.04	742.35	682.40	871.01	805.43	960.35	885.14	977.03
turbine nozzle angle	6.793	9.195	7.100	10.589	9.654	10.864	10.680	11.230
turbine efficiency	0.753	0.774	0.755	0.775	0.774	0.767	0.775	0.767
output shaft speed (rpm)	1500.00	1500.00	2000.00	1500.00	2000.00	1500.00	2000.00	2000.00
output shaft power (kw)	90.99	273.47	112.75	556.96	334.45	745.25	548.04	775.25
output shaft torque (n./m)	579.20	1740.2	538.1	3544.3	1596.2	4742.4	2615.6	3700.0
output thermal efficiency	0.363	0.265	0.347	0.238	0.258	0.234	0.236	0.228
engine fuel flow (kg/min)	0.2296	0.3144	0.2402	0.3506	0.3235	0.3558	0.3541	0.3652
pressure loss in pipe a (bar)	0.551	1.209	0.652	2.208	1.437	2.912	2.152	2.951
pressure loss in pipe b (bar)	0.00324	0.00391	0.00324	0.01601	0.00874	0.01942	0.01374	0.01798
pressure loss in pipe c (bar)	0.00391	0.00700	0.00559	0.01300	0.00928	0.00870	0.01464	0.01002
pressure loss in pipe d (bar)	0.00523	0.01462	0.00570	0.02797	0.01590	0.03540	0.02529	0.03422

Table 2

RR C6 DCE 1000hp with centrifugal compressor (inc. pipe losses(10cm i.d.))

ambient temperature (deg k)	300.0	inlet valve closing (deg)	223.0	compressor scale factor 1.00
compression ratio	10.00	ambient pressure (bar)	1.00	cooler effectiveness 0.8000
		engine diagram factor	0.9500	turbine flow loss factor 0.8000

63   2   3   2   3   3

	1	2	3	4	5	6	7	8
engine speed(r.p.m)	1022.86	1134.91	1429.02	1709.14	1345.44	1540.32	1751.60	1891.66
boost pressure ratio	1.897	2.842	4.733	6.628	1.897	3.314	4.733	5.680
delivered air to fuel ratio	34.974	25.667	23.381	24.043	38.209	26.035	23.944	24.369
delivery ratio	0.966	0.967	0.966	0.966	0.966	0.966	0.966	0.966
manifold temp (deg k)	320.251	330.677	344.567	355.037	320.251	334.638	344.567	349.626
engine power (k.w.)	71.20	188.25	438.65	665.41	92.37	314.63	536.37	659.30
engine torque (n.m.)	658.15	1590.11	2928.48	3718.90	658.15	1961.38	2928.48	3327.63
b.m.e.p (bar)	6.3983	15.2465	28.1758	35.7848	6.3102	18.7744	28.1458	32.0347
s.f.c. (kg/kw hr)	0.321	0.266	0.253	0.263	0.298	0.246	0.247	0.252
b.thermal eff.	0.2599	0.3132	0.3300	0.3171	0.2801	0.3396	0.3377	0.3306
fuel / rev (kj.)	3.724	7.362	12.914	17.070	3.407	8.360	12.603	14.654
max cyl pressure (bar)	81.32	147.95	146.32	150.43	81.91	150.75	148.26	148.90
exhaust temperature(deg k)	654.89	852.78	1041.95	1125.66	658.98	906.62	1045.95	1085.02
mass flow (kg/min)	13.321	21.446	43.148	70.143	17.514	33.524	52.858	67.551
percentage heat to coolant	41.24	31.27	20.85	15.80	35.06	24.05	18.48	16.07
compressor speed (r.p.m.)	25000.0	29000.0	39500.0	49500.0	25000.0	31957.1	39500.0	44500.0
compressor pressure ratio	2.000	3.000	5.000	7.000	2.000	3.500	5.000	6.000
mass flow (kg/min)	25.996	49.991	86.985	111.981	25.996	60.420	86.985	99.983
compressor power (kw.)	44.20	129.15	328.00	523.58	44.20	176.46	328.00	420.61
compressor torque (n.m)	16.88	42.51	79.26	100.96	16.88	52.71	79.26	90.22
delivery temperature (deg k)	401.25	453.39	522.84	575.19	401.25	473.19	522.84	548.13
compressor efficiency	0.650	0.720	0.780	0.800	0.650	0.743	0.780	0.800
turbine speed (r.p.m)	30000.0	40500.0	53500.0	60000.0	31000.0	46000.0	55000.0	59000.0
turbine pressure ratio	1.992	2.976	4.949	6.935	1.992	3.469	4.949	5.941
mass flow (kg/min)	26.409	50.864	88.938	115.062	26.489	61.750	89.305	102.905
turbine power (kw)	32.10	113.89	348.54	608.44	34.86	178.24	375.43	506.69
turbine torque (n.m)	10.21	26.84	62.18	96.80	10.73	36.99	65.16	81.98
inlet temperature (deg k)	536.97	638.18	801.21	940.19	579.74	728.61	860.17	928.93
turbine nozzle angle	6.195	8.429	9.975	10.006	6.457	9.410	10.401	10.389
turbine efficiency	0.750	0.773	0.778	0.764	0.752	0.777	0.775	0.768
output shaft speed (r.p.m)	500.00	500.00	500.00	500.00	1000.00	1000.00	1000.00	1000.00
output shaft power (kw)	48.47	155.81	419.53	688.72	69.51	289.89	538.33	687.50
output shaft torque (n./m)	925.3	2974.4	8009.1	13148.1	663.5	2767.1	5138.5	6562.4
output shaft sfc (kg/kw.hr)	0.471	0.322	0.264	0.254	0.396	0.267	0.246	0.242
output thermal efficiency	0.1769	0.2592	0.3160	0.3282	0.2108	0.3129	0.3390	0.3448
engine fuel flow (kg/min)	0.381	0.836	1.845	2.917	0.458	1.288	2.208	2.772
pressure loss in pipe a (bar)	0.00324	0.01798	0.01798	0.00324	0.00324	0.01134	0.01798	0.02068
pressure loss in pipe b (bar)	0.00155	0.00310	0.00674	0.00275	0.00275	0.00623	0.01085	0.00730
pressure loss in pipe c (bar)	0.00083	0.00295	0.00462	0.00340	0.00039	0.00236	0.00291	0.00231
pressure loss in pipe d (bar)	0.00442	0.01250	0.02796	0.03856	0.00480	0.01777	0.03005	0.03557

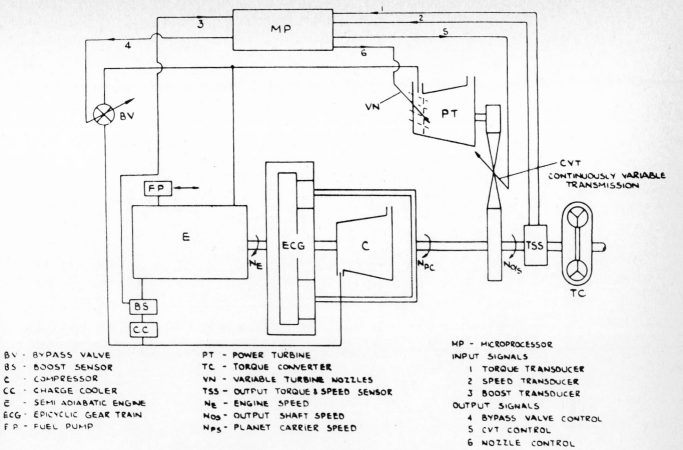

BV - BYPASS VALVE
BS - BOOST SENSOR
C - COMPRESSOR
CC - CHARGE COOLER
Ē - SEMI ADIABATIC ENGINE
ECG - EPICYCLIC GEAR TRAIN
FP - FUEL PUMP

PT - POWER TURBINE
TC - TORQUE CONVERTER
VN - VARIABLE TURBINE NOZZLES
TSS - OUTPUT TORQUE & SPEED SENSOR
N_E - ENGINE SPEED
N_{OS} - OUTPUT SHAFT SPEED
N_{PS} - PLANET CARRIER SPEED

MP - MICROPROCESSOR
INPUT SIGNALS
  1 TORQUE TRANSDUCER
  2 SPEED TRANSDUCER
  3 BOOST TRANSDUCER
OUTPUT SIGNALS
  4 BYPASS VALVE CONTROL
  5 CVT CONTROL
  6 NOZZLE CONTROL

Fig 1   Differential compound engine (DCE) layout — final version

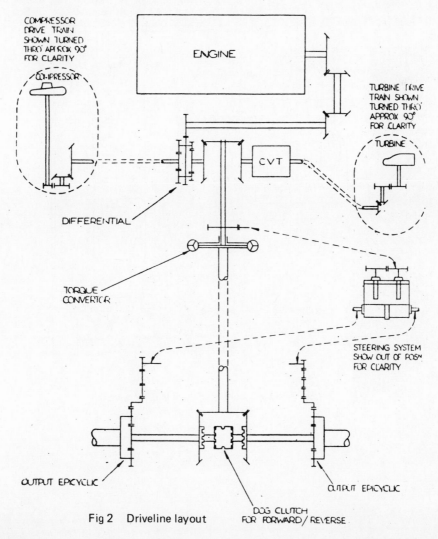

Fig 2   Driveline layout

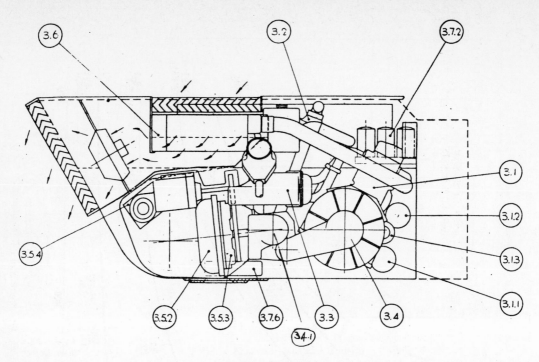

Fig 3a Side view

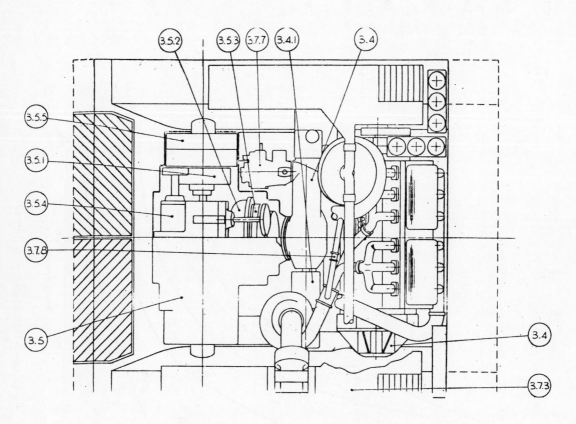

Fig 3b Plan view (with cooling group removed)

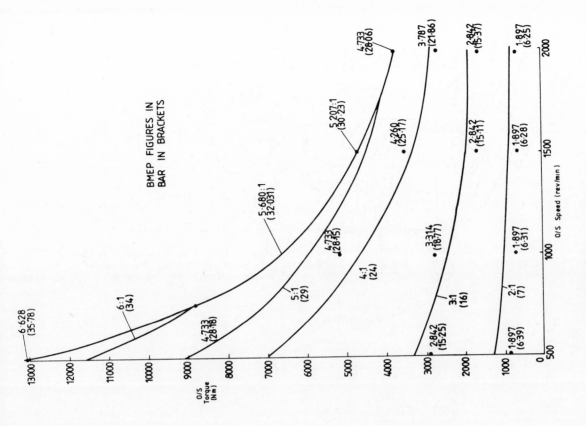

BMEP FIGURES IN
BAR IN BRACKETS

Fig 4b Boost and b.m.e.p. contours

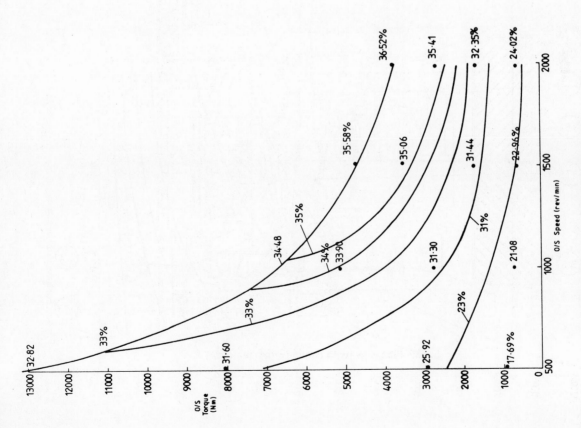

Fig 4a Brake thermal efficiency contours

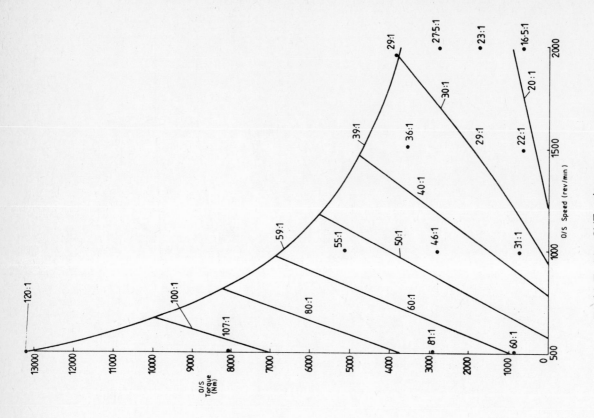

Fig 4d Turbine CVT ratio

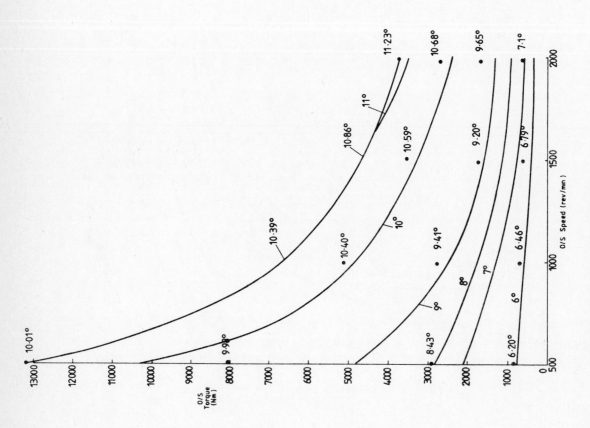

Fig 4c Turbine nozzle angle

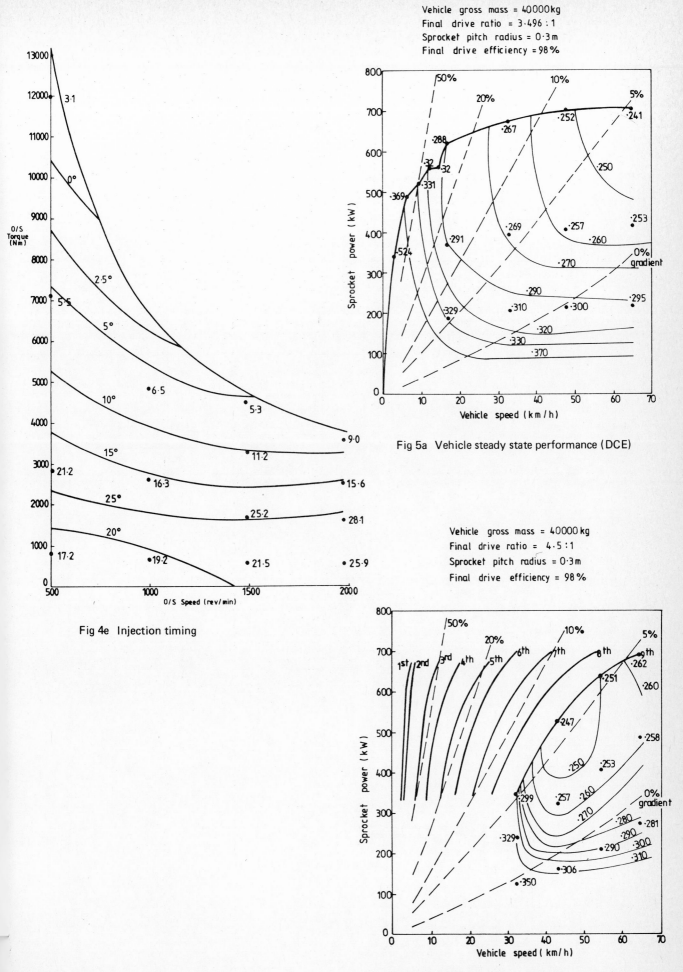

Fig 4e Injection timing

Vehicle gross mass = 40000kg
Final drive ratio = 3·496 : 1
Sprocket pitch radius = 0·3 m
Final drive efficiency = 98%

Fig 5a Vehicle steady state performance (DCE)

Vehicle gross mass = 40000 kg
Final drive ratio = 4·5 : 1
Sprocket pitch radius = 0·3 m
Final drive efficiency = 98%

Fig 5b Steady state characteristics of two-stage turbocharged conventional gearbox

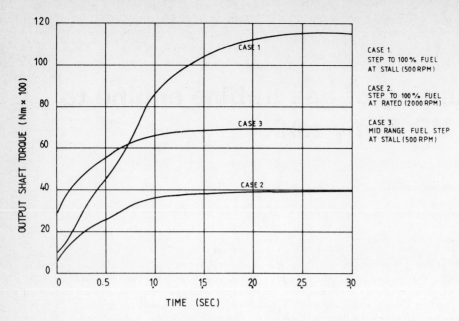

CASE 1.
STEP TO 100% FUEL
AT STALL (500 RPM)

CASE 2.
STEP TO 100% FUEL
AT RATED (2000 RPM)

CASE 3.
MID RANGE FUEL STEP
AT STALL (500 RPM)

Fig 6a Output shaft torque response

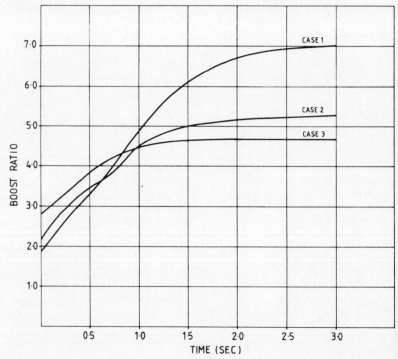

Fig 6b Boost response (course grid)

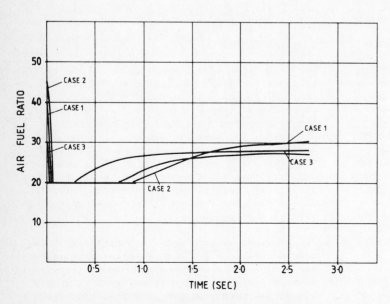

Fig 6c Air—fuel ratio response

C201/86

Transverse mounting of gas turbine engine to transmission in US Army tank

C BANTHIN, MSME, BSME
Avco-Lycoming Textron, Stratford, Connecticut, USA

SYNOPSIS   Presented is a description of proposed changes to the turbine engine propulsion system of the U.S. Army's M1 Abrams tank. The method of transversely mounting and integrating the gas turbine engine to the hydrokinetic transmission is described. Objectives of the program were to reduce propulsion system size, improve fuel economy and reduce maintenance, while retaining maximum parts commonality with the present system. Changes to the engine and transmission are enumerated. Reconfigured propulsion sub-systems and their contribution in enhancing the powerpack are included. Gains achieved by transverse mounting are quantified. Drawings of the powerpack and photographs of a full size mockup are presented.

1.   INTRODUCTION

The U.S. Army's M1 Abrams main battle tank is the first, and presently the only, military land vehicle that is solely gas turbine powered. This 60-ton, 1500 horsepower vehicle entered full scale production in 1980. Presently over three thousand tanks have been built. An equal number more will be completed by 1990. At this stage of maturity, early on problems associated with the fielding of the new turbine propulsion system are overcome. It is now fitting that significant engineering efforts be directed towards improvement.

Unlike aircraft, where weight reduction of the propulsion system is of prime consideration, in military tracked vehicles space is at a premium. Fuel economy is also important as it effects vehicle range, space, and the logistics of supply.

The propulsion system of the M1 tank was originally planned to accommodate either a large Diesel or smaller gas turbine engine. The larger Diesel engine required in line or fore and aft mounting in the vehicle with a rear power take-off entering the front of an aft located transmission. This is known as a conventional (T) configuration. The gas turbine, which was the winning powerplant, simply replaced the Diesel to give the present gas turbine (T) configuration in today's production M1.

Studying options for saving space, an opportunity became evident. Due to the small size, particularly length of the gas turbine engine, sidewise or transverse orientation of the gas turbine engine was possible. The challenge was to find an attractive method of transferring power from the turbine to the transmission with the engine mounted in this manner.

In the course of making changes to the transmission and engine to accomplish their integration, an opportunity to improve efficiency of the powerpack with relatively little additional changes became evident. These changes resulted in significant fuel saving.

The following Text describes this activity, including modifications made to powerpack sub-components, necessary for the high density packaging and overall efficiency of the system.

The transverse engine program was initiated by an Army inquiry to AVCO Lycoming TEXTRON, builder of the AGT1500 turbine engine, and Detroit Diesel Allison (DDA), producer of the tank's X1100 transmission. Shortly thereafter, General Dynamics Land Systems (GDLS), producer of the tank joined the team.

A propulsion system preliminary design was completed and a full size mock-up produced. A proposal to build and test a demonstration unit was submitted to the U. S. Army, the long term goal being consideration of this propulsion system for future M1 Abrams tank production.

2   BACKGROUND

The propulsion system compartment of the M1 tank is sized for a (T) configured engine and transmission requiring a length of 120 inches. The AGT1500 gas gurbine, selected for the tank, is easily placed in the compartment which could also allow for a larger Diesel. In time, the need for extra space in the tank evolved. Space for additional ammunition, electronic counter measures, auxiliary power units (APU), nuclear/biological/chemical (NBC) protection, or additional fuel would improve the combat effectiveness of the vehicle.

Reduced vehicle fuel consumption also became desirable. A 15 to 20 percent reduction was considered attractive. 30 to 40 percent reduction would be a significant gain, and possible only if the vehicles idle fuel rate was addressed.

A third desire was to reduce the powerpack's operational and support (O & S) costs. In this category, servicing, maintenance, and durability of the powerpack are important, and certainly critical to availability of the fighting vehicle during combat.

The challenge was to achieve these benefits for the M1 vehicle with relatively minimal changes in order to retain the production base, keep development costs low, and minimize risk.

3   APPROACH

The architecture of the transverse mounted engine propulsion system evolved after several iterations. Having found room to turn the engine sideways and move it aft against the transmission, linking the power from the engine to the transmission in an attractive manner was critical to the success of the venture. Several approaches were pursued, all of which employed some form of turning the power link through two right angles: first from the engine's aft end (which is now located at the side of the tank) and secondly when turning into the transmission's centrally located power input section. This involved at least one large bevel gear set, a costly and often sensitive piece of hardware.

Several schemes were studied. All of these approaches, classified as "dog leg" adapters, had a space savings compromise. A shaft is required between the engine and transmission to enter the power input module. This limits the extent to which the engine can be moved aft against the transmission. A more direct route was possible by locating a bevel gear within the AGT1500 engine between the power and gas producer turbines. This would allow direct inline shaft entry to the transmission from the bevel gear. This approach was eventually discarded as it would have required extensive engine changes, and judged too risky due to engine heat surrounding the bevel gear.

All approaches using bevel gears seemed inherently wrong. Since the power output shaft of the engine is transverse to the vehicle, and the internal works of the transmission is transverse, why the intermediate step of an inline shaft for power input? This requires a bevel gear to get into the transmission and then another bevel gear immediately within the transmission to get back to transverse shafting. This reasoning lead to the final "side door entry" approach.

Through the efforts of DDA, an attractive solution was devised. The front power input module of the transmission was completely eliminated and the left side output housing was modified to accept power input via a transverse shaft. Power link from engine to transmission was then handled by simple spur gears stepping the engine power aft. The power input shaft lead directly to the transmission rangepack. In addition, elimination of the transmission's front mounted power input module, which contained the torque converter and main bevel gears, allowed even further aft placement of the engine.

To complete the package, a new engine air filter system was devised in order to fit the small space provided at the engine inlet. This unit contains a compact self-cleaning rotating drum filter mated to and encompassing the engine inlet.

4   ENGINE/TRANSMISSION MECHANICAL DESCRIPTION

4.1   External Layout

A plan view of the transverse mounted engine and transmission located in the rear of the M1 tank hull is shown in Figure 1A. Included is the transfer gear case which links power between the two through spur gears. The engine is mounted to the transmission by an aft mount to the transfer case and a centermount to the transmission front face. The air filter, mounted to the engine inlet, completes the picture. The present production M1 tank layout is shown in Figure 1B for comparison.

Approximately 1/3 of the propulsion system compartment space is freed (roughly 40 inches in length or ≃ 50 cubic feet under armor space) with the transverse mounting arrangement. A comparison of transmissions shows the power input module has been eliminated with transverse mounting, its function being served by the transfer gear case. Removal of the power input module allowed an additional 12 inches aft placement of the transverse engine. The bevel gear set in the power input module was completely eliminated, and the lock-up torque converter was relocated to the transfer gear case. The transfer gear case serves a multi-purpose:

(1)   Links power from engine to transmission

(2)   Serves as a rear engine mounting structure

(3)   Houses the torque converter and transfer gearing

(4)   Acts as an accessory gearbox

(5)   Replaces the engine as a powerpack third mount point

Item (2) above, rear engine mounting to the transfer gear case, is shown in Figure 2. This engine mount (at the aft end of the recuperator housing) is the same as with present production engines. A second attachment is to the transmission's front cover plate near the "system C.G.". This holds the engine in the vehicle's fore and aft, and vertical directions. This mount is configured to allow free thermal expansion of the engine in the transverse direction, eliminating strains on the transfer case.

The engine/transmission package is mounted to the tank hull at three points: The left and right final drive trunnions, and a third mount at the transfer case forward end which counters final drive torque. The engine has no mounts to the vehicle, unlike the present inline production engine where final drive torque is countered through the engine to the vehicle floor.

There are accessory pads located on the

transfer gear case to drive the alternator, oil cooling fans, hull hydraulic pump, and NBC/air filter air pump. The hull hydraulic pump is mounted to the hull wall with a quick disconnect drive shaft to the transfer case. This arrangement allows powerpack removal without breaking hydraulic lines. Locations of the accessories on the transfer case are shown in Figure 3.

A redesign of the engine air filter was necessary to fit in the narrow space between the engine inlet and hull right sidewall. This filter is critical to the space saving achievement of the transverse propulsion system. An innovative self-cleaning rotating drum barrier filter surrounded directly by precleaner vortex tubes was evolved. The filter, shown in Figure 4, encompasses and mounts directly to the engine inlet. The barrier portion of this air-filter is much more compact than the present production unit. Mounting directly to the engine allows removal with the engine. The advantage is safe ground testing of the engine without special 'carry along' adapter filters, and avoidance of inadvertent leaks due to disconnect joints.

4.2   Internal Description

4.2.1   Transfer Gear Case

The gearing in the transfer case is shown schematically in Figure 5. The engine power input is at 3,000 rpm. Spur gears transfer power aft to the torque converter located in the transfer case near center section of the transmission. The torque converter is a lock-up type having the same hydrodynamic components as the present production unit. The torque converter is different mechanically, however, in that the converter turbine shaft does not go through the pump element and stator as in most torque converter assemblies. The torque path through the converter is:to a ring gear bolted to the OD of the converter pump housing, the pump/stator/turbine elements (or lockup clutch when applied), turbine shaft and gear set to the transmission rangepack.

Two small bevel gear sets in the transfer case transmits power to the accessory drives. PTO pads are located on the transfer case housing. Three pads will have vertical drives off the top of the housing while a fourth will be a horizontal drive off the front face of the housing. A schematic of these drives is shown in Figure 5. The top three pads will drive the oil cooling fans, NBC/SCAF air pump, and alternator. The first two are hydraulic pump drives, the pump being mounted on the transfer case housing and the hydraulic motor remotely located at the unit receiving power. The alternator is direct shaft driven. The front facing PTO will drive the hull (turret) hydraulic pump. This unit was removed from the production engine accessory gear box to improve the engine's idle operation, allow a smaller size accessory gear box, and eliminate hydraulic line disconnects when removing the powerpack. A gear train to drive the relocated transmission main oil pump is also contained within the transfer case.

The transfer case housing is integral with the new transmission left output housing. The

housing will be cast in several high strength aluminum alloy sections similar to the main transmission housing. The castings will have cored passages for lube oil to gears and bearings, and to service the torque converter and its clutch lock-up feature.

4.2.2   Transmission

An exploded view of the X-1100 transmission showing modules removal and those replaced for the transverse mounting of the engine is given in Figure 6. The major modifications are:

(1) Replacement of the power input module with a cover assembly

(2) Replacement of the left output module with the transfer gear case housing combined with an output module

(3) Replacement of hydraulic controls with electronic controls

The main bevel gear assembly within the power input housing has been discarded. A majority of the transmission components including the four-speed rangepack, hydrostatic steering, and brakes were retained, including the main housings and internal structure. In the process of adapting the transmission for side entry power input, more subtle improvements to the internal works were possible. Included is a reduced size main pump to take advantage of recently achieved system leakage improvements. Less pump input power will result. Transmission performance is also improved through less drag from improved lube flow and increased clearance in the rangepack, clutches and service brakes. A new modulated output pump is also employed. This unit requires less power to the pump when less than full power is being transmitted through the transmission. The new electronic control will eventually communicate directly with the engine electronic control. Past experience with other heavy vehicles has shown dramatic improvement in drive quality and performance using this match up of electronics.

4.3.2   Engine

Modifications to the AGT1500 turbine engine for the transverse propulsion package includes internal component improvements for performance gains as well as external changes to accommodate the mounting. The engine is shown in Figure 7. Both externally and internally, the visible changes to the engine are not obvious. The external changes are: removal of a bottom mount (to the vehicle floor), the addition of mid-engine mount to connect to the transmission, and a reduced size accessory gear box. The gear box size reduction was made possible by the re-location of the vehicle hydraulic pump to the transfer gear case. The smaller gearbox was instrumental in allowing room for the new airfilter. The filter also required the inlet of the engine to be cut back 2 inches in length and 4 inches in diameter to accommodate its mounting. The basic engine is 2 inches shorter but is not perceptable with the airfilter mounted.

Internal changes to the engine contribute approximately 15 percent stand alone fuel savings.

These engine fuel saving components were developed by AVCO over the past few years under a U.S. Army fuel economy program and with in-house research and development funds. The Transverse Mounted Engine Program presented an opportunity to employ these fuel saving developments. Starting from the front of the engine, changes include:

(1) Compressor rotor blade shroud tip treatment to reduce air bypass losses.

(2) High pressure compressor bleed closure at idle for fuel economy.

(3) Compressor diffuser manifolding for surge line relief.

(4) Single crystal high pressure gas producer turbine blades requiring less cooling air.

(5) Turbine blade tip trenching for improved aerodynamic efficiency.

(6) Turbine nozzle area changes for more optimum engine component matching.

(7) Redesigned power turbine blade/vane profiles optimized for higher efficiency at part powers, and a greater range variable first-stage power turbine stator to cover lower power needs.

(8) A "High Density" recuperator that achieves greater effectiveness and lower gas-side pressure drop through increased surface area within the same envelope.

The location of these engine improvement items are shown in the cut-away photograph in Figure 7. The engine (and the transmission) will also incorporate new digital fuel controls. More precise powerpack and vehicle control will result particularly when integrated with each other through the military designated 1553 bus system. The integration of engine/transmission digital controls could result in an additional 5 to 10 percent fuel savings above that presently predicted.

5   POWERPACK SUB-SYSTEMS

In integrating the engine and transmission for space savings and fuel economy, changes to other powerpack sub-systems were possible or necessary. Notable are the changes to the oil coolers, and engine airfilter.

With the incorporation of a transfer gear case, an alternate means of driving the oil cooling fans was studied to reduce cooling power drain and eliminate long drive shafts. Shafts, although efficient in transferring power, would be cumbersome in the transverse powerpack due to space limitations. A hydraulic drive was chosen. Not only are the hydraulic lines easily placed but more importantly modulated speed can be used to save power. Since the cooling fans of the vehicle are sized for a maximum steady load of .7 tractive effort over gross weight (which occurs in first gear at approximately

half engine speed), the fans must satisfy cooling demand at this condition. Wasted fan power results when vehicle tractive effort is much lower or engine speeds (and thus fan speeds) are higher which occurs most of the time. Based on the cube law of fan power with speed, eight times the power would be required by the fans at 100 percent engine speed versus 50 percent speed when actually less cooling may be needed. Use of a hydraulic drive allows modulation of the cooling fan speed to satisfy only the cooling needs. Despite the lower efficiency of power transfer through a hydraulic system, the total power saved could be as much as 100 horsepower at maximum engine speed, and typically 25 to 50 horsepower over the normal range of operation.

As described earlier, a new airfilter was required with the transverse mounted engine due to the very limited space allowed. The uniqueness of the filter is its rotating drum barrier filter. The rotating drum has an intermittent operating self-cleaning feature with 200 hours projected life, 10-fold greater than the present engine filter. Surrounding and mounted closely to the drum are annular arranged precleaners which result in space savings due to minimal ducting needs. The size of this self-cleaning filter system and ducts has been reduced to half of the present production engine filter and ducts. A comparison of the different filters is seen in Figure 1. Figure 4 shows the internal parts of the TME filter.

6   POWERPACK MOCK-UP

A full size mock-up of the transverse mounted propulsion system was built after preliminary design and installation drawings of the system were completed. The mock-up serves to verify space claims, clearances, mounting features and external details on new components. It is also used to install lines, piping, wiring and the like. AVCO constructed the mock-up at its facility with major components built at different shops; transmission at DDA, engine at AVCO, transfer gear case and airfilter sub-contracted to vendors. After assembly and finishing at AVCO, the mock-up was shipped to GDLS for installation in an M1 tank hull, and the mock-up did fit nicely as planned.

Photographs of the mock-up after build but prior to installation into the tank hull are shown in Figures 8 and 9. Figure 8 is a quartering view looking aft from the left front side of the powerpack. Seen to the left in the picture is the airfilter, the outer bank of small round precleaner vortex tubes being evident. The airfilter is encompassing the inlet of the turbine engine. Extending out from the filter is the engine compressor section with piping, lines, and accessories. The dome shaped part is the engine burner. The large aft casing of the engine encompasses the recuperator core. The aft end of the recuperator casing is attached to the transfer gear case. The other end of the transfer gear case is attached to the side of the transmission. Oil cooler fans normally located over the transmission, and the engine exhaust duct leading aft from the top of the recuperator casing have not been installed in these photos to allow better visability of the major components. Photo 9 is a left rear quarter view of the powerpack. The accessories on top of the transfer gear case and close proximity of the engine to the transmission are noted.

7 REVIEW OF BENEFITS ACHIEVED

The transverse mounting and integrating of the gas turbine engine to the hydrokinetic transmission in the M1 Abrams tank gives the following benefits:

○ Propulsion System Compartment Space Savings

One third (1/3) of the propulsion system compartment has been freed making room for combat critical equipment. This space amounts to approximately 40 inches in length forward of the engine or ≃ 50 cubic feet of under armor space. This space can be utilized in several ways. Combinations of ammunition, fuel, APU, NBC protection and electronic countermeasures are possible. If all fuel is selected for instance, the combat range of the vehicle could be increased by close to 100 percent. If all ammunition is selected up to 50 percent increase in the number of rounds is possible. A likely candidate for the space is an APU to minimize idle fuel consumption.

○ Mission Fuel Savings

With 15 percent fuel savings from the engine, plus improved efficiency of the transmission, reduced cooling fan power and the employment of an APU, the vehicle will achieve 20 percent mission fuel saving over a typical battlefield day. 40 percent fuel saving during peacetime training is achieved by using the APU in lieu of the main turbine engine during the many hours spent at idle.

○ Other Improvements

- Easier service of maintenance intensive items like hydraulic pumps, alternator, self-cleaning airfilter

- Easier powerpack removal due to vertical lift from the hull versus presently required shoe-in action.

- No air filter disconnects or leaks. The airfilter is permanently secured to the engine.
- Reduced Operational and Support (O&S) costs in terms of supporting fuel trucks, cost of fuel, and reduce running hours on the engine when using an APU

8 CONCLUSION

A proposed transverse mounting of an AGT1500 gas turbine engine to the X1100 transmission in the M1 Abrams U.S. tank has been presented. The system was made possible by an innovative method of combining the engine and transmission with a transfer gear case. Including relocation of the powerpack sub-components and devising a unique self cleaning air filter, a compact propulsion package was achieved resulting in a significant compartment space savings. Improvements in the engine, transmission and other components give sizable gains in fuel economy. These benefits are achievable with relatively modest changes to the present M1 propulsion system hardware.

ACKNOWLEDGEMENT

The author wishes to thank Mr. Edward Such of Detroit Diesel Allison and his team of engineers for their contributions to this program.

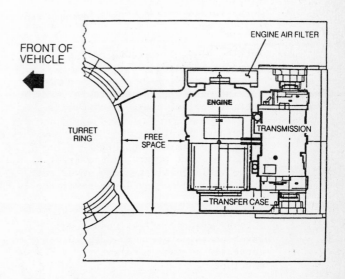

Fig 1a   Transverse engine in M1 hull

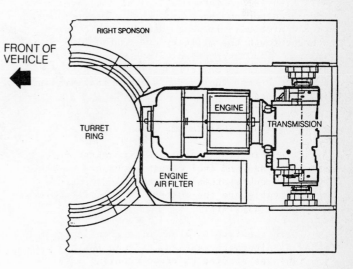

Fig 1b   Production engine in M1 hull

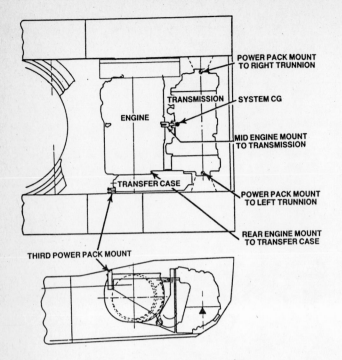

Fig 2   Power pack mounting

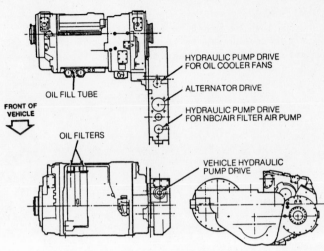

Fig 3   Transmission and transfer case showing accessory drives

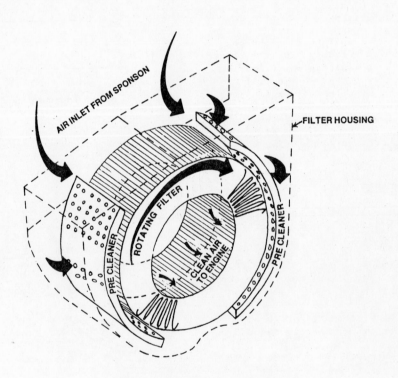

Fig 4   Isometric view of air filter

ACCESSORY DRIVES

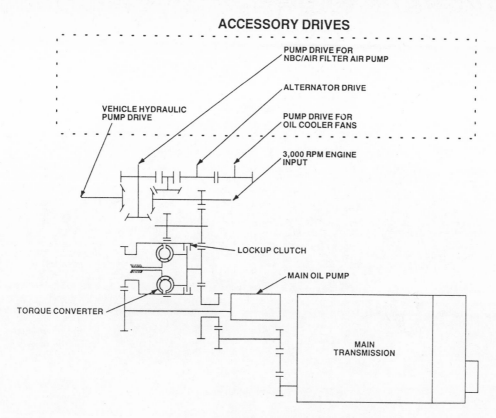

Fig 5   Transfer case gear schematic

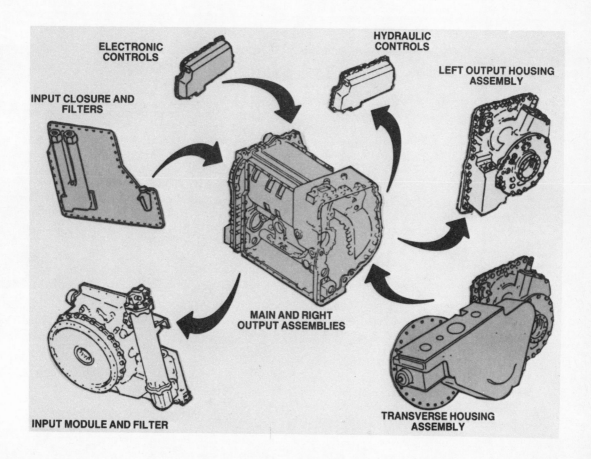

Fig 6   Transmission modifications

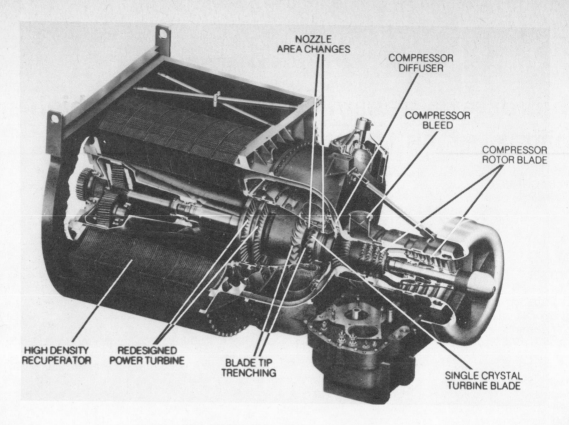

Fig 7   AGT 1500 turbine engine modifications

Fig 8   Transverse mounted propulsion system — front view

Fig 9   Transverse mounted propulsion system — aft view

C199/86

Hydrostatic transmission for steering high speed military track laying fighting vehicles

F W BAGGETT, CEng, FIMechE
Consulting Engineer to Commercial Hydraulics, Hucclecote, Gloucester

ABSTRACT

The concept of steering high speed track laying vehicles is briefly reviewed and some examples of mechanical and hydrostatic transmission steering systems outlined.

Progress in improving the power to weight ratio of compact axial piston transmissions is reported with examples and reference made to the application of separate high performance pumps and motors.

A novel brake-assisted steering system, under development, is described which attempts to exploit the high efficiency point of a mechanical brake system with the infinitely variable steering obtained from a hydrostatic transmission.

1.0 INTRODUCTION

The steering of high speed track laying military vehicles has been the subject of many ingenious designs since the armoured fighting vehicle was first used in the 1914-18 War in Europe.

Essentially it is performed by slowing or stopping the track on one side of the vehicle and increasing the speed of the track on the other side. This results in a slewing couple about the vehicle centre so that a negative force arises at the inner track and a positive force at the outer, these forces being the same magnitude but of opposite sense. However the positive force applied to the outer track is in addition to the force already applied for forward propulsion and in terms of power at high vehicle speeds is several times that available from the engine. In order to sustain the turn without slowing the vehicles' forward speed, power must be transferred from the inner to the outer track by as efficient a means as practicable.

When the vehicle is in a turn skidding of the tracks occur and the turning force at the tracks is dependent upon the distance between the tracks for a given track length on the ground. A factor 'K' derived from the ratio of this distance C to the track length, L is used to modify the turning effort μW and its value can be obtained from a graph $\overline{2}$ as shown in figure 1.

The calculation for steering power is given by:-

$$Power = F \times TSD \qquad (1)$$

where F = steer force per track $\left(\dfrac{\mu KW}{2}\right)$

TSD = track speed difference

μ = co-efficient of adhesion between the track and ground

W = weight of vehicle

and K = factor obtained from the graph shown in figure 1

The value of μ is dependent upon the surface of the ground and is generally taken at a higher value for the initiation of the turn, reducing for a sustained turn. The values chosen are usually a matter of judgement and experience on the part of the designer of the steering mechanism.

A full analysis of the above is given by MERRITT (1) and STEEDS (2) and later workers have suggested modifications to the basic formula to take into account the re-distribution of the weight on the tracks due to centrifugal forces during high rate turns and the variation of coefficient of adhesion at different turn rates. Nevertheless with judgement the basic formula provides a satisfactory value for the sizing of the steer transmission.

2.0 STEERING TRANSMISSIONS

Steering mechanisms or transmissions fall into two broad categories viz

(a) Mechanical
(b) Hydrostatic

Whilst this paper is concerning itself with hydrostatic transmissions a brief description of a typical mechanical system will serve to illustrate some of the points made later.

2.1 Mechanical Systems
The most well known version is the MERRITT triple-differential system - an example of which is shown in figure 2, in which a 3 element epicyclic is part of each output assembly.

The sun wheels, which carry the steer brake discs, are interconnected by a two part primary shaft with differential driven by the engine. Each annulus is connected by a secondary shaft which takes its drive from the output of the gearbox. In the configuration shown, for reasons unconnected with steering, the sun wheels rotate in the opposite direction by the insertion of an idler gear. The planetary carrier is the output drive to the sprockets.

In the straight ahead mode each epicyclic is rotating at the same speed. (Providing the torque resistance from the tracks is the same on each output shaft.)

Application of a disc brake reduces the speed of its associated sun wheel, speeding up its output carrier. At the same time, by means of the two part primary shaft and differential, the sun wheel in the other epicyclic increases speed and reduces the speed of the output carrier. Thus the output shafts are differentially rotating at a speed dependent upon the input speed from the range change pack to the annuli and the speeds of the sun wheel. At all times the mean speed of the output shafts in straight ahead is half the sum of the two outputs when steering.

A moments reflection will enable the reader to understand that by operating the disc brake as an "on-off" device, at any given input speed, the output shaft will only rotate at the same number of discrete speeds as the number of speed steps in the range change pack, although the maximum side-to-side speed difference is constant in all gears. The vehicle will therefore steer in a series of polygonal paths which approximate to a radius of steer. In practice of course, in order to approximate to a true radius of turn, the steer brakes are allowed to slip with a consequential high loss of power through heat generation. Thus it becomes necessary to design these steer brakes for thermal capacity as well as for torque transmission. At the point of no slip of course there is no loss and the steer mechanism becomes very efficient, the only losses being gear contact and bearing losses. This is an important point which is referred to elsewhere in the paper.

There are many other types of mechanical steering systems in current use but they all use disc, band or clutch brakes and all suffer from the disadvantages outlined above, while at the same time enjoying the high efficiency at each discrete minimum radius turn.

2.2 Hydrostatic Transmission Systems

In the previous chapter it was pointed out that steering by a mechanical braking system produces a series of polygonal paths which approximate to a radius of turn unless slipping of the brake occurs, which produces excessive heat and power loss. If however the range of speed difference between the output shafts can be produced in an infinitely variable manner, variable true radii of turn will be achieved with improved driver control.

Figure 3 shows a typical null shaft steering system using a hydrostatic trans-

mission to provide infinitely variable track speed difference. It will be seen that the variable capacity, over-centre pump is driven by the engine (in some cases the pump is driven by the output of the torque converter, but this is a separate discussion outside of the scope of this paper) and the motor drives a null shaft which engages the sun wheels of the output epicyclics by means of a two gear and three gear train.

In the vehicle straight ahead mode, the motor, null shaft and sun wheels are stationary, the drive from the gear change assembly is to the annuli connected by a secondary through shaft, as previously, and the output to the track sprockets is via the carriers.

Rotation of the hydrostatic motor causes the sun wheels to rotate in opposite directions, increasing and decreasing the speed of the carriers by equal amounts.

The choice of steering to the left or right is made by selecting the direction of rotation of the motor by the over-centre pump. As in the previous arrangement regenerated power is transferred through the secondary shaft connecting the annuli.

While this system works well and is in widespread use it suffers from a high power loss at the point of minimum geared and pivot turn radius, when compared to the mechanical braking system. Improvements in efficiency can be made, at the expense of increased complexity, by the use of gears and clutches to form a "shunt" around the hydrostatic transmission and figure 4 shows this in diagrammatic form. Figure 5 shows the system coupled to the sun wheels in a null shaft arrangement previously described. Gibson, Cockeram and Sheldon (3) explain the case for shunted transmission very fully.

Many other combinations of hydrostatic transmissions, gears and clutches are possible and several are in use to provide infinitely variable steering systems. Those shown here merely serve to illustrate the principles involved.

At the present time hydrostatic transmissions for military use are either of axial piston type using high pressure and low swept volume, or radial piston type using medium pressure and high swept volume. Axial piston machines generally do not exceed 246 cc/rev (15 CIR) but operate at pressures up to 690 bar (10,000 lbf/in^2), radial piston machines generally have a swept volume of 328 cc/rev (20 CIR) to 492 cc/rev (30 CIR) and operate at pressures in the order of 207 bar (3000 lbf/in^2).

Axial piston machines are of course cylindrical in general shape while radial machines are more akin to a thick disc. Since they are comparable in control and performance but dissimilar in shape the choice is often determined by the shape of the gearbox, which is often governed by the shape of the vehicle. Vehicle shape is determined by the need for a low height, high ground clearance, position of engine/gearbox assembly, position of the driver and crew and above all the need for the vehicle to have high mobility, maximum armour plating for crew safety, maximum gun firing power and ammunition storage. Together with a few other "goodies" such as N.B.C. systems, electronics etc., there is little room for automotive components and no sympathy from the vehicle designer.

3.0 COMPACT AXIAL PISTON TRANSMISSION

Having set some of the scene the paper will now discuss some of the design aspects of Axial Piston Transmissions. As an example a heavily armoured battle tank weighing some 60 tonnes requires about 450 kW (600 HP) at the tracks in order for it to execute a pivot turn of 180° in about 5 to 6 seconds. In a typical null shaft steering system as shown in figure 3 around 510 kW (680 HP) is required as an output power from the hydrostatic motor. If we take a typical industrial hydrostatic transmission efficiency of say 84% then our battle tank steer transmission would take around 600 kW (800 HP) from the engine. However this efficiency assumes an oil temperature of 50°C, an oil viscosity of 30 centistokes, oil pressures in the range 140-210 bar and input and output speeds in the order of 2000 rpm. In practice the oil temperature will be between 100° and 120°C, will have an oil viscosity between 4.5 to 24 centistokes, an oil pressure between 415 bar (6000 psi) and 690 bar (10,000 psi) and input speeds between 3000 to 5000 rpm. The efficiency under these conditions is likely to be in the order of 60% to 70%. Thus the input power required for our battle tank steer transmission is likely to be about 750 kW (1000 HP).

The steer transmission is generally an integrated part of the propulsion transmission and is contained within the casing of the gearbox. This means of course that not only does the steer transmission have to perform on the gearbox oil at its sump temperature but it lives in a hot oil mist environment with no opportunity of convection cooling. In addition because of lack of space in the vehicle the gearbox generally has a shallow sump. This leads to problems when the vehicle is negotiating slopes and sometimes on combined slopes of 30° and greater, the boost pump may run out of oil. Not only does it run out of oil, but it may draw in air/oil mist for periods of time lasting around 5 seconds, at a time when the engine and steer transmission may be running at maximum speed. Other problems include contamination from gears and clutch debris together with high vibration levels coming from the vehicle tracks and rough terrain at high speed. These requirements demand that steer transmissions must be rugged machines and yet of light weight and small volume in comparison to the power transmitted.

Figure 6 shows a compact transmission having an input power of 450 kW (600 HP) at a speed of 2500 rev/min which was developed in 1973. It has a 246 cc/rev (15 CIR) variable displacement over-centre pump and a fixed displacement motor of similar capacity. Its maximum operating pressure is 415 bar (6000 psi) and its weight is 272 kg (600 lbs), giving a power to weight ratio of 1.65 kW/kg

(1:1 HP/lb). The unit is used in a 30 tonne armoured vehicle.

However the need to improve power to weight ratios was obvious and a move was made to increase speeds of rotation, lift operating oil pressures and reduce casing weight by using aluminium.

It was clear that to do this a more detailed knowledge of structural deflection, machine dynamics and fatigue was required together with a better understanding of the materials we were using or proposed to use.

The Company therefore set up a methodical programme of development to achieve its aims, one of which was to examine in more depth the use of Tufftriding.

3.1 Tufftriding

The transmission outlined above uses low carbon steel rotating elements which are Tufftrided. Tufftriding allows steel to run on steel as bearing material with high unit loading. However, it does not like edge loading and if the control of the process is not maintained to a very high level the surface breaks down under load with consequential failure of the components. High unit loading was an important part of the Company strategy for increased performance but it was important to determine that these process controls could be maintained on a production basis before proceeding to its final adoption.

Tufftriding was developed by Degussa, West Germany and is licenced in both the U.K. and U.S.A. together with a number of other countries. Components are suspended in a molten bath of cyanide compound at 570°C for 2 hours, which results in diffusion of additional carbon and nitrogen into the surface of the material. The salt bath treatment is preceded by a hot air pre-heat at 300°C. After treatment, a low temperature oil quench is followed by an agitated water wash and a final clean water spray. The components which are jigged are allowed to stand until they are cool enough to handle. The total cycle time is around 4 hours. The advantages of this treatment are:-

(a) Considerably enhanced fatigue properties.
(b) Much improved resistance to wear.

Considerable evaluation outside the scope of this paper was done before adopting the process but finally after concluding that the controls necessary to ensure product reliability could be guaranteed, the Company decided to install its own plant.

To maintain these required quality standards the plant has been dedicated to the material used in the steer transmission and scrupulous attention is given to all aspects of the process. Both microsection checks and X-Ray diffraction is used routinely "in-house" on each batch of components processed.

Heat treating complex shapes even at the modest temperature of 570°C brings with it problems of movement of the component. Additionally with tufftriding there is some small growth in dimension. Considerable attention is therefore given at the design stage to the shape of components to prevent distortion as finishing by machining after tufftriding is not possible. However by attention to detail it is possible to hold the flatness of components to within 5 μm (0.0002").

Removal of the dried salts after tufftriding requires considerable care and for example high pressure water is used to clean the orifices in pistons together with very gentle aqua blasting of working surfaces. Of course all debris must be removed because of its abrasive nature.

3.2 Computer Aided Design

In improving power-desities both speeds and pressures increase in order to contain volumes and weight to an acceptable level. However this must not be at the expense of efficiency and both mechanical and volumetric losses must be kept to a minimum. Higher pressures impose both increased deflection and reduced fatigue life. Deflection leads to high slip loss and reduced fatigue life to unreliability, neither being acceptable.

The trick therefore is to contain the deflection and maintain the fatigue life without increasing weight, by skill in design. To do this meant a more detailed knowledge of the loads imposed when transmitting maximum power. A number of in-depth studies were set in motion which resulted in computer packages covering the finite element analysis of the structural deflection of the porting region of the case, portplate, cylinder block and swashplate, optimum geometric design of the rotating assembly, oil film thickness, dynamic forces and pressures across the portplate, behaviour and lubrication of the slippers and etc. The result of this work was written up as a pump feasibility and design programme by Clarke (4) and later described by Hannan (5). The computer output, figure 7, shows how a number of basic geometrical and stress restrains labelled 1 to 5 limit the possible choices of number of pistons, swash angle, piston diameter and piston p.c.d. for a pump of given capacity, speed and pressure. The restraints include items such as slipper separation, piston neck stress, adequate separation of piston bores and adequate flow areas.
The programme suggests to the designer a range of sizes of components but lets him choose the actual size so that he is not constrained by the computer. Hydrodynamic journal bearing calculations can be performed before the programme moves onto the initial portplate design. At the end of this stage of the design the programme has enough information to produce the initial scale sketch of the running gear, figure 8. If the designer feels the overall size is unsuitable, he can quickly change his input dimensions and repeat the process until satisfied. From this point he can move forward into the discrete areas of analysis some of which are mentioned above.

3.3 Enhanced Design

Figure 9 shows in isometric view of a steer unit developed using the programme described above. It is used to steer a modern battle tank of 62 tonnes and weighs 212 kg (466 lbs).

This unit has twinned 92 cc/rev (5.6 CIR) variable displacement over-centre pumps driven from a common gear in the gearbox, driving twinned 92 cc/rev (5.6 CIR) fixed displacement motors connected by a through shaft. Reference to figure 3 shows the steer unit and gearbox in matchstick diagram form.

At maximum engine speed this unit has an input speed of 3700 rev/min with occasional overspeed excursions up to 4200 rev/min. When it rotates the vehicle in a full rate pivot turn, i.e. tracks rotating at maximum steer speed in opposite direction an oil pressure of 690 bar (10,000 psi) is reached and at this point 750 kW (1000 HP) is being taken from the engine. With a weight of 212 kg, this gives a power to weight ratio of 3.54 kW/kg (2.14 HP/lb), a significant improvement over the 1.65 kW/kg (1:1 HP/lb) ratio mentioned previously.

All the rotating elements are tufftrided steel and the casings forged high duty aluminium. Figure 10 shows the computer network mesh around the port area of the case and figure 11 shows the distortion under pressure in exaggerated form.

The forged steel swashplates tufftrided to give enhanced fatigue life are keyed together to operate as a unit and are actuated by differential area servo pistons. An overriding control sensing pressure, limits the output torque and backs the swashplates off to prevent engine stall.

The portplate is of unique design, also tufftrided steel, but with a high temperature plastic facing across the thrust pads. The cylinder block is designed for minimum deflection at the portplate face and the pistons for fatigue. Internal interconnecting oil passageways are gun drilled to give a fine surface finish to reduce stress concentrations.

Particular attention is given to the intersections of these drillings to ensure that all burrs are removed. This is very important as at high rotating speed with large oil flow small burrs can become detached and as the pumps and motors are hydraulically closed-coupled the debris may remain in circulation with catastrophic effects.

To meet these stringent performance requirements, manufacture and quality control must be of the highest order. Each steer unit is unique and has a log book containing qualitative information concerning the critical components, assembly, production test data and etc., providing a complete record, with traceability back to material supplier. Figure 12 shows a typical computer output after the inspection of a component. Included in the read-out is a histogram giving statistical information. The hard copy is filed in the steer unit log book as part of the quality control programme.

The maintenance of a lubricating oil film of adequate thickness is a major problem with military steer transmissions. In Europe the highest oil temperatures are generally in the order of 100°C, but in desert conditions in other parts of the world temperatures are in the order of 100°C-120°C. This particular transmission uses a Polyalkylene Glycol fluid having a viscosity of 24 centistokes at 100°C. At 120°C this falls to 15 centistokes. Figure 13 shows the viscosity - temperature relationship of a number of oils including that above.

As mentioned earlier in the paper the shape of a steer transmission is governed by the shape available in the gearbox which itself is constrained by the vehicle shape. In this case the only space available was above the range change pack, but the height was restricted by the need to keep the top of the gearbox low to accommodate the engine/gearbox cooling group between the gearbox and the top of the engine compartment. Whilst a swept volume of some 180 cc/rev (11 CIR) was required at 690 bar (10,000 psi) to meet the power requirement there was insufficient height available. As a result twinned 92 cc/rev (5.6 CIR) rotating elements were chosen. The banana shape of the transmission in side view again is to suit the space available.

Although the transmission in this particular application is equivalent to a single pump and motor it can be used, with modification to the controls, as a two line system and some early experiments along these lines are currently in progress in a fighting vehicle.

A more recent product taking advantage of the current level of technology is shown in figure 14. This unit, suitable for steering vehicles up to 20 tonnes has an input speed range from 3800 to 4300 rev/min. The maximum pressure reached on the initiation of turn is 480 bar (7000 psi). The transmission has a power rating of 180 kW (240 HP) and a weight with controls of 48 kg (105 lbs), thus giving a power to weight ratio of 3.75 kW/kg (2.3 HP/lb). It is capable of running on engine oil with a viscosity of 4.5 centistokes at 120°C, and with enhanced ratings in slightly modified form and using a higher viscosity oil.

4.0 SEPARATE AXIAL PISTON PUMPS AND MOTORS

The steer transmissions so far described are built into propulsion gearboxes. For various reasons, such as weight distribution in a vehicle with a road/swim role, for example, requiring the disposition of the engine, gearbox and steering system as discrete units for packaging, the pump and motor may be separated and connected by high pressure hose. As another example, figure 15 shows a typical arrangement used in a personnel carrier of 18 tonnes weight. Current high performance technology is used with pressures of up to 480 bar (7000 psi). The oil reservoir is part of the steering gearbox and 20 micron filtration is used as standard. Again a pressure sensing stroke controller is used to limit output torque and prevent engine stall under maximum turn rate conditions.

5.0 HYBRID MECHANICAL-ASSISTED STEERING SYSTEM

An application of unique design using separate pumps and motors is described by Booth and Baggett (6). This system is a combination of mechanical braking as shown in figure 2 and a hydrostatic transmission of different operating mode. Figure 16 shows the system in diagrammatic form.

Earlier in the paper it was pointed out that at pivot and minimum geared turn radius the mechanical brake when fully applied provided the most efficient way of producing a track speed difference, the only losses being those associated with gear tooth contacts and bearings. By comparison the null shaft hydrostatic transmission has its maximum power loss at this point and at all other turn radii above minimum it is oversized for the role it plays. It is worth noting that these latter comments apply to all currently known forms of hydrostatic transmissions and mechanical infinitely variable speed devices.

The concept invented by Booth (7), is an attempt to overcome the disadvantages of the hydrostatic transmission at minimum geared turn radius but taking advantage of its infinitely variable output speed to give variable and smooth steering to the vehicle. At the point of minimum or pivot turn the hydrostatic transmission is no longer operational and the steer brake is fully locked.

The system comprises the MERRITT type of triple-differential mechanical steering system shown in figure 2, but with the addition of a variable displacement hydraulic pump/motor in geared association with each sun wheel in the output epicyclics. These hydraulic units are connected in closed circuit either in compact or by hydraulic hoses in the usual way with make-up boost supply.

When the vehicle is travelling in the straight ahead mode with the output epicyclics rotating at the same speed the rotating sun wheels each drive a hydraulic unit which is at full displacement. Because these displacements are equal, oil in the circuit is circulated without pressure but with some small flow loss. Steering is performed by reducing the displacement of one of the units in the usual way which causes a pressure rise and torque reaction onto the sun wheels. The unit with the smaller displacement now starts to increase in speed acting as a motor, while the increased torque from the large displacement unit causes a reduction in speed. Since these units are connected through the primary shaft and differential they increase and decrease in speed equally. The vehicle has now commenced to turn, further reduction of displacement of the hydraulic unit increasing the amount of vehicle turn up to a point where insufficient torque from the hydrostatic transmission is available. At a pre-determined point the steer brake is applied by means of a pressure signal from the hydrostatic transmission, which on increasing demand eventually brings the sun wheel and hydrostatic transmission to rest. Steer power from the engine is now running through the geared steering system with minimum loss, with the vehicle turning either in pivot or at minimum geared turn radius. Figure 17 shows a comparison between the power losses of the MERRITT all-mechanical braking system and the hybrid system described.

The sizing of the hydrostatic transmission is one of experience and judgement but the vehicle being trialled for evaluation weighs 50 tonnes and uses two 92 cc/rev (5.6 CIR) units. Some initial problem with the control system occurred but an improved and novel type of control now provides the stability required.

The system described above relates to a gearing arrangement where the sun wheels of the output epicyclic gears are rotating except at minimum geared and pivot turns. However, alternative configurations are shown in figures 18 and 19 which use a null shaft system similar to that described earlier, where the sun wheels are normally stationary and counter-rotate during steering.

In these alternative arrangements a smaller hydrostatic transmission is used than that shown in figure 3 and the torque from the motor supplemented at a pre-determined point by clutch brakes which eventually bring the pump and motor to the same speed and the null shaft in direct geared association with the engine. Again the benefit is obtained of improved steering of the vehicle during most of its duty cycle, together with the highly efficient minimum geared and pivot turn gearing arrangement.

There are of course many system arrangements which can be used to accommodate the available space within the gearbox and the diagrams shown serve to illustrate the principles involved.

THE FUTURE

Demands from the user, that is, the Army, will continue to be made for armoured vehicles of low profile, higher speeds and mobility, enhanced power to weight ratios and increased firepower.

This in turn will increase the pressure on the designer of the automotive components to provide smaller, lighter and more efficient units.

As stated earlier in the paper the choice between radial and axial piston pumps and motors is a matter of packaging and there is no single solution. Opportunities therefore exist for imaginative designs and development both of components and systems.

Oil formulations must not be forgotten and the need for improvements in viscosity at elevated temperatures continues.

The competition to the hydraulics industry is from mechanical systems and improved mechanical and electrical variable speed devices. Whilst these latter transmissions are not an immediate threat there are signs of considerable improvements in some areas.

The message is as always that we cannot afford to be complacent but must pursue the technology to give improved power to weight ratios without sacrificing reliability.

ACKNOWLEDGEMENTS

The author wishes to thank his colleagues for the invaluable help given in preparing this paper. Todays' technology is no longer the work of one person but of a team of highly competent people. The preparation of this paper is the same.

The author also wishes to thank the Directors of Commercial Shearing Incorporated for permission to publish the contents.

REFERENCES

1 Merritt, H.E., "The Evolution of a Tank Transmission", published by The Institution of Mechanical Engineers, PROC. 1946, Vol. 154, p 257.

2 Steeds, W., "Tracked Vehicles – An Analysis of the Factors Involved in Steering", published by Automobile Engineer, pp 143-148, April 1950.

3 Gibson, P., Cockeram, D., and Sheldon, D.F., "Application of Shunt Transmission for Fighting Vehicles", published by The Institution of Mechanical Engineers, 1981.

4 Clarke, A., "Rationalisation and Improvements of a Company's Engineering Design Procedures", Thesis submitted for award of PhD, University of Aston in Birmingham, 1978.

5 Hannan, D.M., "Experience with Computers in a hydraulics company", I.Mech.E. Seminar Computer aided design in high pressure hydraulic systems, Paper 8, November 1983.

6 Booth, S.H., and Baggett, F.W., "A Hybrid Brake-Assisted Hydrostatic Steering System for High Speed Tracked Vehicles", published by C.S.I. for A.D.P.A. Conference, Indianapolis, 1984.

7 Booth, S.H., Patent No. 1122268.

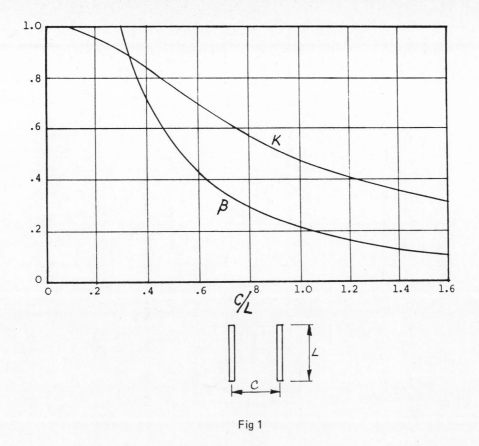

Fig 1

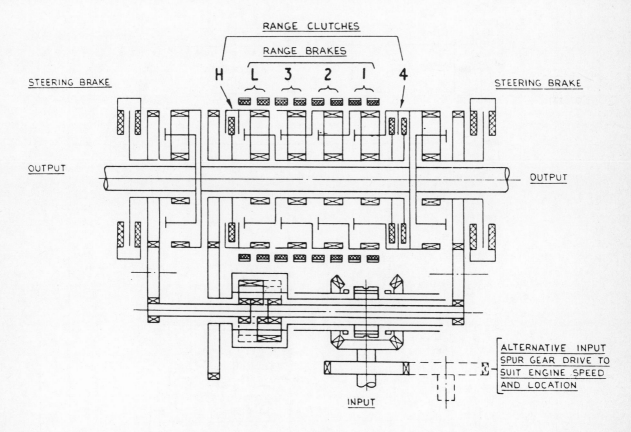

Fig 2

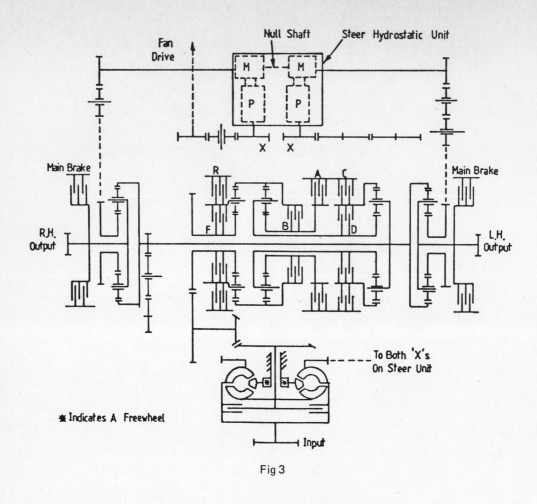

Fan Drive

Null Shaft

Steer Hydrostatic Unit

M   M

P   P

X   X

Main Brake

R   A   C

F   B   D

Main Brake

R.H. Output

L.H. Output

To Both 'X's On Steer Unit

✳ Indicates A Freewheel

Input

Fig 3

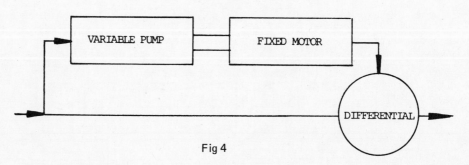

VARIABLE PUMP

FIXED MOTOR

DIFFERENTIAL

Fig 4

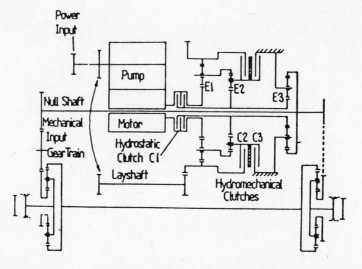

Power Input

Pump

E1   E2   E3

Null Shaft

Motor

C2 C3

Mechanical Input Gear Train

Hydrostatic Clutch C1

Layshaft

Hydromechanical Clutches

Fig 5

Fig 6

Fig 9

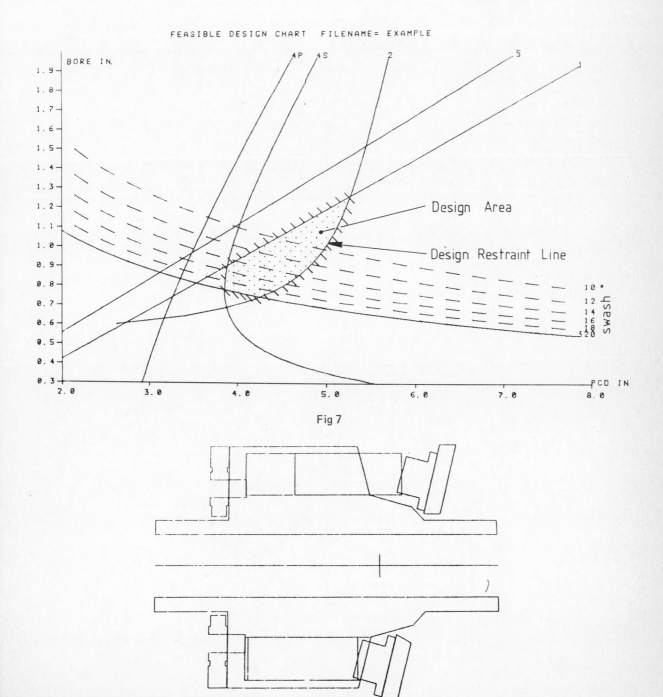

FEASIBLE DESIGN CHART   FILENAME= EXAMPLE

Fig 7

Fig 8

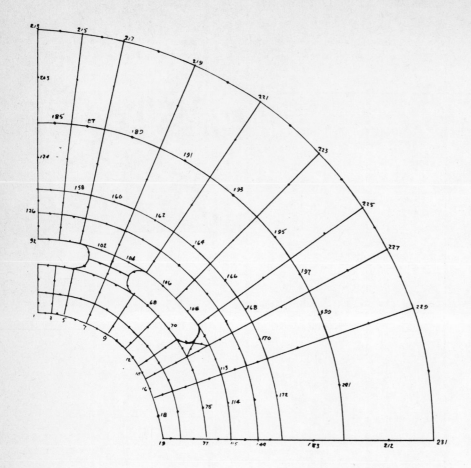

Fig 10

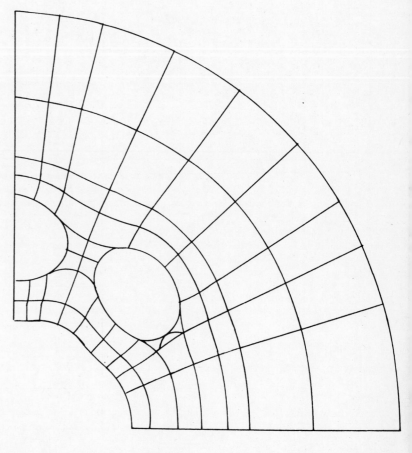

Fig 11

172

```
IDENT. ............... 772D
OPERATORS NAME........ HE
STATION NUMBER........  0
DATE................. 30/6/83
```

				MINIMUM SEPARATION	MAXIMUM SEPARATION
A	B	C	D	E	F
+00.2	+00.6	+03.4	+03.3	+02.7	+03.1
+00.3	+00.9	+03.3	+03.3	+02.4	+03.0
+00.7	+01.5	+03.7	+03.6	+02.2	+03.0
+00.9	+01.3	+03.5	+03.7	+02.4	+02.8
+01.0	+01.4	+03.8	+03.5	+02.4	+02.7
+00.9	+01.3	+03.5	+03.6	+02.3	+02.7
+00.5	+00.9	+03.7	+03.5	+02.8	+03.1
+00.3	+00.8	+03.5	+03.6	+02.8	+03.3
+00.0	+00.4	+04.0	+03.6	+03.6	+04.0
+00.0	+00.6	+04.1	+03.8	+03.5	+04.1
+00.1	+00.4	+04.0	+03.7	+03.6	+03.9
+00.5	+00.7	+03.8	+03.7	+03.1	+03.2
+00.5	+00.5	+03.7	+03.5	+03.1	+03.2
+00.5	+00.2	+03.7	+03.6	+03.2	+03.5
+00.6	+00.3	+03.6	+03.6	+03.0	+03.3
+00.5	+00.7	+03.4	+03.4	+02.7	+02.9
+00.5	+00.7	+03.3	+03.2	+02.6	+02.7
+00.3	+00.7	+03.1	+03.3	+02.6	+03.0

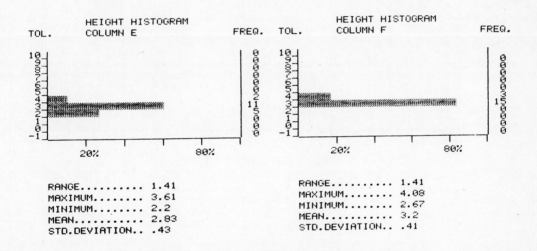

```
         HEIGHT HISTOGRAM                          HEIGHT HISTOGRAM
  TOL.      COLUMN E          FREQ.    TOL.          COLUMN F          FREQ.
  10 _|                         0      10 _|                            0
   9  |                         0       9  |                            0
   8  |                         0       8  |                            0
   7  |                         0       7  |                            0
   6  |                         0       6  |                            0
   5  |                         0       5  |                            0
   4  |                         2       4  |                            3
   3  |                        11       3  |                           15
   2  |                         5       2  |                            0
   1  |                         0       1  |                            0
   0  |                         0       0  |                            0
  -1 _|                         0      -1 _|                            0
        20%         80%                      20%            80%
```

RANGE.......... 1.41	RANGE.......... 1.41
MAXIMUM........ 3.61	MAXIMUM........ 4.08
MINIMUM........ 2.2	MINIMUM........ 2.67
MEAN........... 2.83	MEAN........... 3.2
STD.DEVIATION.. .43	STD.DEVIATION.. .41

Fig 12

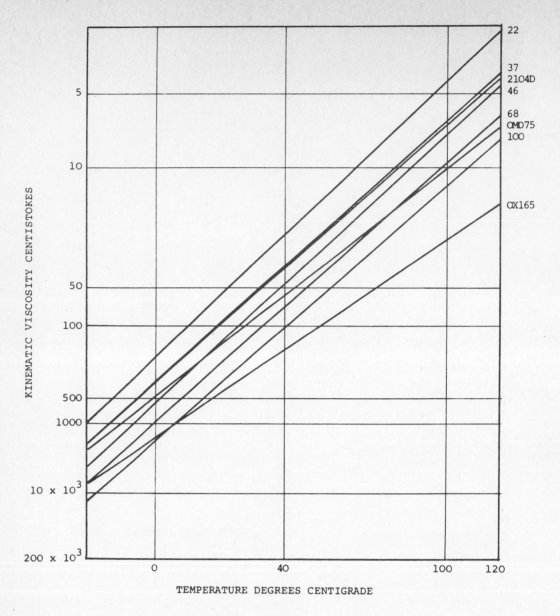

Fig 13

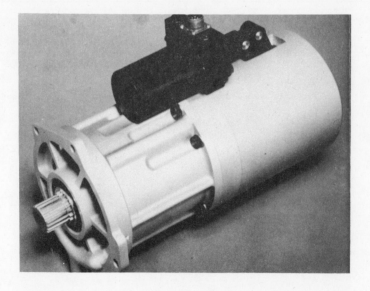

Fig 14

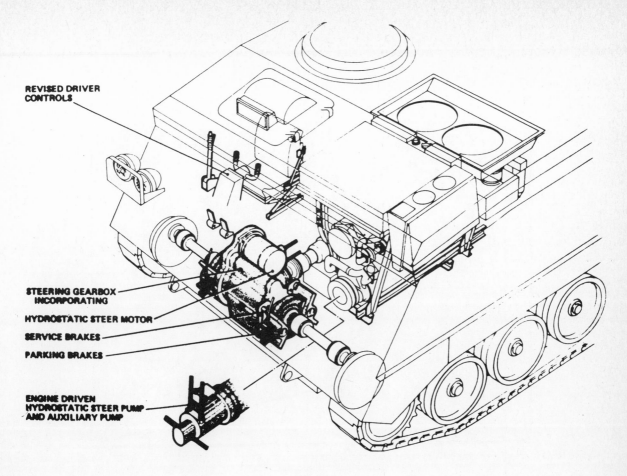

Fig 15

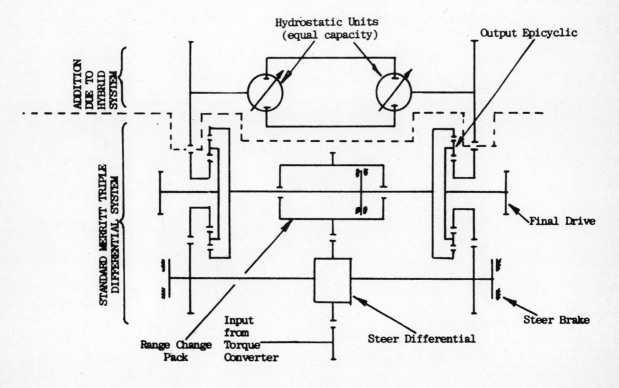

Fig 16

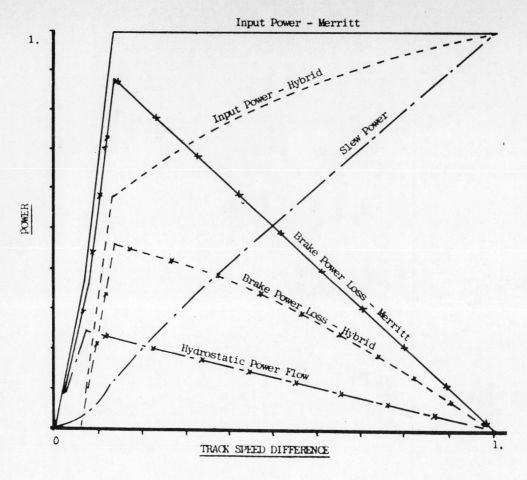

Fig 17

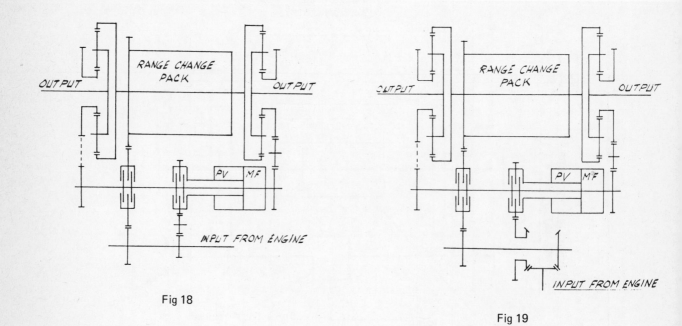

Fig 18

Fig 19